the po•e•try dic•tion•ar•y

second edition

1: Defines key terms that should be in the vocabulary of every poet.

2: Includes over 250 illustrative poems from Homer to the present day.

John Drury
with foreword by Dana Gioia

WRITER'S DIGEST BOOKS
Cincinnati, Ohio
www.writersdigest.com

APR   2010

Visit our Web site at www.writersdigest.com for information on more resources for writers.

To receive a free weekly e-mail newsletter delivering tips and updates about writing and about Writer's Digest products, register directly at our Web site at http://newsletters.fwpublications.com.

11 10 09   6 5 4 3

Distributed in Canada by Fraser Direct, 100 Armstrong Avenue, Georgetown, ON, Canada L7G 5S4, Tel: (905) 877-4411.

Distributed in the U.K. and Europe by David & Charles, Brunel House, Newton Abbot, Devon, TQ12 4PU, England, Tel: (+44) 1626 323200, Fax: (+44) 1626 323319, E-mail: postmaster@davidandcharles.co.uk.

Distributed in Australia by Capricorn Link, P.O. Box 704, Windsor, NSW 2756 Australia, Tel: (02) 4577-3555.

Library of Congress Cataloging-in-Publication Data

Drury, John, 1950-
  The poetry dictionary / by John Drury.-- 2nd ed.
      p. cm.
  Includes index.
  ISBN-13: 978-1-58297-329-6 (pbk. : alk. paper)
  ISBN-10: 1-58297-329-6 (pbk. : alk. paper)
  1. Poetry--Dictionaries. I. Title.
  PN1021.D78 2006   2005015113
  808.1'03--dc22

Edited by Michelle Ruberg Ehrhard
Designed by Grace Ring
Production coordinated by Robin Richie

fw
F+W PUBLICATIONS, INC.

ABOUT THE AUTHOR

John Drury is the author of two poetry collections: *The Disappearing Town* and *Burning the Aspern Papers*, both published by Miami University Press. He is also the author of *Creating Poetry*, published by Writer's Digest Books. His poems have appeared in many literary magazines, including *The American Poetry Review*, *The Hudson Review*, *The New Republic*, *The Paris Review*, *Ploughshares*, *Poetry*, and *The Southern Review*. He has won the Bernard F. Conners Prize for Poetry and two Ohio Arts Council grants, as well as the Dolly Cohen Award for Distinguished Teaching. He teaches poetry writing and poetics at the University of Cincinnati.

ACKNOWLEDGMENTS

I want to thank a number of people for their advice, suggestions, and corrections of entries in this revised version of *The Poetry Dictionary*: Stephen Burt for ELLIPTICAL POETRY; Thomas Carper for SCANSION; Allison Joseph for OCCASIONAL VERSE; David Lehman for ANAGRAM; Sarah Perrier for SPEAKER and VOICE; Jim Simmerman for DIALOGUE; and C.D. Wright for ABECEDARIUM.

My colleagues at the University of Cincinnati have been generous with their time and assistance. Professor Lowanne Jones of Romance Languages gave my translation of Arnaut Daniel's sestina from the Provençal a close reading and offered many suggestions and corrections that have made my English version more accurate. Professor Pearl Chao of Asian Languages corrected my translation of the poem by Li Bai. Professor Edgar Slotkin of the English Department helped me with the entries DRÓTTKVAETT, RANN, and WELSH POETIC FORMS.

Jim Cummins helped me immeasurably on both editions, offering astute comments and useful suggestions, providing me with the phone numbers and addresses of poets and other information I couldn't find elsewhere, and lending me noncirculating books from the Elliston Poetry Room of Langsam Library.

Julie Gonnering, my graduate assistant, helped me with the difficult, time-consuming task of seeking and securing permissions to reprint poems. She also read through the entire manuscript and offered proofreading corrections, editing suggestions, and savvy advice. I'm grateful for her attentiveness, good humor, and intelligent way of examining things.

I also want to thank my colleague Joanie Mackowski for reading the final draft of this revision and giving it a friendly, critical look.

Dana Gioia, Jack Heffron, Laurie Henry, Heather McHugh, Donna Poehner, and Laura Smith helped me with the first edition in 1995. Michelle Ruberg Ehrhard edited this revision, and I'm grateful for her patience and expertise. Jane Friedman helped make a revised edition possible. I want to thank Grace Ring for her beautiful design and sensitive layout of this book. Special thanks to Annie Wright for her help in securing permissions.

Leaves from my teaching at the University of Cincinnati gave me some crucial free time to work on both editions of this book. Grants from the Charles Phelps Taft Memorial Fund have supported the work. Students in my workshops have offered helpful responses about this dictionary and suggestions for how to improve it. I'm grateful for the assistance.

Finally, I want to thank LaWanda Walters, to whom this new edition is dedicated.

FOREWORD

Why would a poet need a poetry dictionary? Conventional wisdom proclaims that poets are spontaneous and emotional creatures who burst forth naturally into song as untutored as birds in a pear tree. General opinion also holds that reference books are impersonal, intellectual compilations utterly at odds with creativity and imagination. Conventional wisdom is, of course, absolutely wrong. A poet's favorite book is nearly always the dictionary. W.H. Auden used his unabridged *Oxford English Dictionary* so frequently that he eventually read its thirteen sturdy volumes to pieces.

I cannot imagine a poet—beginning or established—who would not want *The Poetry Dictionary* on his or her bookshelf. All writers, even those with Ivy League degrees, are largely self-taught, and the process of learning goes on a lifetime. When formal education ends, the challenge of continued learning falls on the individual. Most people find the burden too great, but genuine writers flourish under such circumstance: They delight in pursuing knowledge according to their own dictates, but they need reliable guides.

John Drury has designed an invaluable book for poets. He has not only provided concise, clear, accurate, and current definitions of the terms and traditions of poetry; he has also presented judiciously selected examples of each form, genre, movement, or period. One can read *The Poetry Dictionary* with equal satisfaction either as an informed guide to the practice and history of verse or as an annotated anthology of model poems. Students learn different things from abstract definitions and specific poems, and they need to see both.

Education fosters self-discovery. By learning about the past, we enhance our understanding of the present; by studying others, we gain better perspective on ourselves. A young writer who explores *The Poetry Dictionary* will—consciously or unawares—be investigating his or her own possibilities as an artist. Reading about *The Movement* among British poets of the 1950s may strike a sympathetic chord of skeptical anti-romanticism. Or coming upon *deep image poetry*, a poet may suddenly recognize the imaginative direction his or her future work needs to take. An ambitious writer will instinctively want to try out many possibilities from the sonnet to surrealism before settling into a personal style. And, as the poet gradually discovers an individual voice, he or she will realize that it grew not merely out of some single source but from the still ongoing process of understanding and assimilating each object of study.

Sometimes what we learn by accident proves more important than what we study by plan. The wonderful thing about dictionaries is the arbitrary juxtapositions the alphabet creates. No surrealist poet excelled *Webster's* unintentionally inspired sequence of neighboring words: *chime in, chimera, chimney, chimp*! In *The Poetry Dictionary* we might diligently look up *kenning* only to discover *kyrielle*. Suddenly we learn something intriguing we had not realized we needed to know. An idea, a departure point, or even a poem might unexpectedly appear.

Learning should mix instruction with delight, accessibility with surprise. *The Poetry Dictionary* opens its subject to the reader with exemplary pride and enjoyment. No lover of poetry will find this book less than a pleasure.

—Dana Gioia

HOW TO USE THIS BOOK

One of the principles of this dictionary is the grouping of related terms, whenever possible, into major entries. For example, RHETORICAL DEVICES contains a list of the figures and tropes of classical rhetoric, with definitions and examples. The most important of these devices, such as *alliteration*, also appear in individual entries. Subordinate terms are placed within larger entries. The term *sestet*, for example, appears in the entry SONNET. In lieu of a welter of tiny entries, there is an index containing all of the terms used in the dictionary. If you need to find a specific term, check the index first.

Many of the entries contain one or more "model poems": examples that show the uses of a poetic form or device, starting with the first instance, if possible, and proceeding to more recent examples, innovations, and perhaps departures from the tradition. Most of the examples are whole poems, but when excerpts from longer works have been unavoidable, I have tried to select enough material to give a good sense of how a poet uses the particular form or device.

Throughout the dictionary, terms that appear elsewhere as individual entries are preceded by asterisks (*). The reader is also referred to related terms through notes in parentheses. For example, in the GEORGIC entry a note reads "(*See* IDYLL *and* PASTORAL)." In PASTORAL there is a poem that is spoken by two characters, a shepherd and the girl he pursues, so that it also serves as an example of *dialogue. One goal of the book is to present a web of connections, to show how the elements of poetry are intertwined.

Many poems included here provide examples for multiple terms and are cross-referenced. Paul Muldoon's "News Headlines from the Homer Noble Farm" appears in TERZA RIMA but also serves as an example of *haiku. Sylvia Plath's "You're" appears in FIGURATIVE LANGUAGE but is also a *list poem that uses its *title as first line.

The pronunciation guides avoid linguistic symbols and use simple equivalents from normal American usage, as in the term *rondeau* (ron-doe´). Accents appear above the accented syllables. The idea is to make it easier for the reader. The disadvantage is that there are often various ways to pronounce different sound combinations in English (such as *ough*). But an array of symbols requiring a key and constant reference by the puzzled reader, who is unlikely to specialize in phonetics, would violate the spirit of this book. I have, in any case, tried to avoid ambiguities in the pronunciation guides. One possible confusion, however, is the vowel sound *ay*, which is pronounced here as in "day."

I have aimed to include the most necessary poetic terms, along with a helpful selection of poems, in this dictionary. Inevitably, choices must be made and material omitted, however reluctantly.

Some of the omissions involve subject matter, such as political poetry and religious poetry. However, both of these kinds, as well as many others, are represented within various categories: political poetry by Langston Hughes's "I, Too" in HARLEM RENAISSANCE and Adrienne Rich's "The Ninth Symphony of Beethoven Understood at Last as a Sexual Message" in LINE BREAK; religious poetry by the poems of Basho and Issa in HAIKU (representing Zen Buddhism), Hafiz's "Where Can I Hear the News" in GHAZAL (representing Sufism, or Islamic mysticism), passages from the Bible in BIBLICAL VERSE and PSALM (representing Judaism), and poems by George Herbert in ECHO VERSE and PATTERN POEM and Gerard Manley Hopkins in CURTAL SONNET and SPRUNG RHYTHM (representing Christianity).

Several abbreviations are used throughout the dictionary:

b. = born

B.C.E. = Before Common Era (also B.C.)

C.E. = Common Era (also A.D.)

tr. = translated by

For whatever kind of poetry the reader may prefer, this dictionary is a way station—a place of maps, fuel, refreshment, first aid—whose purpose is to lead the reader back to reading and to encourage the writer to venture forth. It represents not a last word but directions along the way, signposts for the journey.

—John Drury

ABECEDARIUM (ab'-eh-suh-dare'-ee-um; Latin, "alphabet" or "primer," from the letters ABCD; plural, *abecedaria*; also called *abecedarius, abecedary, alphabet poem*) A poem arranged according to the alphabet, so that the first line begins with the letter A. It is really an *acrostic that proceeds according to alphabetical order instead of spelling out a name or a message.

Geoffrey Chaucer's "An ABC" is an early example in English, although his authorship of the poem is doubtful. Inger Christensen's book-length poem *alphabet* begins with the letter *a* ("apricot trees exist, apricot trees exist") and devotes whole sections to different letters of the alphabet, as in the third part, whose last line is "cicadas, cedars, cypresses, the cerebellum." In Carolyn Forché's *Blue Hour*, successive lines begin with one particular letter before the poem moves on to the next letter. C.D. Wright's "Arkansas Towns," a section of "The Ozark Odes," is a *list poem that begins with Acorn and ends with Zent, repeating some letters of the alphabet (as in Okay and Ozone) and omitting others (K, P, Q, V, and X).

In *The White Goddess: A Historical Grammar of Poetic Myth*, Robert Graves discusses the Irish "tree alphabets." He points out that "in all Celtic languages *trees* means *letters* ... and that the most ancient Irish alphabet, the Beth-Luis-Nion ('Birch-Rowan-Ash') takes its name from the first three of a series of trees whose initials form the sequence of its letters."

A

David Young's poem "A Lowercase Alphabet" is actually an exercise in metaphor, commenting on how the letters look.

A LOWERCASE ALPHABET / David Young (b. 1936)

a   snail going up the wall
b   hang up the little dipper
c   mouth, moon, riverbend
d   the dipper in the mirror
e   tiny eye of the whale
f   oil well, skate, old pistol
g   what did you do to your glasses?
h   a chimney for every hut
i   the levitation of the spot
j   landscape with fishhook and planet
k   where three roads almost meet
l   romance of the periscope
m   comb from the iron age
n   the hut that lost its chimney
o   simplification of the blood
p   the dipper dead and buried
q   its mirror buried with it
r   geyser that goes off crooked
s   little black love seat
t   the portable cross
u   cross section of a trough
v   the hawk above the valley
w   a graph for winter, pigsfoot
x   dancer, hourglass, black suspenders
y   the root begins to sprout
z   path of the rabbit

ABSTRACT LANGUAGE Words that represent ideas, concepts, and intangible things, such as "beauty" and "truth."

When John Keats uses those two words at the end of his "Ode on a Grecian Urn," they follow four and a half stanzas that describe the scenes depicted on the urn, images fixed in time, unchanging—and the urn itself utters the abstractions:

> "Beauty is truth, truth beauty,"—that is all
> Ye know on earth, and all ye need to know.

Most contemporary poets prefer *concrete language (words that represent particular, tangible things, such as "woodchuck" or "telescope" or "bungalow") to abstractions—or at least use a larger proportion of concrete to abstract words. In many poems, the abstraction may be what all the concrete details add up to, although there is usually no existing word that can sum them up. (If there is, the poem will be a kind of *allegory.)

ABSTRACT POETRY Poetry that aims to use its sounds, textures, rhythms, and rhymes to convey an emotion instead of relying on the meanings of words.

Edith Sitwell coined the term, and poems in her *Façade* exemplify it. Abstract poetry does not represent any particular object or focus on any definite subject. Instead, it proceeds the way an abstract painter paints, creating not portraits or landscapes but arrangements of pigments, blocks of color, slashes and swirls of paint. Abstract poetry aspires to be similarly nonrepresentational.

In "Notes Toward a Supreme Fiction," Wallace Stevens asserts, "It Must Be Abstract." John Ashbery's poems are typically abstract in a painterly way. Jorie Graham's "Soul Says" (in FRAGMENTATION) and William Carlos Williams's "The Descent" (in TRIADIC LINE) use abstract language prominently and effectively.

ACADEMIC VERSE Poetry that adheres to the accepted standards and requirements of some kind of "school." Poetry approved, officially or unofficially, by a literary establishment.

Originally, "the Academy" referred to Plato's school for advanced education. The Greek critics in Alexandria, Egypt, codified the terms of poetry and commented on the works of ancient poets such as Sappho. The French Academy, founded in 1635, formulated rules for

3

poetry. Today, universities serve as headquarters for poetry workshops, where students have their poems critiqued by a teacher (who is usually a published poet) and other student poets. Although there is really no central "authority" that stipulates what kinds of poems are acceptable, the workshop poem is a recognizably homogenized product of the system. Contemporary academic verse tends to be low-key, conversational, imagistic, autobiographical, and written in *free verse of medium-length lines. Of course, many fine poems fit that description, but some readers object to the proliferation of poems that seem safe and formulaic. In the early twentieth century, Ezra Pound called for "breaking the pentameter" of what was the academic verse of its time: rhymed *iambic pentameter.

Another sense of academic verse seizes upon the bookish nature of such poems. We may properly call poems that display learning (from John Milton's *Paradise Lost* to Ezra Pound's *The Cantos*) academic. Anthony Hecht's early poems, which are elaborately formal, exemplify how impressive such a professorial style can be. The use of difficult forms (such as the double *sonnet), elevated diction, and strict meter may be the poetic equivalents of cap and gown.

Usually, however, the term *academic* is pejorative. We dismiss a poem by saying it is academic, suggesting that it slavishly follows a current fashion or smacks of the classroom.

ACCENT (ak'-sent; Latin, "song added [to speech]," a direct rendering of the Greek term that is the root of the word *prosody) A syllable that is emphasized (usually marked by ´ when scanning a poem); also called *stress or *beat. (*See* SCANSION.)

In a polysyllabic word, accent is inherent in the pronunciation of a word and can be verified in a dictionary: *pattern*, for example, has an accent on the first syllable (*pat*); *conglomeration* has accents on the second and fourth of its five syllables (*glom* and *ra*); *altitude* has a strong accent on its first syllable (*al*) and a weak accent, or secondary stress, on its third (*tude*). The accenting of monosyllabic words, however, depends on the context and position in a line. Nouns and verbs are more likely to be accented than articles and prepositions, but any word that falls on a metrical stress can be emphasized, however slightly. The actual effect of an accent is often a rise in pitch and volume, more of a push or a punch than an unstressed syllable will have. Accent represents a peak as opposed to a dip, a burst as opposed to a lull.

ACCENTUAL METER (ak-sen′-choo-ul) A rhythmic pattern based on a recurring number of accents (or stresses) in each line of a poem or section of a poem.

In *accentual-syllabic meter, some weak syllables may be accented, however slightly, if they are surrounded by even weaker syllables. But in accentual verse, a stress must have a definite "thump." It must be heard and felt. The number of unstressed syllables is not counted, but it should vary from line to line.

The earliest English poetry was accentual. Robert Graves, in his essay "Harp, Anvil, Oar," suggests that the rhythm of accentual meter comes from the strokes of rowing over rough seas. It may also come from the prevalence of burly, monosyllabic words in Anglo-Saxon, from which we now draw much of our basic vocabulary of physical words, such as *rock*, *boat*, *thrash*, and *burst*. (See ALLITERATIVE METER.)

The following accentual poem by Donald Justice is written in two-stress lines. The syllable count varies from line to line, ranging from three ("End of piers") to six ("And offers to show you"). A couple of lines may seem to have extra stresses, like the word "bar" in "The cozy ship's-bar." However, the phrase "ship's-bar" works as a single unit (like "wet-bar"), with the primary accent on "ship's." In the line "I hear a great splashing," "great" could be accented, but "splash" is even more emphatic, and the swing of the two-stress meter, already well established, forces us to hear two primary stresses. Still, the near accent of "great" does have a pleasingly ambiguous sound effect. It makes the line stand out, weighted more heavily than the others, and leads to the climax of the poem, an image of grandfathers lolling in tubs.

DREAMS OF WATER / Donald Justice (1925–2004)

A

1.

An odd silence
Falls as we enter
The cozy ship's-bar.

The captain, smiling,
Unfolds his spyglass
And offers to show you

The obscene shapes
Of certain islands,
Low in the offing.

I sit by in silence.

2.

People in raincoats
Stand looking out from
Ends of piers.

A fog gathers;
And little tugs,
Growing uncertain

Of their position,
Start to complain
With the deep and bearded

Voices of fathers.

3.

The season is ending.
White verandas
Curve away.

The hotel seems empty
But, once inside,
I hear a great splashing.

Behind doors
Grandfathers loll
In steaming tubs,

Huge, unblushing.

ACCENTUAL-SYLLABIC METER (also called *syllable-stress meter*) A rhythmic pattern based on a regular count of both syllables and *accents (or *stresses) in a line of poetry.

The metrical system used most commonly in English emerged as a combination of the *accentual meter of Anglo-Saxon and the *syllabic meter of French, as in these lines by Geoffrey Chaucer from *The Canterbury Tales*:

Ă Knyght | thĕr wás, | ănd thát | ă worth-| y̆ mán,

Thăt fró | thĕ tým-| ĕ thát | hĕ fírst | bĭgán

Tŏ rí-| dĕn oút, | hĕ lóv-| ĕd chív-| ălríĕ.

NOTE: When reading Chaucer's Middle English—which doesn't get much easier than this—the reader should pronounce any final "-e" not followed by a vowel or "h" in the next word; "-ed," as in "lovèd," is also pronounced.

Chaucer's lines are in *iambic pentameter. The pattern stipulates ten syllables (or eleven if the last one is unstressed) and five accents (generally on the even-numbered syllables) in each line. The poet can vary the strict iambic pattern in many ways (by substituting different feet for some of the iambs, for example), but all such changes really involve playing off the expected number of syllables against the position and relative strength of the accents.

Specific varieties of accentual-syllabic meter depend upon two factors: the kind of *foot (arrangement of stressed and unstressed syllables) and the number of feet per *line. Here are lists of (1) the most common feet used in English verse and (2) the terms identifying the number of feet in a line:

A

Pattern of syllables	Foot	Example	Feet per line
˘ ˘ ´	*anapest, anapestic	(ascertain´)	1 monometer
´ ˘ ˘	*dactyl, dactylic	(par´asol)	2 dimeter
˘ ´	*iamb, iambic	(debate´)	3 trimeter
˘ ˘	*pyrrhic	(of a)	4 tetrameter
´ ´	*spondee, spondaic	(fast´ food´)	5 pentameter
´ ˘	*trochee, trochaic	(cro´cus)	6 hexameter
´	*monosyllabic foot	(hit´)	7 heptameter
˘	*feminine ending (extra unstressed syllable)	(last syllable of demand´ing)	8 octameter

Not all of these feet, however, can work as a metrical basis for a line. Since the pyrrhic foot consists of two unstressed syllables, any noun, verb, adjective, or polysyllabic word will require an accent, which will leap up and overwhelm the lowly pyrrhic foot. Spondaic meter might occur on occasion, in a particular line, but it would not work as the basis for a poem, since minor words (such as articles, conjunctions, and most prepositions) will be unstressed, and polysyllabic words will usually contain unstressed syllables. Meter based upon two-syllable feet (iambic and trochaic) is called duple meter, while meter based upon three-syllable feet (anapestic and dactylic) is called triple meter. Pyrrhic and spondaic feet are useful as *substitutions to vary the rhythm of a particular meter so it doesn't sound mechanical.

The most common accentual-syllabic meter in English verse is iambic. Pentameter is the most common line length, followed by tetrameter, then trimeter and hexameter (used in the *alexandrine).

Trochaic meter is most often tetrameter, as in William Blake's "The Tyger." The first line of Edgar Allan Poe's "The Raven" is trochaic octameter, but it *sounds* like two tetrameter lines: "Once upon a midnight dreary, || while I pondered, weak and weary." The *internal rhyme reinforces the sense of two separate parts.

Triple meter (such as anapestic or dactylic) tends to sound overly light or overly powerful. The rhythmic swing makes it hard to be subtle or to reproduce the natural rise and fall of speech, unless the poet introduces enough substitutions (iambs, trochees, spondees, monosyllabic feet) to let the melody overcome the metronome.

(*See* ANAPEST, DACTYL, FOOT, IAMB, METER, MINOR IONIC, PYRRHIC, SCANSION, SPONDEE, *and* TROCHEE.)

ACROSTIC (uh-cros'-tik; Greek, "tip, point" + "line, verse, stich") Poem in which the initial letters of the lines, read downward, spell out a name or message. Other possibilities exist for hiding the acrostic, such as moving the letter one space over in each succeeding line. Acrostics are usually used for *light verse, *riddles or puzzles, and *occasional verse. The following poem commemorates a "golden afternoon" of boating and storytelling. The first letters spell out a girl's name.

from *THROUGH THE LOOKING-GLASS* / Lewis Carroll (1832–1898)

A boat, beneath a sunny sky
Lingering onward dreamily
In an evening of July—

Children three that nestle near,
Eager eye and willing ear,
Pleased a simple tale to hear—

Long has paled that sunny sky:
Echoes fade and memories die:
Autumn frosts have slain July.

A

Still she haunts me, phantomwise,
Alice moving under skies
Never seen by waking eyes.

Children yet, the tale to hear,
Eager eye and willing ear,
Lovingly shall nestle near.

In a Wonderland they lie,
Dreaming as the days go by,
Dreaming as the summers die:

Ever drifting down the stream—
Lingering in the golden gleam—
Life, what is it but a dream?

NOTE: On July 4, 1862, Rev. Charles Lutwidge Dodgson and Rev. Robinson Duckworth took the three young Liddell sisters on a boat ride up the Thames River, one of many rowing expeditions with the girls. Alice Pleasance Liddell, whose name is encoded in this acrostic, was then ten years old. During this afternoon, as Dodgson (whose pseudonym was Lewis Carroll) later wrote, "I told them the fairy-tale of Alice's adventures underground. ..."

ALCAICS, ALCAIC STANZA (al-kay′-ix, al-kay′-ik) A stanza form named after the Greek poet Alcaeus, a contemporary of Sappho in the late seventh to early sixth century B.C.E. Its metrical pattern (with the symbols for long and short syllables used in Greek *quantitative meter) is the following:

	Number of syllables	Short syllables that can be long
◡ – ◡ – ◡ – ◡ ◡ – ◡ –	11	1st or 5th
◡ – ◡ – ◡ – ◡ ◡ – ◡ –	11	1st or 5th
◡ – ◡ – ◡ – ◡ – ◡	9	1st, 5th, or 9th
– ◡ ◡ – ◡ ◡ – ◡ – ◡	10	10th

A poet writing in English *accentual-syllabic meter can change the long syllables to accents (or stresses) and the short ones to unstressed syllables. If a poet counts only the number of syllables, the pattern is 11-11-9-10. In Greek, the stanza is unrhymed. Horace uses alcaics in many of his odes, which were originally in Latin. Alfred, Lord Tennyson's "Milton" is also in alcaics. (*See* ODE *and* SAPPHICS.)

STORM IN THE STATE / Alcaeus (Seventh to sixth century B.C.E.; tr. Richmond Lattimore)

I cannot understand how the winds are set
against each other. Now from this side and now
    from that the waves roll. We between them
       run with the wind in our black ship driven,

hard pressed and laboring under the giant storm.
All round the mast-step washes the sea we shipped.
    You can see through the sail already
       where there are opening rents within it.

The forestays slacken. ...

ALEXANDRINE (al-ek-zan'-drin; deriving perhaps from the name of Alexandre Paris, a French poet, or from Alexander the Great, the subject of heroic poems in this form) A line in *iambic hexameter, or six iambic feet (˘ ´ | ˘ ´ | ˘ ´ | ˘ ´ | ˘ ´ | ˘ ´); a line consisting of twelve syllables.

In its syllabic form, the alexandrine is the most important kind of line in French poetry, which requires a *caesura (or pause) in the middle, after the sixth syllable. Sometimes, in English verse, it is inserted in an otherwise pentameter poem, as in the final line of the *Spenserian stanza. Here is an example from Edmund Spenser's *The Faerie Queen*:

And Shame his ugly face did hide from living eye.

English poems entirely in alexandrines are relatively uncommon, probably because the line tends to split into two distinct parts, usually containing three feet each.

A

ALLEGORY (al'-eh-gore-ee; Greek, combining the words for "other" and "speak," meaning to speak of one thing in terms of something else)

1. Figurative language in which characters, images, and events stand for something abstract. Themis, the courtroom's representation of a blindfolded woman holding a sword and a set of scales, is an allegory for Justice. Allegory differs from *symbolism in that it represents more of a one-to-one correspondence and is used systematically and extensively. A true symbol is often hard to define in words other than the poem's. The image resonates so powerfully that it suggests other meanings, as with William Blake's "tyger," which represents a kind of intense force in the unconscious, or an electric power from the underworld, or a creative fire in the murky cosmos. If the tiger were merely an allegory, one might reduce it to a kind of equation: tiger = evil.

2. A poem or other literary work that uses allegories. Edmund Spenser's *The Faerie Queen* is perhaps the best-known allegory in English poetry. In Book III, for example, Sir Guyon (Temperance) charges a knight who knocks him off his horse; the knight turns out to be Britomart, a lady, who represents Chastity. (Her lance is enchanted.) Characters in an allegory serve more as chess pieces than as human beings. Or perhaps they are concepts masquerading as people.

ALLITERATION (uh-lit'-ur-ay'-shun; Latin, "to letter") Generally, the repetition of consonant sounds (also called *consonance). More precisely, the repetition of initial consonant sounds, as in this song from William Shakespeare's *As You Like It*:

> It was a lover and his lass—
> With a hey, and a ho, and a hey nonino—

In this song "l" is alliterated in the first line, "h" in the second. Alliteration is essential in *alliterative meter (also called Anglo-Saxon strong-stress meter), but it occurs frequently in much later English poetry. It is usually a prominent aural effect and can sound ridiculous if used carelessly or indiscriminately. In *Love's Labour's Lost*, Shakespeare parodies it when Holofernes "affects the letter" (or practices alliterating) in Act IV, Scene II: "The preyful princess pierc'd and prick'd a pretty pleasing pricket." Over-alliterating may lead to similar tongue-twisters: "Peter Piper picked a peck of pickled peppers" or "She sells seashells by the seashore."

Here are the particular terms for various kinds of "letter" repetition:

Kind of Alliteration	Repeats
alliteration (also beginning, head, or initial rhyme)	initial consonants (roof/righteous: *r*) (brain/brush: *br*)
consonance (final alliteration)	consonants at the end of words (thick/creek: *k*)
parallel (or cross) alliteration	interwoven consonants (big time/bus trip: *b*, *t*)
hidden (or internal) alliteration	consonants in the middle of words (runner/flannel: *n*)
bracket alliteration	initial and final consonants (grain/groin: *gr*, *n*)
submerged (or thesis) alliteration	unstressed syllables of words (mailbox/carob: *b*)
suspended alliteration	reversal of a consonant-vowel combination found in one word in another word that follows (tawny/aeronautics: *t*, *aw*, *n*)

The repetition of vowel sounds is usually called *assonance, although it too is sometimes considered a kind of alliteration. Although *alliteration* and *consonance* are both used loosely to encompass various kinds of consonant repetition, it is perhaps useful to distinguish between them.

The repetition of a whole syllable in nearby words is called *polyptoton* ("The man manages manuscripts"). The repetition of suffixes is called *homoeoteleuton* (Greek for "similar endings"), as in "The valley is lovely."

Alliteration differs from *rhyme in several respects. It repeats an isolated sound at several points within one or more lines and does not usually appear at any particular point. Rhyme, however, usually repeats at least two sounds together, a vowel and a consonant, and usually appears at the end of a line or (in the case of *internal rhyme) at rhythmic points within a line. Although it is common enough to find *slant rhyme that repeats only the final consonants of its rhyme words, it is unusual (and unconvincing) to find true alliteration passed off as rhyme.

Alliteration depends for its success or failure on the poet's ear. Since, except in Anglo-Saxon meter, there are no rules dictating where and when (or even if) to alliterate, the poet must pace these repetitions carefully. Alliteration can be especially striking in adjacent words, but it can also rise like a series of wave crests if non-alliterating words intervene. After a certain amount of time, a consonant ceases to resonate. Even though it may be repeated, it will not sound like a repetition. Exactly what that interval may be is hard to determine, except by trial and error, but rhyme sounds persist much longer in the ear than does alliteration. (Assonance seems to last somewhere between the two.) We can wait several lines for a rhyme to recur, but the gap of a single pentameter line without an echoing consonant pretty much muffles the effect of alliteration. Often, instead of sticking to a single alliterating sound, the poet will braid or interweave two or more consonants, alternating them and making the effect richer, more colorful, not so monochromatically emphatic.

Alliteration is used primarily as a sound effect, either euphonious, cacophonous, or onomatopoeic, something pleasant or plangent for its own sake, but it also serves to link associated words, to tighten the structure of a poem, and to formalize the language, making it more highly wrought (which may or may not be desirable).

INVERSNAID / Gerard Manley Hopkins (1844–1889)

This darksome burn, horseback brown,
His rollrock highroad roaring down,
In coop and in comb the fleece of his foam
Flutes and low to the lake falls home.

A windpuff-bonnet of fáwn-fróth
Turns and twindles over the broth
Of a pool so pitchblack, féll-frówning,
It rounds and rounds Despair to drowning.

Degged with dew, dappled with dew
Are the groins of the braes that the brook treads through,
Wiry heathpacks, flitches of fern,
And the beadbonny ash that sits over the burn.

What would the world be, once bereft
Of wet and of wildness? Let them be left,
O let them be left, wildness and wet;
Long live the weeds and the wilderness yet.

NOTE: *coop*: water cooped up; *comb*: water moving over stones; *twindle*: a portmanteau word combining "twists," "twitches," and "dwindles" (possibly taken from an obsolete word meaning "twin"); *degged*: sprinkled; *heathpacks*: heather; *flitches*: ragged, russet tufts.

ALLITERATIVE METER (uh-lit'-ur-uh-tiv; also called *Anglo-Saxon meter, Old English meter,* and *strong-stress meter*) The accentual, alliterative meter of Anglo-Saxon England before the effects of the Norman Conquest of 1066—and in particular the assimilation of French vocabulary and poetics—finally took hold in the work of Geoffrey Chaucer.

A line of alliterative meter contains four stresses, with a noticeable pause or *caesura in the middle of the line. Three of the four stresses are usually alliterated (but sometimes two, sometimes two different pairs, and sometimes all four). Each half-line to the left and right of the caesura is called a *hemistich.* Alliteration usually occurs from one hemistich to the other, across the caesura. In Anglo-Saxon practice, alliteration includes not just repeated consonants but also vowels (any vowel or diphthong with any other).

Alliterative verse often uses parallelism and *kennings, figurative expressions used repetitively, such as "whale road" instead of "sea"— much like the epithets of Homeric epics ("Earth-shaker" instead of "Poseidon").

Beowulf is the best-known example of alliterative meter, but Chaucer's contemporary William Langland was still using it in *Piers Plowman*. Chaucer can draw on the alliterative tradition when he chooses, even in lines that adhere to the prevailing pattern of rhymed *iambic pentameter couplets:

> The **helm**es *they* to**hew**en *and* to**shred**e;
> Out **brest** the **blood** with **stierne** strem**es** *rede*;
> With **myght**y mac**es** the **bon**es *they* to**brest**e.
> He **thurgh** the **thikk**este *of* the **throng** gan **threst**e;
> Ther **stomb**len **steed**es **strong**e, *and* *doun* gooth *al*;
> He *roll*eth *un*der *foot* as *dooth* a *ball*
> He **foyn**eth *on* his **feet** with *his* tron*choun*,
> And **he** hym **hurt**leth *with* his **hors** a*doun* ...

(*The Knight's Tale*, lines 2609–16)

NOTE: *tohewen*: hew into pieces; *toshrede*: cut into shreds; *brest*: burst; *stierne*: violent; *tobreste*: break into pieces; *threste*: thrust; *foyneth*: thrust and parry; *tronchoun*: truncheon.

In this passage, alliterated stresses are printed in boldface, while non-alliterated stresses are italicized. Yet the lines also rhyme in couplets (*toshrede/rede*) and scan, with acceptable variations, as *iambic pentameter.

It isn't hard to see why accentual-syllabic meter, such as iambic pentameter, won out over alliterative meter. One is flexible enough to contain the other. From the example, however, it is clear that alliterative meter is strong and aggressive. It conveys physical force, such as fighting, powerfully and memorably.

Although Gerard Manley Hopkins used alliteration with great frequency and force in his poems in the nineteenth century, alliterative meter was not revived until Ezra Pound imitated it loosely in his translation of an Anglo-Saxon poem, "The Seafarer," and in "Canto I." W.H. Auden uses alliterative meter in a long poem, *The Age of Anxiety*, whose first line is "My deuce, my double, my dear image." Other twentieth-century poets have used alliterative meter on occasion: Richard Wilbur ("Junk" and "The Lilacs"), C. Day Lewis ("As One Who Wanders into Old Workings"), James Dickey ("Mary Sheffield"), Richard Eberhart ("Brotherhood of Men"), Fred Chappell ("My Grandfather's Church Goes Up"), and Joanie Mackowski, whose "Lullaby" begins "Trumpet vine, heliotrope, || trouble, your footsteps ..." (*See* ACCENTUAL METER *and* BOB AND WHEEL.)

from *PIERS PLOWMAN* / William Langland
(fourteenth century)

> In a somer seson,   whan soft was the sonne,
> I shope me into shroudes,   as I a shepe were;
> In habite as an heremite   unholy of workes
> Went wide in this world,   wondres to here.
> Ac on a May morninge   on Malverne hulles
> Me bifel a ferly,   of fairy me thoughte:
> I was wery forwandred   and went me to reste
> Under a brode banke   by a bornes side,
> And as I lay and lened   and loked on the wateres,
> I slombred in a sleping,   it sweyed so merye.
> Thanne gan I to meten   a merveilouse swevene,
> That I was in a wildernesse,   wist I never where.

NOTE: The space in each line indicates the caesura. These are the first twelve lines of a long visionary poem in Middle English. Pronounce each final "e"; also pronounce the "gh" in "thoughte" like "ch" in the Scottish *loch*.

    shope: dressed; *shepe*: shepherd; *here*: hear; *ac*: but; *bifel*: befell; *ferly*: marvel; *wery*: weary; *forwandred*: from wandering; *bornes*: brook's; *lened*: rested; *sweyed*: sounded; *gan*: began; *meten*: to dream; *swevene*: dream; *wist*: knew.

THE LILACS / Richard Wilbur (b. 1921)

Those laden lilacs
>> at the lawn's end
Came stark, spindly,
>> and in staggered file,
Like walking wounded
>> from the dead of winter.
We watched them waken
>> in the brusque weather
To rot and rootbreak,
>> to ripped branches,
And saw them shiver
>> as the memory swept them
Of night and numbness
>> and the taste of nothing.
Out of present pain
>> and from past terror
Their bullet-shaped buds
>> came quick and bursting,
As if they aimed
>> to be open with us!
But the sun suddenly
>> settled about them,
And green and grateful
>> the lilacs grew,
Healed in that hush,
>> that hospital quiet.
These lacquered leaves
>> where the light paddles
And the big blooms
>> buzzing among them
Have kept their counsel,
>> conveying nothing
Of their mortal message,

                         unless one should measure
         The depth and dumbness
                              of death's kingdom
         By the pure power
                         of this perfume.

NOTE: The tenth line of "The Lilacs" is not alliterated but uses initial assonance (vowel repetition).

ALLUSION (uh-loo'-zhun; Latin, "playing with, touching upon") Reference to a literary work, myth, Biblical story, historical event, or some other cultural artifact.

Although excessive allusion can seem pedantic and may perplex and dishearten some readers, allusion is still one of the great means of compression (and therefore power) in poetry. The mere mention of certain names, places, and events can shoot an electric current through a poem, linking the distant past to the present. A *symbol is, perhaps, another kind of allusion, not a reference to names but to images or details that go back in human history and deep in the human psyche: garden, cross, ship, labyrinth.

The following poem is spoken in the voice of Sidney Lanier, nineteenth-century American poet and Confederate veteran. The speaker alludes to the Greek myth of Danae.

THE YELLOW STEEPLE / Andrew Hudgins (b. 1951)

On my way home from work, I jumped the fence
and cut across the Baptist cemetery.
As I walked over Sarah Pratt,
I saw a workman standing on a scaffold
and swatting a coat of yellow paint
over the peeling whitewash on the steeple.
He dropped a can of paint, and as it fell
the paint dispersed into a mist
and spread a rain of yellow dots
across a corner of the cemetery—
the bushes, trees, headstones, and me.

A

It ruined my coat. I didn't care:
I felt like Danae when she
was loved by Zeus in the golden rain.
Then, looking up, I saw a hawk.
It didn't move at all—not once—
but hung arrested in the air
till I released the breath I held
in awe of its pinpoint, predatory grace.
Still watching it as I walked home,
I barked my shins on a marble angel,
slid down a bank of slick white mud,
fell in the creek, and came up laughing.

It was one of those sustaining days
when you're absolutely sure you have a soul.

NOTE: "Perseus, / conceived by Danaë in a rain of gold." (Ovid, *Metamorphoses*, Book IV, tr. Charles Martin).

AMBIGUITY (Latin, "driving both ways") A word, phrase, image, or idea whose meaning is unclear or which signifies more than one thing, like a pun or a double entendre.

"Dark leaves," for example, could signify a tree's leaves that are dark in color, shady, mysterious, or sinister. It could also mean that darkness is departing. The word *dark* might suggest nighttime or a period of ignorance (like the so-called Dark Ages).

In *Seven Types of Ambiguity*, William Empson describes ambiguity as "any verbal nuance, however slight, which gives room for alternative reactions to the same piece of language." The basic type of ambiguity involves "a word or a grammatical structure [that] is effective in several ways at once." Empson discusses the ambiguity of a line from William Shakespeare's Sonnet 73 (which begins "That time of year thou mayst in me behold"):

> To take a famous example, there is no pun, double syntax, or dubiety of feeling, in
>
> *Bare ruined choirs, where late the sweet birds sang,*

but the comparison holds for many reasons; because ruined monastery choirs are places in which to sing, because they involve sitting in a row, because they are made of wood, are carved into knots and so forth, because they used to be surrounded by a sheltering building crystallised out of the likeness of a forest, and coloured with stained glass and painting like flowers and leaves, because they are now abandoned by all but the grey walls coloured like the skies of winter, because the cold and Narcissistic charm suggested by choir-boys suits well with Shakespeare's feeling for the object of the Sonnets, and for various sociological and historical reasons (the protestant destruction of monasteries; fear of puritanism), which it would be hard now to trace out in their proportions; these reasons, and many more relating the simile to its place in the Sonnet, must all combine to give the line its beauty, and there is a sort of ambiguity in not knowing which of them to hold most clearly in mind.

Empson also asserts that "the machinations of ambiguity are among the very roots of poetry."

In poetry, ambiguity can be like a "forking" move in chess (so one piece, such as a knight, can threaten two or more enemy pieces at once). Ambiguous language can suggest doubleness, opposites merging, paths branching out. It can be a way of speaking with the proverbial "forked tongue" or with "tongue in cheek." It is also a way to compress the language of poetry, to make it richer, denser, more resonant.

On the other hand, ambiguity can be a serious fault in writing that requires clarity. In logical prose (such as a legal document), this kind of ambiguity ruins the text. In poetry, however, the poet may want to use words that perform several tasks concurrently, like a one-man band strumming a banjo, tooting a kazoo, kicking a bass drum, and crashing cymbals between his knees. And the language may lead beyond the poet's original intent into less conscious, more mysterious associations. Ambiguity that muddles is bad; ambiguity that magnifies is good.

AMPHIBRACH (am'-fih-brak; Greek, "short at each end") A foot consisting of a stressed syllable surrounded by two unstressed syllables (˘ ´ ˘). Words that are amphibrachic include "alluring," "deliver," and "commotion." In a sense, it is very common in English verse, as the last foot in an iambic line with a feminine ending (Emily Dickinson's "Thĕ aúc- | tiŏneér | ŏf pártiňg," for example), but that extra unstressed syllable is usually considered extrametrical, a coda to the iambic line, not really part of its final foot. The amphibrach, however, is sometimes found in the *limerick. Along with the *anapest and the *dactyl, it occurs in lines written in triple meter, as in Robert Browning's "Ĭ spráng tŏ | thĕ stirrŭp …"

ANACRUSIS (an-uh-croo'-sis; Greek, "striking up a tune") Unstressed syllable or syllables prefixed to a line, but not part of its metrical pattern.

There is anacrusis in the second of the following *trochaic lines from William Butler Yeats's "Under Ben Bulben":

> Under bare Ben Bulben's head
> In Drumcliff churchyard Yeats is laid.

The meter throughout the poem is trochaic tetrameter, but many lines begin with an unstressed syllable. Out of its metrical context, such a line would be *iambic tetrameter. However, the anacrusis follows a trochaic line, one that lacks a final unstressed syllable (making it catalectic or truncated). That initial unstressed syllable serves merely as a bridge, a repositioning of the syllable omitted from the trochaic line above. To test this practice, which sounds complicated but is in fact simple, imagine moving "In" from the start of Yeats's second line to the end of his first. (Ben Bulben, incidentally, is a mountain in Ireland.)

The term *anacrusis* was borrowed from music, in which it indicates a note just before the melody's first bar. (*See* CATALEXIS.)

ANAGRAM (an'-uh-gram, Greek, "transposition of letters") A word or phrase that is rearranged to form another word or phrase.

Anagrams for "live" include "evil," "vile," "veil," and the name "Levi." Anagrams in which words are spelled backwards, like "devil" and "lived," are useful in constructing palindromes (*see* OULIPO), which read the same in both directions, like "Devils lived."

In the glossary of his anthology *Ecstatic Occasions, Expedient Forms*, David Lehman cites many anagrams, including those of his own *villanelle, "Wystan Hugh Auden," in which every line is an anagram of the poet's name, such as the refrains "Why shun a nude tag?" and "Hug a shady wet nun." Lehman uses the anagrams "rose" and "Eros" in a line of his poem "The Gift": "She gave him a red rose and a little statue of Eros." Heather McHugh makes an anagram when she writes that SHAME "has me."

In the fourth section of "Eight Bits," James Merrill draws anagrams from the last name of the film director and poet Pier Paolo Pasolini, splitting it into two pairs of words: "PAIN" and "SOIL" in English and "PAIN" (meaning bread) and "LOIS" (meaning laws) in French.

ANAPEST, ANAPESTIC (an'-uh-pest, an-uh-pes'-tik; Greek, "beaten back") A *foot consisting of two unstressed syllables followed by a stress (˘ ˘ ´).

Single words can be anapestic ("unaware," "imprecise," "serenade"), but secondary stress in the first syllable often plays tricks in actual lines, seizing more accent than it would command outside of the context of a poetic line. Phrases can also be anapestic ("in the house," "if a book"), but the same tendency, in English, to impose a relative stress on an otherwise unstressed syllable bordered by other weak syllables ("and *in* the *house*," "but *if* a *book*") makes a series of anapests hard to continue in any natural way.

Anapestic meter, like *dactylic, is called triple meter (because each foot contains three syllables). Here is an anapestic line from Herman Melville's "The Maldive Shark":

From his saw-pit of mouth, from his charnel of maw,

In English, anapestic meter often starts galloping and becomes hard to restrain, as in Lord Byron's "The Destruction of Sennacherib,"

whose first stanza is perfectly regular (if the "-ian" of "Assyrian" is
elided into one syllable):

> The Assyrian came down like a wolf on the fold,
> And his cohorts were gleaming in purple and gold;
> And the sheen of their spears was like stars on the sea,
> When the blue wave rolls nightly on deep Galilee.

Byron's lines are powerful, but their expressive range is limited by
the anapestic onrush. Making the feet less predictably anapestic can
help, either by omitting an occasional unstressed syllable or replacing an unstressed syllable with a stress (as Byron does with
"wave" and "rolls" in the fourth line). In fact, it's unusual to find a
poem entirely in anapestic feet. The first foot will frequently be
*iambic, but a mere preponderance of anapests will make a line
sound anapestic—or at least like some sort of triple meter. Often
amphibrachic, anapestic, and dactylic meter are hard to distinguish
in English. A dactylic line can end on a *catalectic foot (one that is
"incomplete," missing its last one or two syllables). And if the line
begins with an unaccented syllable, the line could still be predom-
inantly dactylic, the extra syllable acting as a kind of prefix. (*See*
AMPHIBRACH, ANACRUSIS, CATALEXIS, *and* DACTYL.)

The speaker of the following poem in anapestic pentameter is
David, the future King of Israel and supposed author of the Psalms.

SAUL (Part V) / Robert Browning (1812–1889)

> Then I tuned my harp,—took off the lilies we twine round
>   its chords
> Lest they snap 'neath the stress of the noontide—those
>   sunbeams like swords!
> And I first played the tune all our sheep know, as, one
>   after one,
> So docile they come to the pen-door, till folding be
>   done.
> They are white and untorn by the bushes, for lo, they
>   have fed

> Where the long grasses stifle the water within the
>   stream's bed;
> And now one after one seeks its lodgings, as star follows star
> Into eve and the blue far above us,—so blue and so far!

ANAPHORA (uh-naf'-or-uh; Greek, "carrying back") A *rhetorical device in which several successive lines, phrases, clauses, or sentences begin with the same word or phrase; the opposite of *epistrophe.

In Part 42 of "Song of Myself," Walt Whitman repeats the word "ever" at the start of each line:

> Ever the hard unsunk ground,
> Ever the eaters and drinkers, ever the upward and down-
>   ward sun, ever the air and the ceaseless tides,
> Ever myself and my neighbors, refreshing, wicked, real,
> Ever the old inexplicable query, ever that thorn'd thumb,
>   that breath of itches and thirsts,
> Ever the vexer's *hoot! hoot!* till we find where the sly one
>   hides and bring him forth,
> Ever love, ever the sobbing liquid of life,
> Ever the bandage under the chin, ever the trestles of death.

Although anaphora can sound monotonous, mechanical, and artificial, it can also bind a group of lines powerfully and memorably. The device is especially well suited to giving a sense of definite, obvious structure to long-lined *free verse. But it is also an important device in metrical verse, as in the first six of these lines from Alexander Pope's *The Rape of the Lock* (Canto IV):

> Not youthful Kings in Battle seiz'd alive,
> Not scornful Virgins who their Charms survive,
> Not ardent Lovers robb'd of all their Bliss,
> Not ancient Ladies when refus'd a Kiss,
> Not Tyrants fierce that unrepenting die,
> Not *Cynthia* when her *Manteau's* pinn'd awry,
> E'er felt such Rage, Resentment, and despair,
> As Thou, sad Virgin! for thy ravish'd Hair.

A

(*See* BIBLICAL VERSE, FREE VERSE, INVENTED FORMS AND STANZAS, *and* RHETORICAL DEVICES.)

ANTHOLOGY (Greek, "bouquet of flowers") A collection of poems or stories by various authors.

Early examples include the *Greek Anthology*, a collection of *epigrams compiled in the tenth century C.E. but reaching back to the seventh century B.C.E., and the *Shih Ching* (*Classic Anthology of Songs*, also called the *Confucian Odes*), a collection of Chinese poems compiled before the fifth century B.C.E.

There are several kinds of poetry anthologies:

• Historical, either comprehensive (*The Norton Anthology of Poetry*) or specific (twentieth-century French, Imagist, and Surrealist poetry)

• Thematic, dealing with topics such as the Old Testament, paintings, dogs, love, jazz, work, and sports

• Celebratory, including the "best" work from a magazine (such as *Shenandoah* and *The Georgia Review*) or an institution (such as the Iowa Writers' Workshop)

• Regional, such as Southern poetry

• Demographic, organized according to gender, race, ethnic background, or sexual preference

• Argumentative, offering a range of poems that represent how an editor thinks poets should write (such as Robert Bly's *News of the Universe* and Donald Allen's *The New American Poetry, 1945–1960*) and sometimes serving as the publicity vehicles for *movements and schools of poetry (such as *Des Imagistes: An Anthology*)

Some anthologies, such as Richard Howard's *Preferences*, include favorite poems chosen by poets (their own or those written by others). And this dictionary contains what might be called a terminological anthology.

ANTI-POEM A text that rebels against the conventions, pretensions, formality, diction, imagery, rhythms, and/or traditions of poetry; a poem in spite of itself (since it can't very well be a non-poem, like a rock or a rutabaga or a jackhammer); a protest or a prank; a parody or send-up of what we think of as a poem; a new kind of poem stripped of fakery, phoniness, and elevated language.

In her poem "Poetry," Marianne Moore remarks, "I, too, dislike it." Nicanor Parra, the Chilean poet and physicist, author of a book called *Anti-Poems*, asserts, "The time has come to bring this ritual up-to-date." He also says, "You can do anything in poetry."

ROLLER COASTER / Nicanor Parra (b. 1914; tr. Miller Williams)

> For half a century
> Poetry was the paradise
> Of the solemn fool.
> Until I came along
> And built my roller coaster.
>
> Go up, if you feel like it.
> It's not my fault if you come down
> Bleeding from your nose and mouth.

APOSTROPHE (uh-pos'-truh-fee; Greek, "turning away") An address, exclamation, or question posed to someone or something, perhaps an absent person (as in a William Wordsworth sonnet, "Milton! thou shouldst be living at this hour") or an abstraction (as in a Wordsworth ode, "O Duty!"). In grammar it is called the vocative, as in "O Rose thou art sick" (William Blake) and "Bright star, would I were steadfast as thou art" (John Keats).

ARGUMENT (Latin, from the verb "to make clear")

1. A prose summary of the plot in a poem or a section of a poem. Each book of John Milton's *Paradise Lost*, for example, begins with a one-paragraph argument. It is similar to a headnote but is generally longer and more of a synopsis.

A

2. The logical sequence of events in a poem. In poetry rooted in rationalism, cause and effect will usually determine the structure of the poem. Argument encompasses narrative (in which it may be the same as the plot), exposition, description, and persuasion. Reacting against the strictures and structures of logic, *Symbolist poets such as Stéphane Mallarmé jettisoned argument from the requirements of poetry. Images became more important in themselves, their connections intuitive and suggested rather than determined by rational connections. Later poets, such as the *Surrealists, sought to explore the unconscious, rejecting logic in the name of psychology.

ARS POETICA (arz' po-et'-ih-cuh; Latin, "the art of poetry") A poem that explores or presents the poet's view of what poetry is and how one should write it. Horace's "The Art of Poetry" is a *verse letter that discusses how to write poems and how to conduct oneself as a poet.

An ars poetica can appear in the guise of prose criticism, like Paul Valéry's *The Art of Poetry*. But poets still use the form in verse, often speaking through *metaphor, as in Norman Dubie's "Ars Poetica." In yet another "Ars Poetica," Archibald MacLeish presents his views in a series of *similes, asserting, for example, that a poem should be "palpable and mute / As a globed fruit." Czeslaw Milosz has written, in more questioning terms, a poem called "Ars Poetica?"

ASSONANCE (ass'-uh-nunce; Latin, "sounding or responding to")

1. The repetition of vowel sounds, like the short "i" repeated in Sylvia Plath's "Strips of tinfoil winking like people" (from "The Bee Meeting," in whose title the long "e" is also assonated). The repetition of consonants is called *alliteration or *consonance.

2. A kind of approximate *rhyme or *slant rhyme that repeats vowels but changes the consonants (*grape/shave, pine/ripe*); also called *vowel rhyme.* Old French and Spanish poetry used assonance regu-

larly in place of rhyme, as in *The Song of Roland* and *The Poem of the Cid*. (*See* RHYME.)

AUBADE (oh-bahd'; French, "dawn poem") A poem set at sunrise, usually about the parting of lovers, like the scene in Act III, Scene V of Shakespeare's *Romeo and Juliet*, in which Juliet says: "Wilt thou be gone? It is not yet near day. / It was the nightingale, and not the lark, / That pierc'd the fearful hollow of thine ear."

AUDIENCE Those who read the poems of a given poet; also those for whom that poet may write. (The two audiences are not necessarily the same.) Walt Whitman asserted, "To have great poets there must be great audiences too."

AUTOMATIC WRITING A process of writing in which the writer does not pause but writes as quickly and unhesitatingly as possible.

Pioneered by the *Surrealists, such as André Breton, it was primarily a means of drawing forth unconscious thoughts, of scaring up mental odds and ends not sorted into rational compartments, of conjuring the disturbing materials of dream and nightmare. In James Merrill's long poem *The Changing Light at Sandover*, the words communicated by the Ouija board (transcribed in capital letters by "DJ," the poet's companion) represent a kind of automatic writing like the words received at a séance—a flow of knowledge from the beyond.

BALLAD (ba'-lud, the "a" pronounced as in "ask"; Latin, "dance") A *song that tells a story; often a *narrative poem in the *ballad stanza. (In popular music, a ballad is a love song played at a slow tempo.)

From 1500 to the early twentieth century, hawkers sold printed broadside ballads at county fairs in England. But more commonly ballads have been sung and passed down by oral tradition. Consequently, they turn up in widely differing versions when copied out or recorded by folk-song collectors. Many Scottish ballads crossed the ocean with settlers who made their homes in the Appalachian Mountains. In an American version of "Barbara Allan," for example, "Sir John Graeme" underwent a name change to "Sweet William" and "Michaelmas" (November 11) became "the merry month of May."

Many poets, imitating the folk tradition, have written literary ballads. Examples include Samuel Taylor Coleridge's "The Rime of the Ancient Mariner," John Keats's "La Belle Dame Sans Merci," Federico Garcia Lorca's *Gypsy Ballads*, Elizabeth Bishop's "The Burglar of Babylon," and Robert Hayden's "The Ballad of Nat Turner."

Although many ballads are written in the *ballad stanza, some appear in different stanzaic forms, sometimes with *refrains or *choruses.

BALLAD STANZA A four-line *stanza in which the first and third lines contain four stresses each and the second and fourth lines contain three stresses each (a pattern of 4-3-4-3) and in which only the even-numbered lines *rhyme (XaXa). "Sir Patrick Spence," which follows, is written in ballad stanzas.

If the first and third lines rhyme as well, this stanza is called the *hymn stanza, common meter,* or *common measure (abab).* The hymn stanza is more regularly *iambic, while the ballad stanza is looser. In practice, however, ballads can be written in the hymn stanza and hymns in the ballad stanza.

Several variations may appear in ballad stanzas. Sometimes the fourth stress from line one or three (or both) is omitted so the line ends on an unstressed syllable. Sometimes *internal rhyme appears in line one or three (or both) so the second and fourth stresses rhyme, as in this stanza from Samuel Taylor Coleridge's "The Rime of the Ancient Mariner":

In mist or cloud, on mast or shroud,	aa
It perched for vespers nine;	b
Whiles all the night, through fog-smoke white,	cc
Glimmered the white Moon-shine.	b

Long meter consists of four tetrameter lines (stressed 4-4-4-4). *Short meter* is primarily trimeter, except for line three, which is tetrameter (stressed 3-3-4-3). (*See* DIPODICS and FOURTEENERS.)

	Ballad Stanza		**Hymn Stanza**	
Line	Stresses	Rhyme	Stresses	Rhyme
1	4	none	4	*a*
2	3	*a*	3	*b*
3	4	none	4	*a*
4	3	*a*	3	*b*
	(loose iambics)		(strict iambics)	

SIR PATRICK SPENCE / Anonymous

The kings sits in Dumferling town,
    Drinking the blood-red wine:
O where will I get a good sailor
    To sail this ship of mine?

Up and spake an elder knight,
    Sat at the king's right knee:
Sir Patrick Spence is the best sailor
    That sails upon the sea.

The king has written a braid letter
    And sign'd it wi' his hand;
And sent it to Sir Patrick Spence,
    Was walking on the sand.

The first line that Sir Patrick read,
    A loud laugh laughèd he:
The next line that Sir Patrick read,
    The tear blinded his e'e.

O who is this has done this deed,
    This ill deed done to me;
To send me out this time o' the year,
    To sail upon the sea?

Make haste, make haste, my merry men all,
    Our good ship sails the morn.
O say not so, my master dear,
    For I fear a deadly storm.

Late, late yest're'en I saw the new moon
    Wi' the old moon in her arm;
And I fear, I fear, my dear master,
    That we will come to harm.

O our Scots nobles were right loath
    To wet their cork-heel'd shoon;

But lang o'er a' the play were play'd,
   Their hats they swam aboon.

O lang, lang may their ladies sit
   Wi' their fans into their hand,
O ere they see Sir Patrick Spence
   Come sailing to the land.

O lang, lang may their ladies stand
   Wi' their gold combs in their hair,
Waiting for their own dear lords,
   For they'll see them no mair.

Half o'er, half o'er to Aberdour,
   It's fifty fadom deep:
And there lies good Sir Patrick Spence,
   Wi' the Scots lords at his feet.

NOTE: *braid*: long, broad; *e'e*: eye; *shoon*: shoes; *aboon*: above; *Aberdour*: Aberdeen, Scotland; *fadom*: fathoms.

BALLADE (buh-lahd'; Latin, "dance") A French fixed form, first popular in the fourteenth century in Europe, consisting of three *stanzas rhymed *ababbcbC* and an *envoi* ("send-off," a kind of coda or postscript) rhymed *bcbC* (the capital letter indicating a refrain).

Through an entire ballade, there are only three different rhyme sounds. The French poet and thief, François Villon, is a master of the ballade, as is the English poet Geoffrey Chaucer. Because of its intricate rhyming and refrains, the form is now often considered most suitable for *light verse, but Villon's ballades demonstrate the great potential for intensity and passion. In our time, Marilyn Hacker has excelled in the form.

Although titled a "ballad" by the translator, Villon's poem below is really a ballade. (*See* UBI SUNT.)

B

THE BALLAD OF DEAD LADIES / François Villon
(1431–1463?; tr. Dante Gabriel Rossetti)

Tell me now in what hidden way is
    Lady Flora the lovely Roman?
Where's Hipparchia, and where is Thais,
    Neither of them the fairer woman?
    Where is Echo, beheld of no man,
Only heard on river and mere,—
    She whose beauty was more than human? ...
But where are the snows of yester-year?

Where's Héloise, the learned nun,
    For whose sake Abeillard, I ween,
Lost manhood and put priesthood on?
    (From Love he won such dule and teen!)
    And where, I pray you, is the Queen
Who willed that Buridan should steer
    Sewed in a sack's mouth down the Seine? ...
But where are the snows of yester-year?

White Queen Blanche, like a queen of lilies,
    With a voice like any mermaiden,—
Bertha Broadfoot, Beatrice, Alice,
    And Ermengarde the lady of Maine,—
    And that good Joan whom Englishmen
At Rouen doomed and burned her there,—
    Mother of God, where are they then? ...
But where are the snows of yester-year?

Nay, never ask this week, fair lord,
    Where they are gone, nor yet this year,
Save with thus much for an overword,—
    But where are the snows of yester-year?

BEAT (also called *accent* or *stress*) Emphasis on a particular syllable. A three-beat line (such as Theodore Roethke's "The hand that held my wrist" from "My Papa's Waltz") contains three accents or stresses (*hand*, *held*, and *wrist*). (*See* SCANSION.)

BEAT POETRY An anti-academic school of poetry that sprang up in the fifties in San Francisco; characterized by fast-paced, associative free verse, a resemblance to jazz, a debt to Walt Whitman, a free-spirited attitude, and irreverent and slangy language.

Beat poetry is best known in the poems of Allen Ginsberg, Gregory Corso, Lawrence Ferlinghetti, and Gary Snyder and in the fiction and poetry of Jack Kerouac. Ferlinghetti's City Lights and James Laughlin's New Directions have been the movement's chief publishers. The term *beat* (popularized as the cartoonish "beatnik") may mean "worn-out" or "beatific," or it may refer to a rhythmic beat, as in the pulse and improvisations of jazz.

The following poem by Allen Ginsberg pays homage to poets Walt Whitman and Federico Garcia Lorca. Although it's presented as a series of prose paragraphs, those paragraphs are cadenced like the long lines of Whitman, with their "enumerations," and like Ginsberg's other oratorical poems, such as "Howl" and "Sunflower Sutra."

A SUPERMARKET IN CALIFORNIA / Allen Ginsberg (1926–1997)

What thoughts I have of you tonight, Walt Whitman, for I walked down the sidestreets under the trees with a headache self-conscious looking at the full moon.

In my hungry fatigue, and shopping for images, I went into the neon fruit supermarket, dreaming of your enumerations!

What peaches and what penumbras! Whole families shopping at night! Aisles full of husbands! Wives in the avocados, babies in the tomatoes!—and you, Garcia Lorca, what were you doing down by the watermelons?

B

I saw you, Walt Whitman, childless, lonely old grubber, poking among the meats in the refrigerator and eyeing the grocery boys.

I heard you asking questions of each: Who killed the pork chops? What price bananas? Are you my Angel?

I wandered in and out of the brilliant stacks of cans following you, and followed in my imagination by the store detective.

We strode down the open corridors together in our solitary fancy tasting artichokes, possessing every frozen delicacy, and never passing the cashier.

Where are we going, Walt Whitman? The doors close in an hour. Which way does your beard point tonight?

(I touch your book and dream of our odyssey in the supermarket and feel absurd.)

Will we walk all night through solitary streets? The trees add shade to shade, lights out in the houses, we'll both be lonely.

Will we stroll dreaming of the lost America of love past blue automobiles in driveways, home to our silent cottage?

Ah, dear father, graybeard, lonely old courage-teacher, what America did you have when Charon quit poling his ferry and you got out on a smoking bank and stood watching the boat disappear on the black waters of Lethe?

Berkeley 1955

BIBLICAL VERSE (also called *Hebraic verse*) Long-lined, unmetrical verse whose *prosody is governed by rhetorical devices, such as the repetition and variation of words and phrases, and by the use of synonyms and antonyms, likenesses and opposites, parallels and antitheses. It appears primarily in the Old Testament of the Bible. (*See* FREE VERSE *and* PSALM.)

Repetition gives the verse power and cohesiveness, while the departure from metrical regularity lets the lines ebb and flow, as in these lines from "The Song of Solomon":

> I am the rose of Sharon, and the lily of the valleys.
>
> As the lily among thorns, so is my love among the daughters.
>
> As the apple-tree among the trees of the wood, so is my beloved among the sons. I sat down under his shadow with great delight, and his fruit was sweet to my taste.
>
> He brought me to the banqueting house, and his banner over me was love.
>
> Stay me with flagons, comfort me with apples: for I am sick of love.
>
> His left hand is under my head, and his right hand doth embrace me.
>
> I charge you, O ye daughters of Jerusalem, by the roes, and by the hinds of the field, that ye stir not up, nor awake my love, till he please.

Walt Whitman depends upon Biblical verse throughout *Leaves of Grass*. Christopher Smart (1722–1771) imitates it in "For I will consider my Cat Jeoffry":

> For he is of the tribe of Tiger.
>
> For the Cherub Cat is a term of the Angel Tiger.
>
> For he has the subtlety and hissing of a serpent, which in goodness he suppresses.
>
> For he will not do destruction if he is well-fed, neither will he spit without provocation.
>
> For he purrs in thankfulness when God tells him he's a good Cat.
>
> For he is an instrument for the children to learn benevolence upon.
>
> For every house is incomplete without him, and a blessing is lacking in the spirit.
>
> (lines 724–730 from *Jubilate Agno*)

BLACK MOUNTAIN SCHOOL A group of poets associated with Black Mountain College, an experimental school in North Carolina, in the 1950s. Much of their early work appeared in *Origin* and *The Black Mountain Review*.

Although the poems of Robert Creeley, Denise Levertov, Charles Olson, and Robert Duncan are very different, they share a belief in what Levertov calls "organic form" (a "sense of seeking out inherent, though not immediately apparent, form," as opposed to the use of "prescribed forms") and a preference for *free verse. They were influenced by William Carlos Williams, Ezra Pound, and Objectivist poets such as Louis Zukofsky. Charles Olson formulated the group's central poetic theory in an essay, "Projective Verse," which insisted that the poet's breath determined the rhythms of a poem, and that the page was an open space in which the poet could transcribe those breath rhythms, a process called "composition by field" or "open composition." Projective verse aims to be a process of registering perception directly on the page, during composition, rather than drawing on previous observations and established forms.

I KNOW A MAN / Robert Creeley (1926–2005)

> As I sd to my
> friend, because I am
> always talking,— John, I
>
> sd, which was not his
> name, the darkness sur-
> rounds us, what
>
> can we do against
> it, or else, shall we &
> why not, buy a goddamn big car,
>
> drive, he sd, for
> christ's sake, look
> out where yr going.

ONE A.M. / Denise Levertov (1923–1997)

The kitchen patio in snowy
moonlight.   That
snowsilence, that
abandon to stillness.
The sawhorse, the concrete
washtub, snowblue. The washline
bowed under its snowfur!
Moon has silenced
the crickets, the summer frogs
hold their breath.
Summer night, summer night, standing
one-legged, a crane
in the snowmarsh, staring
at snowmoon!

LA CHUTE / Charles Olson (1910–1970)

my drum, hollowed out thru the thin slit,
carved from the cedar wood, the base I took
when the tree was felled

o my lute, wrought from the tree's crown

my drum, whose lustiness
was not to be resisted

                my lute,
from whose pulsations
not one could turn away

                They
are where the dead are, my drum fell
where the dead are, who
will bring it up, my lute
who will bring it up where it fell in the face of them
where they are, where my lute and drum have fallen?

NOTE: *la chute:* fall.

BLANK VERSE Unrhymed *iambic pentameter, invented in sixteenth-century England by the Earl of Surrey for his translation of two books of Virgil's epic *The Aeneid*.

Instead of trying to translate Virgil's Latin into unrhymed *dactylic hexameter lines, like the original's, Surrey shortened the line from six to five feet, a more natural length for English, and used iambs instead of dactyls. So much was not new. Gavin Douglas had already translated the entire epic into *heroic couplets. Surrey, who owes much to Douglas' version, kept the iambic pentameter but omitted the rhymes. The result was blank verse. William Shakespeare and Christopher Marlowe made it great in their plays, establishing Surrey's invention as one of the most important forms in English poetry.

Blank verse is flexible, not bound by the recurring sound effects and structural webbing of rhyme. It is an effective form for talk (as in the monologues of Robert Browning) and storytelling (as in the narratives of Robert Frost), the human voice conversing. It started with a translation of a Latin epic but made possible an original epic in English, John Milton's *Paradise Lost*. And, perhaps because of the importance of blank-verse soliloquy in Elizabethan drama, it underlies some of the best meditative poetry by William Wordsworth and Wallace Stevens.

from *THE AENEID, BOOK TWO* / Virgil (tr. Henry Howard, Earl of Surrey, ca. 1517–1547)

> The Grekes chieftains, all irked with the war
> Wherein they wasted had so many years
> And oft repulst by fatal destinie,
> A huge hors made, hye raised like a hill,
> By the divine science of Minerva;
> Of cloven firre compacted were his ribbs;
> For their return a fained sacrifice,
> The fame whereof so wandred it at point.
> In the dark bulk they closde bodies of men
> Chosen by lot, and did enstuff by stealth
> The hollow womb with armed soldiars.

There stands in sight an isle hight Tenedon,
Rich and of fame while Priams kingdom stood:
Now but a bay, and rode unsure for ship.
Hether them secretly the Grekes withdrew,
Shrouding themselves under the desert shore.
And, wening we they had ben fled and gone,
And with that winde had fet the land of Grece,
Troye discharged her long continue dole.
The gates cast up, we issued out to play,
The Grekish camp desirous to behold,
The places void and the forsaken costes.
Here Pyrrhus band, there ferce Achilles pight,
Here rode their shippes, there did their battels joyne.
Astonnied some the scathefull gift beheld,
Behight by vow unto the chaste Minerve,
All wondring at the hugenesse of the horse.

(lines 18–44)

NOTE: Aeneas, the Trojan warrior and refugee who would eventually lead his followers to Italy and establish the city of Rome, is telling the story of the Trojan horse. The final *-ed* of verbs should be pronounced. "Soldiars" consists of three sylables here: *sol'-di-ars.*

Minerva: Roman goddess of wisdom (Athena to the Greeks); *firre:* fir; *fained:* feigned; *enstuff:* furnish with soldiers; *hight:* named, called; *rode:* harbor; *hether:* hither; *wening:* thinking; *fet:* arrived at; *dole:* sorrow, grief; *Pyrrhus and Achilles:* Greek heroes; *pight:* pitched camp; *scathefull:* harmful, injurious; *behight:* promised.

from *THE TEMPEST* / William Shakespeare (1564–1616)

Our revels now are ended. These our actors,
As I foretold you, were all spirits and
Are melted into air, into thin air;
And, like the baseless fabric of this vision,
The cloud-capp'd towers, the gorgeous palaces,
The solemn temples, the great globe itself,
Yea, all which it inherit, shall dissolve,
And, like this insubstantial pageant faded,
Leave not a rack behind. We are such stuff
As dreams are made on, and our little life

Is rounded with a sleep. Sir, I am vex'd.

Bear with my weakness. My old brain is troubled.

Be not disturb'd with my infirmity.

If you be pleas'd, retire into my cell

And there repose. A turn or two I'll walk

To still my beating mind.

(Act IV, Scene I, lines 148–163)

NOTE: The speaker is Prospero, the magician and rightful Duke of Milan who rules the island where the castaways land in the play. See FRAGMENTATION for "Soul Says," a poem by Jorie Graham in the voice of Prospero.

A trimeter line, like the last one here, may occasionally be used in a passage otherwise in pentameter, whether rhymed or not. John Milton uses the variation effectively in "Lycidas." However, Prospero's last line of trimeter is followed by an indented two-foot line, spoken by Ferdinand and Miranda, completing the pentameter: "We wish your peace." This technique of completing iambic pentameter lines by indenting the continuations (often, in plays, spoken by different characters) also occurs in lyric poems such as the sonnet, "The Troll's Nosegay," by Robert Graves. The stepwise appearance resembles the *triadic line invented by William Carlos Williams.

BLASON (blay'-zun; German, "shield"; also *blazon*) 1. A love poem that lists the beauties of the beloved. Sir Philip Sidney's "Pyrocles Praises Philoclea" begins, "What tongue can her perfections tell / In whose each part all tongues may dwell?" The opposite is a *contre-blason (con'-tra-blay'-zun)*, a catalogue of ugliness, like Sidney's "A Contreblason," which ends "As for those parts unknown, which hidden sure are best, / Happy be they which well believe, and never seek the rest." Shakespeare's Sonnet 130 (which appears in SONNET) is a contreblason.

2. A poem composed in lines of eight to ten syllables, concluding with an *epigram, on a theme of praise or blame, usually about a single part of a woman's body. The term comes from 1536, when French poet Clément Marot wrote his "Blason de Beau Tétin" ("Blason of a Beautiful Nipple").

BLUES An African-American song form, derived from the field hollers of slaves in the South. It can refer either loosely to a song about being blue, about loss and hard times, or more specifically to a song in three-line blues form, in which the first two lines are roughly identical and the third line rhymes with them.

W.C. Handy, who popularized the form, discovered the blues while touring with his Knights of Pythias Band in the Mississippi Delta around 1903. His "St. Louis Blues" (1914) begins:

> I hate to see de evenin' sun go down,
> Hate to see de evenin' sun go down,
> 'Cause ma baby, he done lef dis town.

In "New St. Louis Blues," the poet Sterling A. Brown updates the story, writing about a "Market Street woman noted fuh to have dark days."

Langston Hughes was a pioneer in adapting the musical form to poetry, dividing each blues line into two shorter lines so his blues stanza contains six lines instead of three. His rhymes come at the end of even-numbered lines.

Sherley Anne Williams varies this way of writing out the blues, staggering her lines in "Any Woman's Blues" so a single line breaks into halves:

> Soft lamp shinin
>   and me alone in the night.

Her stanzas contain three of these two-part lines.

In his "Con/tin/u/way/shun Blues," Etheridge Knight quotes Mary Helen Washington, who says, "Blues are more than cries of oppression." He then continues:

> They say the blues is just a slave song
> But I say that's just a lie
> Cause even when we be free, baby—
> Lord knows we still have got to die
>   lovers will still lie
>   babies will still cry

One way to vary the blues form is to make the second line rhyme differently from the first (as in the third stanza of Sandra McPherson's

"Bad Mother Blues," which is included below). Another is to omit the repeated line, which is essentially what Knight does in the example above. (Like Hughes, he splits the blues line into two shorter ones.) Knight also adds two indented, even shorter lines, a kind of coda, to the stanza, the way a blues singer might improvise extra phrases and rhymes before continuing to the next verse.

MORNING AFTER / Langston Hughes (1902–1967)

I was so sick last night I
Didn't hardly know my mind.
So sick last night I
Didn't hardly know my mind.
I drunk some bad licker that
Almost made me blind.

Had a dream last night I
Thought I was in hell.
I drempt last night I
Thought I was in hell.
Woke up and looked around me—
Baby, your mouth was open like a well.

I said, Baby! Baby!
Please don't snore so loud.
Baby! Please!
Please don't snore so loud.
You jest like a little bit o' woman but you
Sound like a great big crowd.

BAD MOTHER BLUES / Sandra McPherson (b. 1943)

When you were arrested, child, and I had to take
        your pocketknife
When you were booked and I had to confiscate
        your pocketknife
It had blood on it from where you'd tried to take your life

It was the night before Thanksgiving, all the family
coming over
The night before Thanksgiving, all the family coming over
We had to hide your porno magazine and put your
handcuffs undercover

Each naked man looked at you, said, Baby who do you
think you are
Each man looked straight down on you, like a waiting
astronomer's star
Solely, disgustedly, each wagged his luster

I've decided to throw horror down the well and wish on it
Decided I'll throw horror down the well and wish on it
And up from the water will shine my sweet girl in her
baby bonnet

A thief will blind you with his flashlight
                    but a daughter be your bouquet
A thief will blind you with his flashlight
                    but a daughter be your bouquet
When the thief's your daughter you turn your eyes the
other way

I'm going into the sunflower field where all of them
are facing me
I'm going into the sunflower field so all of them are
facing me
Going to go behind the sunflowers, feel all the sun that
I can't see

BOB AND WHEEL A five-line stanza, rhymed *ababa*, in which the first line (the "bob") contains one or two metrical stresses and each of the next four lines (the "wheel") contains three. A bob may also occur by itself as a *refrain—what George Saintsbury calls a "short-line pivot."

B

The stanza occurs in Middle English poetry, most notably in the anonymous *Sir Gawain and the Green Knight*. In each section of this long narrative poem, the bob and wheel serve as the "tail" at the end of a series of unrhymed lines written in Anglo-Saxon *alliterative meter. The last alliterative line is *enjambed into the bob, which rhymes with the second and fourth lines of the wheel that follows. Each line of the wheel contains *alliteration. Here is John Gardner's translation of the eighth section of Part Two of *Sir Gawain and the Green Knight* (Anonymous, fourteenth century). The last five lines form the bob and wheel:

> He struck the steed with his spurs and sprang on his way
> So swiftly that Gringolet's shoes struck fire on the stone;
> And all who saw that sweet knight sighed in their hearts,
> And each man there said the same to every other,
> Grieving for that knight: "By Christ, it's sad
> That you, lad, must be lost, so noble in life!
> It would not be easy to find this man's equal on earth.
> It would have been wiser to work more warily;
> We might one day have made him a mighty duke,
> A glowing lord of the people in his land;
> Far better that than broken like this into nothing,
> Beheaded by an elf for undue pride.
> Who ever heard of a king who'd hear the counsel
> Of addle-pated knights during Christmas games?"
> Many were the warm tears that watered their eyes
> When that handsome hero rode from the high hall
>   that day.   ◀— bob
>   He paused at no abode   ⎫
>   But swiftly went his way   ⎬ wheel
>   Down many a devious road,   ⎭
>   As all the old books say.

BURNS STANZA (also called *habbie stanza, Scottish stanza*) A six-line *stanza rhyming *aaabab*, with a metrical count of 4-4-4-2-4-2 feet (or accents) for the six lines.

The stanza was a favorite of the Scottish poet Robert Burns. The four *a* rhymes in each stanza require some virtuosity, and the two shorter lines give each stanza a neat musical flip, a quickening, at its end. Here is the opening stanza of Burns's "To a Mouse, on Turning Her Up in Her Nest, with the Plough, November, 1785":

> Wee, sleeket, cowran, tim'rous beastie,
> O, what a panic's in thy breastie!
> Thou need na start awa sae hasty,
> > Wi' bickering brattle!
> I wad be laith to rin an' chase thee,
> > Wi' murd'ring pattle!

NOTE: *sleeket*: sleek; *cowran*: cowering; *na*: not; *brattle*: clatter, hurry; *wad*: would; *rin*: run; *pattle*: spade used to clean a plough.

CADENCE (kay'-dunce; Latin, "falling") The rising and falling of spoken language, the rhythmic shape made by a flow of words.

Cadence may consist of either the alternation of stressed and unstressed syllables or the swelling and subsiding of phrases. *Rhythm is the pattern made by these cadences. When Ezra Pound discusses composing "in the sequence of the musical phrase, not in sequence of a metronome," he is arguing for the rhythmic primacy of cadence. Though the term has musical associations, it also applies to conversation. Although cadence is necessarily present in metrical verse (as it is in prose and speech), it is crucial to free verse, especially in long lines like those of Walt Whitman's poetry, which is sometimes called *cadenced verse*. Here is a stanza from his "Out of the Cradle Endlessly Rocking":

> The aria sinking,
> All else continuing, the stars shining,
> The winds blowing, the notes of the bird continuous echoing,
> With angry moans the fierce old mother incessantly moaning,
> On the sands of Paumanok's shore gray and rustling,
> The yellow half-moon enlarged, sagging down, drooping,
>   the face of the sea almost touching,
> The boy ecstatic, with his bare feet the waves, with his
>   hair the atmosphere dallying,
> The love in the heart long pent, now loose, now at last tu-
>   multuously bursting,

The aria's meaning, the ears, the soul, swiftly depositing,
The strange tears down the cheeks coursing,
The colloquy there, the trio, each uttering,
The undertone, the savage old mother incessantly crying,
To the boy's soul's questions sullenly timing, some drown'd
    secret hissing,
To the outsetting bard.

The cadences vary, depending on the phrase lengths, from a single isolated word ("drooping") to a whole uninterrupted line ("On the sands of Paumanok's shore gray and rustling"). In this passage, as in much of Whitman's verse, the commas neatly delineate many of the cadences. In short-lined *free verse, however, a cadence may be interrupted by a *line break (an effect called *enjambment* or "run-on line"). In metrical verse, cadence will be joined and perhaps controlled by *meter (a regular pattern of stressed and unstressed syllables). Here is the opening stanza of William Wordsworth's "Resolution and Independence":

There was a roaring in the wind all night;
The rain came heavily and fell in floods;
But now the sun is rising calm and bright;
The birds are singing in the distant woods;
Over his own sweet voice the Stock-dove broods;
The Jay makes answer as the Magpie chatters;
And all the air is filled with pleasant noise of waters.

The first six lines are *iambic pentameter (a pattern of five feet, each consisting of an unstressed and a stressed syllable); the last line is hexameter (one extra foot); the rhyme scheme is *ababbcc.* There is considerable rhythmic variety from line to end-stopped line (because the heavier stresses fall in different places and the natural cadences vary), but the iambic meter is powerful and controlling in itself; cadence serves at the meter's pleasure.

In the absence of rhyme and meter, cadence simply becomes more noticeable. Cadence and line breaks are the chief compositional tools of the free-verse poet—along with rhetorical devices such as *anaphora (repetition of the first word or phrase in successive lines).

CAESURA (sih-zhoor'-uh or sih-zoor'-uh; Latin, "cut") A pause or break in the middle of a line; marked with ‖ when scanning a poem. The caesura in each of these lines from Shakespeare's Sonnet 18 is indicated by a comma:

> So long as men can breathe, or eyes can see,
> So long lives this, and this gives life to thee.

Poets composing in *iambic pentameter usually try to vary the place where the caesura occurs from line to line. There can be, of course, more than one in a line, and some lines seem to rush along without much of a pause at all. But the absence of punctuation does not necessarily mean there is no caesura. In the first line of the same sonnet—"Shall I compare thee to a summer's day?"—there is a slight pause after "thee."

CANTO (can'-toe; Italian, "song"; the Italian plural is "canti," but in English "cantos" is acceptable) A section or chapter in a larger poem, like the one hundred cantos of Dante Alighieri's *The Divine Comedy*.

Edmund Spenser's *allegorical epic, *The Faerie Queen*, consists of six books, each divided into twelve cantos. Alexander Pope's *The Rape of the Lock* and Lord Byron's *Don Juan* are also divided into cantos. Ezra Pound's major work, an epic in search of its form, never found a title beyond the provisional one, *The Cantos*. But as a title for a work seeking a Confucian order beneath the apparent fragmentation of modern consciousness, it is fitting, like a novel called *The Chapters*.

CANZONE (can-zoh'-nee, can-zone' or cahn-tsoh'-nay; Italian, "song") An Italian lyric form of varying length, metrical patterns, and rhyme schemes, intended to be set to music and appropriate for serious subjects like beauty, valor, love, and virtue.

Dante, who called the canzone "a composition of words set to music," divided the canzone into two parts, the "head" and the "tail," but he further divided the head into two formally identical parts, making the form both two- and three-part. Stanza length varies from seven to twenty lines. Lines usually contain seven or eleven syllables.

It often concludes with a *commiato* (valediction). According to Dana Gioia, the canzone "tends to be lyric and obsessive."

One early canzone, "Within the Gentle Heart" by Guido Guinizelli (c. 1235–1276), exerted a powerful influence on the Italian poets, including Dante, who followed him. Here, in Dante Gabriel Rossetti's translation, is the first of Guido's six stanzas, each one rhymed *ababcdcede*, with an *accentual-syllabic pattern of 5-5-5-5-3-5-3-5-3-5 in its ten lines:

> Within the gentle heart Love shelters him
> As birds within the green shade of the grove.
> Before the gentle heart, in nature's scheme,
> Love was not, nor the gentle heart ere Love.
> For with the sun, at once,
> So sprang the light immediately; nor was
> Its birth before the sun's.
> And Love hath his effect in gentleness
> Of very self; even as
> Within the middle fire the heat's excess.

Although the form of a canzone can vary widely, two particular patterns deserve mention. The first, taken from a canzone by Dante Alighieri ("*Amor, tu vedi ben che questa donna*," or "Love, very well you notice how this woman"), is now considered the fixed form of the canzone in English. It resembles the *sestina, in that end-words, not rhymes, are repeated in a circular pattern. There are five twelve-line stanzas, using five end-words in a fixed pattern, with a six-line tornada. (*See the chart below.*) Later poets, such as W.H. Auden, John Ashbery, and Marilyn Hacker, in poems called "Canzone," have used a tornada of five lines—one for each end-word. In Dante's first stanza, translated here by Joseph Tusiani, the word "Love" refers to Cupid or Eros:

> Love, very well you notice how this woman
> scorns and ignores your power all the time,
> deeming herself the only lovely woman.
> Oh, since she saw she was my only woman,

for this your ray that fills my face with light,
she was more cruelty than she was woman,
so that her heart, no more a heart of woman,
is that of some wild beast, hateful and cold;
for, though the weather be quite warm or cold,
with these my eyes I only see a woman
carved not of flesh but of a lovely stone
by the most skillful artisan of stone.

Here is the pattern of end-words that Dante uses (the Italian originals are *donna*, *tempo*, *luce*, *freddo*, and *petra*):

Line	Stanza 1	Stanza 2	Stanza 3	Stanza 4	Stanza 5	Tornada
1	woman	stone	cold	light	time	woman
2	time	woman	stone	cold	light	stone
3	woman	stone	cold	light	time	cold
4	woman	stone	cold	light	time	cold
5	light	time	woman	stone	cold	light
6	woman	stone	cold	light	time	time
7	woman	stone	cold	light	time	
8	cold	light	time	woman	stone	
9	cold	light	time	woman	stone	
10	woman	stone	cold	light	time	
11	stone	cold	light	time	woman	
12	stone	cold	light	time	woman	

A different pattern appears in a *canzon* form invented by the twelfth-century Provençal poet Arnaut Daniel. He uses isolated rhyme, called *rimas dissolutas (reé'-mahs dee-so-loo'-tahs)*, so that a rhyme word does not recur within a stanza but appears in succeeding stanzas. All the first lines of different stanzas, for example, use the same rhyme. Ezra Pound's translation of the first two stanzas of Arnaut's "Canzon: Of the Trades and Love" shows the pattern:

Though this measure quaint confine me,   a
And I chip out words and plane them,   b
    They shall yet be true and clear   c

When I finally have filed them.	d
Love glosses and gilds them knowing	e
That my song has for its start	f
One who is worth's hold and warrant.	g
Each day finer I refine me	a
And my cult and service strain them	b
Toward the world's best, as ye hear,	c
"Hers" my root and tip have styled them.	d
And though bitter winds come blowing,	e
The love that rains down in my heart	f
Warmeth me when frost's abhorrent.	g

The next four stanzas continue the pattern (the first lines, for example, rhyming "resign me," "entwine me," "assign me," and "malign me"). The *tornada* uses the rhymes of the last three lines of the stanza: "doing," "ox-cart," and "torrent." Sylvia Plath's "Black Rook in Rainy Weather" is a twentieth-century poem that uses *rimas dissolutas*.

Canzone 1 Each letter represents the same word repeated:	**Canzone 2** Each letter represents a rhyme (which repeats from stanza to stanza):
Stanza 1: ABAACAADDAEE	Stanza 1: *abcdefg*
Stanza 2: EAEEBEECCEDD	Stanza 2: *abcdefg*
Stanza 3: DEDDADDBBDCC	Stanza 3: *abcdefg*
Stanza 4: CDCCECCAACBB	Stanza 4: *abcdefg*
Stanza 5: BCBBDBBEEBAA	Stanza 5: *abcdefg*
Tornada: AEDCB	Stanza 6: *abcdefg*
	Tornada: *efg*
(used by Dante, who adds a line in the tornada: AEDDCB)	(used by Arnaut Daniel)

CARMEN (car'-men; Latin, "song"; plural *carmina*, car-meen'-uh)
A lyric poem or song in Latin, such as the carmina of Catullus. (*See* TRANSLATION *for several versions of his Carmen 85.*)

CAROL (Greek, "choral dance") Generally, a song of joy or praise, such as a Christmas carol.

More specifically, it is a form in which early English carols were composed. It consists of four-line stanzas rhymed *aaab*. Usually the rhymes of the first three lines change from stanza to stanza, while the *b* rhyme remains the same throughout the carol, so several stanzas will rhyme *aaab cccb dddb*, etc. Furthermore, these recurring *b* rhymes can be alternating *refrains, and those refrains can precede the carol as a rhymed *couplet. However, in the following three stanzas taken from an anonymous carol, the *a* lines rhyme together from stanza to stanza, and the *b* lines are not refrains:

> Now is Yole comen wyth gentil chere—
> Of myrthe and gamen he hath no pere;
> In every lond wher he cometh nere
>   Is myrthe and gamen, I dar wel seye.
>
> Now is comen a messager
> Of thy lord, Sir Newe Yeer;
> Biddeth us alle ben myrie heer
>   And make as myrie as we may.
>
> Ther-fore every man that is heer
> Synge a carole on his manere;
> If he can non we shullen him lere,
>   So that we ben myrie alwey.

NOTE: *lere*: teach.

CATALEXIS, CATALECTIC (cat'-uh-lex'-iss, -lek'-tik; Greek, "left off") The omission of one or more unstressed syllables at the end or at the beginning of a metrical line; also called *truncation*.

In William Blake's "The Tyger," the last *foot of each *trochaic tetrameter line is catalectic:

Týgĕr, | týgĕr, | búrnĭng | bríght

By contrast, Henry Wadsworth Longfellow's *Hiawatha* retains the final unstressed syllable in its trochaic tetrameter and is called *acatalectic* (metrically complete, with no syllables omitted from the pattern):

Bý thĕ | shí-nĭng | bíg sĕa | wá-tĕr

If two unstressed syllables are omitted from a final foot in *dactylic meter, the foot is more properly called *brachycatalectic* (the Greek prefix *brachy-*, meaning "short").

In *iambic meter, catalexis can occur in the first foot, cutting off the initial unstressed syllable. Such a line is also called *headless*.

If a syllable is added to a metrical line, the line is *hypermetric*, as in the *feminine ending in iambic meter:

Tŏ bé | ŏr nót | tŏ bé: | thăt ís | thĕ qués- ti̇̆on.

The extra syllable is not counted as a separate foot, nor is it part of the fifth foot.

If an unstressed syllable is prefixed to a line of trochaic meter (whether catalectic or not), the addition is called *anacrusis*, as in the second of the following catalectic lines (also from Blake's "The Tyger"):

Whát ĭm-| mórtăl | hánd ŏr | éye

[̆]
Cŏuld fráme thy̆ | féarfŭl | sým-mĕ-| trý?

CENTO (sen'-toe; Latin, "patchwork") A poem made up of passages from poems by one or more authors; a patchwork of quotations; a literary collage; a pastiche (in the sense of being a mixture of poetic excerpts).

Originally a cento was composed entirely of quotations from a single source, in particular the works of the Roman poet Virgil. Although it began as a game for scholars, it has become an *allusive, postmodernist, intertextual form, as in John Ashbery's "To a Waterfowl" and Charles Tomlinson's "A Biography of the Author: A Cento." The end of T.S. Eliot's *The Waste Land*, with its barrage of quoted fragments, becomes a cento. Marianne Moore's liberal interpolation of quotations in her poems is similar in method. (*See* FOUND POEM, OULIPO, *and* PARODY.)

CHANCE POETRY (also called *aleatory poetry*) Poetry written using chance methods, such as words written on cards and drawn at random to furnish an order for a poem's vocabulary. The leading American proponents of chance poetry have been Jackson MacLow and John Cage (an important avant-garde composer who also experimented with chance methods, or indeterminacy, in music).

Surrealists invented a game called *cadavre exquis* (French, "exquisite corpse") in which a player fills in an assigned grammatical blank in a sentence without knowing what words others have contributed—similar to the American game Mad Libs.

One of the easiest ways to use chance as a stimulus for writing poems is to open a dictionary—or any book—at random and put your finger on a word, and then incorporate that word, along with other strokes of luck, into a poem.

To write the following poem on the assassination of Robert F. Kennedy, Donald Justice chose words and grammatical indicators, wrote them on cards, and drew them randomly as he composed his lines. To write a series of poems on several Presidents of the United States, Jackson MacLow assigned the Phoenician meanings of the alphabet to letters of the Presidents' names and developed the poems from what came up. Here is the alphabetical key: A (ox), B (house), C (camel), D (door), E (window or Look!), F (hook), H (fence), I (hand), K (palm of the hand), L (ox-goad), M (water), N (fish), O (eye), P (mouth), Q (knot), R (head), S (tooth), T (mark), V (hook), X (prop), Y (hook), and Z (weapon). Letters developed after the Phoenicians include G (camel), J (hand), U (hook), and W (hooks).

THE ASSASSINATION / Donald Justice (1925–2004)

It begins again, the nocturnal pulse.
It courses through the cables laid for it.
It mounts to the chandeliers and beats there, hotly.
We are too close. Too late, we would move back.
We are involved with the surge.

Now it bursts. Now it has been announced.
Now it is being soaked up by newspapers.
Now it is running through the streets.
The crowd has it. The woman selling carnations
And the man in the straw hat stand with it in their shoes.

Here is the red marquee it sheltered under,
Here is the ballroom, here
The sadly various orchestra led
By a single gesture. My arms open.
It enters. Look, we are dancing.

June 5, 1968

from THE PRESIDENTS OF THE UNITED STATES
OF AMERICA / Jackson MacLow (1922–2004)

1789

George Washington never owned a camel
but he looked thru the eyes in his head
with a camel's calm and wary look.

Hooks that wd irritate an ox
held his teeth together
and he cd build a fence with his own hands
tho he preferred to go fishing
as anyone else wd
while others did the work *for* him
for tho he had no camels he had slaves enough
and probably made them toe the mark by keeping an eye
    on them
for *he* wd never have stood for anything fishy.

1801

Marked by no fence
farther than an eye cd see
beyond the big waters

57

Thomas Jefferson saw grass enough for myriads of oxen
to grind between their teeth.

His farmer hands itched
when he thought of all that vacant land and looked about
    for a way to hook it in for us
until something unhooked a window in his head
where the greedy needy teeth & eyes of Napoleon shone
eager for the money which
was Jefferson's bait to catch the Louisiana fish.

CHANT ROYAL A French form consisting of five eleven-line *stanzas (rhymed *ababccddedE*) and a five-line *envoi*, or "send-off" (rhymed *ddedE*). The *E* line is a *refrain (and in this form rhymes with the ninth line of each stanza).

Originally, no rhyme word could appear twice, the subject had to be heroic, the audience had to be royal, and the language had to be suitable for regal ears. It is similar to the *ballade.

CHILDREN'S POETRY 1. Poetry written for children, usually by adults. *Nursery rhymes are the most familiar kind of children's poetry, but Robert Louis Stevenson's *A Child's Garden of Verses* contains poems written by a professional poet and intended for children. The writer of children's poems will usually simplify the language and ideas and highlight the rhythms and sound effects. In these particulars, the same process applies to songs (and many nursery rhymes are, in fact, singable). William Blake's *Songs of Innocence and of Experience*, while symbolic and profound, are at the same time simple and musical, full of what might be called "primary images" (on the analogy of primary colors): archetypes such as "lamb," "tiger," and "rose." Nancy Willard invokes Blake's songs in her contemporary book for children, *A Visit to William Blake's Inn*.

2. Poetry written by children. The explosion of Poetry-in-the-Schools programs has encouraged children and teenagers to become involved in poetry in the most compelling way—by writing it. Kenneth Koch,

a poet and one of the earliest, most energetic teachers in the schools, has written and edited *Wishes, Lies, and Dreams* and *Rose, Where Did You Get That Red?* These books discuss how to teach children to read and write poems and present generous samples of their work.

W.H. Auden remarks that there are often prodigies in music and mathematics, seldom in poetry. The greatest teenage poets include Arthur Rimbaud and Dylan Thomas. Usually it takes experience—in language, literature, and life—to make a poet. The child's fresh view of the world is a start, but not enough in itself. (Even as teenagers, Rimbaud and Thomas had read widely.)

CHINESE POETIC FORMS The rhymed song forms in which most Chinese poetry has been composed. In English, we know Chinese poems mainly through the free-verse translations of Ezra Pound, Arthur Waley, and others. But most Chinese poems are rhymed, their meter governed by the number of characters in each line. The meter is syllabic, each character equaling a single syllable. At the same time, it is governed by arrangements of two categories of tones: level (long and keeping the same pitch) and deflected (relatively short, in which the pitch moves upwards or downwards). There are three kinds of deflected tone: rising, falling, and entering. The tone pattern, free in early Chinese poetry, was later fixed in specific arrangements.

There are several major poetic forms in Chinese:

• Four-syllable verse: four (occasionally five) characters per line, rhymed *aaXa bbcc cdcd*

• Ancient verse: five- or seven-syllable lines, in which even-numbered lines rhyme, using either a single rhyme throughout or changing it at will; no fixed tone pattern

• Regulated verse: eight lines, all five syllables or seven syllables, rhyming even lines (and sometimes line one) on the same rhyme sound, with two acceptable tone patterns for each line length, the four lines in the middle forming two pairs of antithetical couplets (For example, if one line says, "In the morning, she lifts the curtain," the other might say, "In the evening, she loosens her hair.")

• Lyric meters (or *Tz'u*): poems written to existing music, in lines of unequal length (as opposed to equal lines, or *shih*, as in the forms listed above)

SONGS IN THE OLD STYLE: 52 / Li Bai (700–762; tr. John Drury)

I started at the rush of spring torrents.
By summer, streams grew thin.
I can't bear seeing fall tumbleweeds
lifting up. At the end, what can I lean on?

A faint breeze extinguishes orchids,
dew sprinkled on beans and sunflowers.
A fine man—not me—hopes for something.
Day by day, the green world scatters.

CHORUS (Greek, "dance, group of dancers") 1. A group of performers, sometimes represented by a leader, who comment on the action in the plays of ancient Greece, singing and moving in a stylized dance. The choral *ode (also called the Pindaric ode) is structured in three parts that represent those movements: turn, counter-turn, and stand (or *strophe*, *antistrophe*, and *epode*).

2. A repeated stanza in a *song, as opposed to the *verse, which is different each time. The pattern can go on indefinitely, but it begins like this:

Verse 1
CHORUS
Verse 2
CHORUS

For example, the little-known first verse of a well-known song begins, "Katie Casey was baseball-mad, / Had the fever and had it bad." The chorus begins, "Take me out to the ballgame." It is a chorus because it is repeated and because everyone may sing along.

The chorus is sometimes called a *refrain, although a refrain usually consists of one line, perhaps two, while a chorus may contain several. The chief difference, however, lies in where the terms are currently used: chorus in songs, refrain in poems. *Burden* is another synonym, an older one that applies to the refrain or chorus in, say, an Elizabethan lute-song.

CINQUAIN (sing-kane'; French, "group of five") A poetic form, inspired by Japanese *tanka, invented by Adelaide Crapsey (who wrote twenty-eight of them), with a syllabic arrangement of 2-4-6-8-2 in its five lines. In her own cinquains, Crapsey allows herself to add or subtract a syllable from any given line. The term is also used for any five-line stanza, along with *quintain, quintet,* and *pentastich.* (*See* QUINTAIN *for a fuller discussion of five-line stanzas.*)

NIAGARA / Adelaide Crapsey (1878–1914)

Seen on a Night in November

How frail
Above the bulk
Of crashing water hangs,
Autumnal, evanescent, wan,
The moon.

CITY POEM A poem about life in a city, or about the city itself; a modern counterpart to poems about rural life variously known as *bucolics,* *eclogues,* *georgics,* *idylls,* and *pastorals.*

A city poem might be called an "urban pastoral" (or perhaps an "urbanic"), probably in an ironic sense. The rise of such poems as William Blake's "London" and William Wordsworth's "Composed upon Westminster Bridge, September 3, 1802" coincides with the Industrial Revolution around the turn of the nineteenth century.

A STEP AWAY FROM THEM / Frank O'Hara (1926–1966)

It's my lunch hour, so I go
for a walk among the hum-colored
cabs. First, down the sidewalk

where laborers feed their dirty
glistening torsos sandwiches
and Coca-Cola, with yellow helmets
on. They protect them from falling
bricks, I guess. Then onto the
avenue where skirts are flipping
above heels and blow up over
grates. The sun is hot, but the
cabs stir up the air. I look
at bargains in wristwatches. There
are cats playing in sawdust.
                                        On
to Times Square, where the sign
blows smoke over my head, and higher
the waterfall pours lightly. A
Negro stands in a doorway with a
toothpick, languorously agitating.
A blonde chorus girl clicks: he
smiles and rubs his chin. Everything
suddenly honks: it is 12:40 of
a Thursday.
                        Neon in daylight is a
great pleasure, as Edwin Denby would
write, as are light bulbs in daylight.
I stop for a cheeseburger at JULIET'S
CORNER. Giulietta Masina, wife of
Federico Fellini, è bell' attrice.
And chocolate malted. A lady in
foxes on such a day puts her poodle
in a cab.
                        There are several Puerto
Ricans on the avenue today, which
makes it beautiful and warm. First
Bunny died, then John Latouche,
then Jackson Pollock. But is the

earth as full as life was full, of them?
And one has eaten and one walks,
past the magazines with nudes
and posters for BULLFIGHT and
the Manhattan Storage Warehouse,
which they'll soon tear down. I
used to think they had the Armory
Show there.
        A glass of papaya juice
and back to work. My heart is in my
pocket, it is Poems by Pierre Reverdy.

NOTE: Pierre Reverdy (1889–1960), French Surrealist poet.

CLERIHEW A *light verse form, rhymed *aabb*; its first line is the name of a famous person and its second forms a comic predicate; lines three and four comment further, comically, on some biographical fact or absurd fancy related to that person.

The *meter in a clerihew tends to be intentionally rough and irregular, shortening or lengthening according to the author's whim. Edmund Clerihew Bentley (1875–1956) invented the form when he was a student at St. Paul's Boys' School in London. His first clerihew follows:

> Sir Humphry Davy
> Abominated gravy.
> He lived in the odium
> Of having discovered sodium.

CLOSURE The way a poem ends.

In Barbara Herrnstein Smith's *Poetic Closure*, the term is reserved for metrical verse, but we can apply it to all poems. Endings can range from the quiet (an easing out or what the Elizabethans called a "dying fall") to the emphatic and dramatic, an orchestra's final thump. Often the last line will, in fact, be the poem's climax, but it could also be a refrain, strong because repeated but not exactly unexpected. Poems can also end on a question, an exclamation, or an ellipsis—like a movie or song fading out. The ending can be a single word, phrase, or sentence. It can be detached, preceded by a stanza break, or connected to the rest of the poem so there's a continual buildup like a wave cresting. Any of these possibilities—and others as well (should the poem end with an image? an aphorism? somebody talking?)—can determine a poem's closure.

COBLA (coe'-bla; Provençal, "verse") Any poem that is one stanza long. It was the troubadours' equivalent of the *epigram, as well as their usual word for *stanza. The current sense of the word comes from *cobla esparsa (eh-spar'-sa)*, a single isolated stanza.

CONCRETE LANGUAGE Words that denote particular, palpable things (such as *boat*, *persimmon*, *flip*, and *jump*), as opposed to *abstract language (such as *truth*, *infinity*, and *perseverance*). Most poets prefer concrete language, words that appeal to the senses and provide *images.

CONFESSIONAL POETRY Work by some mid-twentieth-century American poets that uses personal and private details from their own lives, material once considered too embarrassing to discuss publicly.

M.L. Rosenthal coined the term in his book *The New Poets*, which deals with poets such as Robert Lowell, Sylvia Plath, Anne Sexton, and John Berryman. These poets may be variously "confessional" in the religious sense of a penitent declaring his sins to a priest, in the psychological sense of a patient revealing secrets to an analyst, or in the judicial sense of an accused person admitting to a crime. At best, this poetry explores previously forbidden subjects with an honesty and directness that electrifies the language; at worst, it indulges in personal gossip, wallows in emotional excess, and confines its vision to egocentric musings, self-pity, and megalomania. Confessional poetry may expose family secrets, sexual affairs, physical abuse (either given or received, or both), cowardice and cruelty, and usually does so in the guise of autobiography. Rosenthal points out, however, that "the private life of the poet himself, especially under stress of psychological crisis ... is felt at the same time as a symbolic embodiment of national and cultural crisis."

MAN AND WIFE / Robert Lowell (1917–1977)

Tamed by *Miltown*, we lie on Mother's bed;
the rising sun in war paint dyes us red;
in broad daylight her gilded bed-posts shine,
abandoned, almost Dionysian.
At last the trees are green on Marlborough Street,
blossoms on our magnolia ignite
the morning with their murderous five days' white.
All night I've held your hand,
as if you had
a fourth time faced the kingdom of the mad—
its hackneyed speech, its homicidal eye—
and dragged me home alive. ... Oh my *Petite*,
clearest of all God's creatures, still all air and nerve:
you were in your twenties, and I,
once hand on glass
and heart in mouth,
outdrank the Rahvs in the heat
of Greenwich Village, fainting at your feet—
too boiled and shy
and poker-faced to make a pass,
while the shrill verve
of your invective scorched the traditional South.

Now twelve years later, you turn your back.
Sleepless, you hold
your pillow to your hollows like a child;
your old-fashioned tirade—
loving, rapid, merciless—
breaks like the Atlantic Ocean on my head.

NOTES: *Miltown*: a tranquilizer; *the Rahvs*: Philip, who edited *The Partisan Review*, and Nathalie.

CONNOTATION The suggested meaning of a word, as opposed to its denotation, or dictionary meaning.

Consider the differences among synonyms: *physician, surgeon, doctor, sawbones, quack*. Each has a different level of respect (or disrespect), an emotional charge. Connotations are the overtones of words, their vibrations—good or bad. One might argue that connotation is to denotation as the figurative is to the literal. Connotation represents the things we associate with a word; it is like an aura, resonance, or electric field around that word. Poets in search of *le mot juste* (the exact word) must weigh these associations that both complicate and enrich.

CONSONANCE 1. The repetition of consonant sounds. The term is often used synonymously with *alliteration (which is, however, usually confined to the repetition of initial consonants).

2. *Slant rhyme that repeats consonants but changes the vowels, such as *book/rack*.

CORRUPTED FORM Intentional flouting, breaking, disregard, or sabotage of a poetic form's rules or conventions.

A corrupted form crosses the line beyond acceptable variations, but such a departure is not necessarily bad. For example, the *villanelle ordinarily contains nineteen lines. Acceptable variations include reversing the order of the final two *refrain lines, omitting two of the middle *tercets (as Leconte de Lisle does), or adding two tercets (as Marilyn Hacker does)—usually in pairs so both refrains can recur. Donald Justice's "Variations for Two Pianos," included below, is a corrupted villanelle. It contains the two refrains that make it a villanelle but transforms the first tercet into a *couplet (the two refrain lines), omitting the inner rhymes of the remaining tercets, and changing the concluding *quatrain to a single line, a repetition of the first refrain.

Corrupted form is effective because it surprises us with the contortions of a familiar pattern. It grabs our attention because we recognize what's there but realize it's been transformed. It makes an old form new. Since it is really a quirk of criticism that one particular *rhyme scheme and refrain pattern became the so-called fixed form of the villanelle, there is much to be said for such corrupting. (And it drives the sticklers crazy.) It may be better to honor the spirit of a poetic form than the letter (which, as scripture tells us, "killeth").

C

VARIATIONS FOR TWO PIANOS / Donald Justice (1925–2004)

There is no music now in all Arkansas.
Higgins is gone, taking both his pianos.

Movers dismantled the instruments, away
Sped the vans. The first detour untuned the strings.
There is no music now in all Arkansas.

Up Main Street, past the cold shopfronts of Conway,
The brash, self-important brick of the college,
Higgins is gone, taking both his pianos.

Warm evenings, the windows open, he would play
Something of Mozart's for his pupils, the birds.
There is no music now in all Arkansas.

How shall the mockingbird mend her trill, the jay
His eccentric attack, lacking a teacher?
Higgins is gone, taking both his pianos.

There is no music now in all Arkansas.

for Thomas Higgins, pianist

COUPLET (cup'-let) A pair of rhymed lines; a two-line stanza.

The couplet is also called a *distich*, especially if unrhymed. The *heroic couplet (a rhymed couplet in iambic pentameter) began with Geoffrey Chaucer but reached its peak of influence in the early eighteenth century, especially in the work of Alexander Pope. The couplet also figures prominently in the Shakespearean *sonnet, whose last two lines rhyme, as in sonnet 116 ("Let me not to the marriage of true minds"):

> If this be error and upon me prov'd,
> I never writ, nor no man ever lov'd.

Couplets are essential to a Middle Eastern form, the *ghazal, and turn up in a great deal of free verse, as a semi-metrical way to introduce a sense of regularity and balance.

(For other poems written in rhymed couplets, like the Robert Herrick poem that follows, see ALLITERATION, ANAPEST, ANAPHORA, CLERI-HEW, DRAMATIC MONOLOGUE, ELEGY, EPIC SIMILE, EPIGRAM, FOUR-TEENER, HEROIC COUPLET, HUDIBRASTICS, IDYLL, ONOMATOPOEIA, PARODY, PASTORAL, QUATRAIN, SATIRE, *and* TROCHEE.*)*

THE POMANDER BRACELET / Robert Herrick (1591–1674)

> To me my Julia lately sent
> A bracelet richly redolent:
> The beads I kissed, but most loved her
> That did perfume the pomander.

THE LAST WOMAN WITH LOTUS FEET / Marilyn Chin (b. 1955)

Locke, CA 1983

> She hobbled down to tell us about the widows
> of gold-diggers no taller than you and me, women
>
> who dragged their men out from under oxcarts and wheel-
> barrows
> while she, still virgin, sat and brewed
>
> Chrysanthemum tea that squealed in a copper kettle.
> Its steam was blue—as lorries passed ...
>
> I saw the bandage darkening around her ankles.
> There was more to tell now, less to show.

CRETIC (kree'-tik; Greek, "Cretan"; also called *amphimacer* [am-fih'-muh-ser] or *amphimac* [am'-fih-mak], Greek, "long at each end") A *foot consisting of two stressed syllables with an unstressed syllable in between them (´ ˘ ´).

The following phrases are cretic: "breakfast bar," "here and there," "what I want." However, in the context of a line in English, a cretic foot is rare. The stresses tend to break off into separate feet: "The break-| fast bár | iš clóšed"; "Hére añd | thére thě | péople | gáthěr"; "Whát Ĭ | wánt nŏw | iš péace."

CURSE An imprecation or damnation in verse, the act of what Robert Graves calls the "left hand" of poetry (while the right hand praises). In a poem by Graves, "Traveller's Curse after Misdirection," the lost speaker rails against those who have misled him, imploring "May they stumble, stage by stage, / On an endless pilgrimage" and hoping that they fall with each step, each time breaking their necks.

CURTAL SONNET (cur'-tul) An abridged *sonnet, containing eleven lines arranged in two stanzas, the first rhymed *abcabc* and the second either *dbcdc* or *dcbdc*, the last line indented and shorter than the others.

Gerard Manley Hopkins invented the curtal sonnet and used it for two poems, "Pied Beauty" in 1877 and "Peace" two years later.

PIED BEAUTY / Gerard Manley Hopkins (1844–1889)

Glory be to God for dappled things—
  For skies of couple-colour as a brinded cow;
    For rose-moles all in stipple upon trout that swim;
Fresh-firecoal chestnut-falls; finches' wings;
  Landscape plotted and pieced—fold, fallow, and plough;
    And all trades, their gear and tackle and trim.

All things counter, original, spare, strange;
  Whatever is fickle, freckled (who knows how?)
    With swift, slow; sweet, sour; adazzle, dim;
He fathers-forth whose beauty is past change:
        Praise him.

NOTE: *brinded*: brindled

DACTYL, DACTYLIC (dak′-tul, dak-til′-ik; Greek, "finger") A *foot consisting of a *stress followed by two unstressed syllables (′ ˘ ˘).

Dactylic words include "harmony," "bigamist," and "precipice." In many cases, however, the third syllable of a dactylic word receives secondary stress. The impulse to alternate stressed and unstressed syllables in English is so powerful, those secondary stresses actually favor *iambic meter, especially when the dactylic word is followed by an unstressed syllable: "harmony and bliss," "bigamist who flees," "precipice of doom."

Dactylic meter, like *anapestic, is called triple meter because each foot contains three syllables. In the original Greek, Homer's *The Iliad* and *The Odyssey* are written in *dactylic hexameter* (six feet, most of them dactyls); so is the Latin verse of Virgil's *The Aeneid*. The pattern of long and short syllables is arranged as follows:

– ˘ ˘ | – ˘ ˘ | – ˘ ˘ | – ˘ ˘ | – ˘ ˘ | – –

NOTE: The fifth foot can be a *spondee (– –), and the sixth foot can be a *trochee (– ˘).

Henry Wadsworth Longfellow imitates dactylic hexameter in a long narrative poem, *Evangeline*, whose first line is:

> This is the forest primeval. The murmuring pines
> and the hemlocks

Rolfe Humphries, who translated Latin poets such as Virgil, Ovid, and Juvenal, says of dactylic hexameter, "This meter, in our usage, tends to gallop if not run away, Buckety, Buckety, Buckety, Buckety, Buckety, Bump down."

In English, dactylic meter can sound too rigid, rhythmically head-strong, and uniformly propulsive if not varied a good deal. Alfred, Lord Tennyson's "The Charge of the Light Brigade" exemplifies this dactylic onrush:

> Half a league, half a league,
> Half a league onward,
> All in the valley of Death
>   Rode the six hundred.
> 'Forward the Light Brigade!
> Charge for the guns!' he said.
> Into the valley of Death
>   Rode the six hundred.

The dactylic impetus becomes so powerful that ordinarily strong words like "league" and "said" grow weak and rushed over, while the usually minor "In-" of "Into" receives a kind of field promotion to the commanding status of "vall[ey]" and "Death" in the same line. It would seem false to the poem not to follow this bumpety-bumpety ride of dactyls as they charge.

To harness the galloping of the meter, the poet can (1) substitute trochees or spondees for dactyls, (2) omit both unstressed syllables from the last foot (*catalexis) or change it to a trochee, (3) begin an occasional line with an extra unstressed syllable (*anacrusis), or (4) change one of the unstressed syllables in a dactyl to a stress. Subject, manner, and tone can help, too, as can pauses and colloquial speech patterns. The first stanza of Paul Laurence Dunbar's "Little Brown Baby," which is written in African-American dialect of the nineteenth century, ends:

> Look at dat mouf—dat's merlasses, I bet;
>   Come hyeah, Maria, an' wipe off his han's.
> Bees gwine to ketch you an' eat you up yit,
>   Bein' so sticky an sweet—goodness lan's!

71

In the poem a father is speaking to his child. Although Dunbar's lines here are metrically strict (allowing for the truncation of the last two unstressed syllables), they sound spoken, not bombastic.

William Carlos Williams asserted that "American speech tends toward dactylic," and poets such as Allen Ginsberg and James Dickey have agreed both in critical remarks and in their own practice. All three of those poets allow themselves great rhythmic leeway in their poems, which are not consistently dactylic at all—nor metrical, in most cases. What they mean by "dactylic" may actually be close to what Robert Frost means by "loose iambics," whose extra unstressed syllables make the verse sound more conversational, natural, and easygoing—perhaps more American.

DEEP IMAGE POETRY Work by poets such as Robert Bly and James Wright, who published, during the 1960s, *free-verse poems about mysterious images drawn largely from rural life and the natural world.

This imagery draws the reader into depths of consciousness, as in the following lines by Wright: "Mother of roots, you have not seeded / The tall ashes of loneliness." Bly also emphasizes darkness as part of this deepening: "Now I want to go back among the dark roots; / Now I want to see the day pulling its long wing." These deep images are like Yeatsian *symbols, talismans strange in their simplicity, or links that connect the physical world to the unconscious or the spiritual.

Bly edited an influential magazine called *The Fifties*, then *The Sixties*, and then (for one issue on "Leaping Poetry") *The Seventies*. The magazine featured translations of Spanish, German, and Norwegian poetry that brought something new—associative, visionary, and passionate—into American poetry. As certain words became connected with this poetry ("dark" and "stone," for example), imitators changed what was striking into something formulaic and stale. By the late seventies, a reaction had set in against the fashion of "deep images," although such images, whatever one calls them, are the roots of poetry.

DRIVING TOWARD THE LAC QUI PARLE RIVER /
Robert Bly (b. 1926)

I

I am driving; it is dusk; Minnesota.
The stubble field catches the last growth of·sun.
The soybeans are breathing on all sides.
Old men are sitting before their houses on carseats
In the small towns. I am happy,
The moon is rising above the turkey sheds.

II

The small world of the car
Plunges through the deep fields of the night,
On the road from Willmar to Milan.
This solitude covered with iron
Moves through the fields of night
Penetrated by the noise of crickets.

III

Nearly to Milan, suddenly a small bridge,
And water kneeling in the moonlight.
In small towns the houses are built right on the ground;
The lamplight falls on all fours in the grass.
When I reach the river, the full moon covers it;
A few people are talking low in a boat.

DENOTATION The dictionary definition of a word, as opposed to
its *connotation or suggested meanings.

While the connotation is like the figurative sense of a word, the denotation is the literal sense. For example, *stallion* means "male horse"
(its denotation), but it suggests something powerful, sexually aggressive, and conceitedly beautiful (its connotation). A poet should be exact
about the denotations of words and sensitive to their connotations.

DIALOGUE, DIALOG (die'-uh-log; Greek, "conversation") A poem in which two voices alternate.

Usually a dialogue involves *speakers conversing, the back-and-forth of voices, verbal sparring, as in the *sonnet below from Shakespeare's *Romeo and Juliet*. But in Andrew Marvell's "A Dialogue Between the Soul and Body," the voices represent the spirit and the flesh.

More recently, Richard Howard has written "two-part inventions," borrowing the title of J.S. Bach's compositions for two musical voices. In these verbal inventions, voices may alternate, as in "Wildflowers" (whose speakers are Walt Whitman and Oscar Wilde), or one character's entire speech or monologue may be answered by another's, as in "After the Facts," which presents a *verse letter and its *response.

Richard Wilbur's "At Moorditch" uses dialogue within the poem (as do a number of Robert Frost's *narrative poems) in the same way that dialogue is used in short stories. Mark Strand's "Answers" (from "Elegy for My Father") and Li-Young Lee's "The Interrogation" (which appears below) use a question-and-answer structure. John Ashbery's "Litany" appears as two columns of text that are meant, as the poet notes, "to be read as simultaneous but independent monologues." (*See* DRAMATIC MONOLOGUE, DRAMATIC POETRY, FUGITIVES, LETTER POEM, *and* PASTORAL.)

Sonnet from ACT I, SCENE V of *ROMEO AND JULIET* / William Shakespeare (1564–1616)

ROMEO.	If I profane with my unworthiest hand
	This holy shrine, the gentle fine is this:
	My lips, two blushing pilgrims, ready stand
	To smooth that rough touch with a tender kiss.
JULIET.	Good pilgrim, you do wrong your hand too much,
	Which mannerly devotion shows in this;
	For saints have hands that pilgrims' hands do touch,
	And palm to palm is holy palmer's kiss.
ROMEO.	Have not saints lips, and holy palmers too?
JULIET.	Ay, pilgrim, lips that they must use in pray'r.

74

ROMEO.   O, then, dear saint, let lips do what hands do!
          They pray; grant thou, lest faith turn to despair.
JULIET.   Saints do not move, though grant for prayers' sake.
ROMEO.   Then move not while my prayer's effect I take.

THE INTERROGATION / Li-Young Lee (b. 1957)

Two streams: one dry, one poured all night by our beds.

I'll wonder
about neither.

The dry one was clogged with bodies.

I'm through
with memory.

At which window of what house did light teach you tedium?
On which step of whose stairway did you learn indecision?

I'm through
sorting avenues and doors,
curating houses and deaths.

Which house did we flee by night? Which house did we flee
     by day?

Don't ask me.

We stood and watched one burn; from one we ran away.

I'm neatly folding
the nights and days, notes
to be forgotten.

We were diminished. We were not spared. There was no pity.
Neither was their sanctuary. Neither rest.
There were fires in the streets. We stood among men, at
     the level
of their hands, all those wrists, dead or soon to die.

No more
letting my survival
depend on memory.

There was the sea; its green volume brought despair.
There was waiting, there was leaving. There was
astonishment too. The astonishment of
"I thought you died!" "How did you get out?"
"And Little Fei Fei walked right by the guards!"

I grow
leaden with stories,
my son's eyelids
grow heavy.

Who rowed the boat when our father tired?

Don't ask me.

Who came along? Who got left behind?

Ask the sea.

Through it all there was no song, and weeping
came many years later.

I'm through
with memory.

Sometimes a song,
even when there was weeping.

I'm through with memory.

Can't you still smell the smoke on my body?

DIDACTIC POETRY (die-dak'-tik; Greek, "skilled in teaching")
Poetry that teaches something; more specifically, poetry whose primary purpose is to instruct.

In "The Art of Poetry," the Roman poet Horace declares that poetry should both delight and instruct. When that instruction is paramount, rather than an outgrowth of imaginative pleasure, the poem may become moral propaganda or something merely handy, such as "Thirty days hath September, / April, June, and November." But some explicitly didactic poems teach practical lessons without sacrificing the poetry. The *Georgics* of Virgil, for example, give instructions in farming and are a pleasure to read. The pejorative sense of didactic poetry derives primarily from the "Art for Art's Sake" movement of the 1890s. But a poem that teaches nothing is worth little. A reader wants at least a sense of encountering something new, of discovering a fresh way to consider human nature and the world.

D

DIPODICS, DIPODIC VERSE (die-pod'-ix) Originally, in Greek and Latin, *meter that counted two *feet as a single unit. In English, however, dipodics are really a kind of *accentual meter. Folk poems such as *ballads and *nursery rhymes tend to give stronger emphasis to every other accent, starting with the first one in a line. Thus, in the ballad "Lamkin," lines that might be scanned as *iambic tetrameter and iambic trimeter emerge as dipodics, with two strong beats in each line: "It's LAMkin was a MASon good / as EVer built wi' STANE." It is, perhaps, not the doubling up of feet so much as the two-stress line that characterizes dipodics in English, as in the nursery rhyme "RING around a ROSy, / POCKet full of POSies."

DISTICH (dis'-tik; Greek, "two" + "line, verse") A two-line stanza; sometimes used synonymously with *couplet. Some critics, however, would confine the term *couplet* to rhymed pairs of lines but allow *distich* to encompass unrhymed pairs as well.

DITHYRAMB, DITHYRAMBIC (dith'-ih-ram, dith-ih-ram'-bic) Originally a Greek choral hymn for Dionysus, god of wine. Later, any poem that is wild and rhapsodic.

DOUBLE DACTYL An eight-line *light-verse form, invented by Anthony Hecht, consisting of two *quatrains of *dactylic dimeter (´ ˘ ˘ | ´ ˘ ˘).

The first line is made up of nonsense words (usually "Higgledy-piggledy"); the second line is the name of a famous person (like the first line in a related form, the *clerihew); at least one line in the second quatrain consists of a single six-syllable word (such as "valedictorian"); the fourth and eighth lines rhyme; the final two unstressed syllables are omitted at the end of each quatrain.

The definitive collection of double dactyls is *Jiggery-Pokery: A Compendium of Double Dactyls*, edited by Anthony Hecht and John Hollander. Here is a double dactyl based on Part IV of Jonathan Swift's *Gulliver's Travels*:

> Higgledy-piggledy
> Lemuel Gulliver
> Wasn't a visitor
> Houyhnhnms would seek.
>
> Horse sense would tell them his
> Anthropomorphical
> Form was the same as a
> Yahoo physique.

DOUBLE FOOT Two metrical feet in combination. In English, the only common double *foot is the *minor ionic or double iamb (˘ ˘ ´ ´), a *pyrrhic foot and a *spondee. The rhythm is endemic to the English language, occurring in many phrases: "the absurd fact," "with a blank look," "an obscene mask."

DRAMATIC MONOLOGUE Poem spoken by a character or through a *persona* (Greek for "mask"), rather than by the poet or an unidentified *speaker.

In a dramatic monologue, the speaker must be identified, although he need not be named. The character who speaks the monologue will usually be human, but it can be an animal (like the pig in Philip

Levine's "Animals Are Passing from Our Lives," which appears in
SYLLABICS), a plant (like "The Red Poppy" by Louise Glück, which
appears below), or perhaps an inanimate object. The speaker can be
a real person, an imaginary character, a historical or literary figure—
anyone except the poet or some neutral voice. Robert Browning's
dramatic monologues essentially lifted the Shakespearean soliloquy
out of the play and presented it without the larger context of a whole
drama, without the actual interaction of characters on a stage. All of
the action is compressed into the monologue, which may either be
spoken or written to another character or spoken in isolation, the
speaker talking to himself. Events before the monologue must be suggested or mentioned. When the speaker is unaware of the implica-
tions of what he says, but the implied listener or the reader
understands them, the monologue contains *dramatic *irony. (See
Richard Howard's "1801" in* VERSE LETTER.*)*

MY LAST DUCHESS / Robert Browning (1812–1889)

FERRARA

That's my last Duchess painted on the wall,
Looking as if she were alive. I call
That piece a wonder, now: Frà Pandolf's hands
Worked busily a day, and there she stands.
Will't please you sit and look at her? I said
"Frà Pandolf" by design, for never read
Strangers like you that pictured countenance,
The depth and passion of its earnest glance,
But to myself they turned (since none puts by
The curtain I have drawn for you, but I)
And seemed as they would ask me, if they durst,
How such a glance came there; so, not the first
Are you to turn and ask thus. Sir, 'twas not
Her husband's presence only, called that spot
Of joy into the Duchess' cheek: perhaps
Frà Pandolf chanced to say "Her mantle laps
"Over my Lady's wrist too much," or "Paint

"Must never hope to reproduce the faint
"Half-flush that dies along her throat": such stuff
Was courtesy, she thought, and cause enough
For calling up that spot of joy. She had
A heart—how shall I say?—too soon made glad,
Too easily impressed; she liked whate'er
She looked on, and her looks went everywhere.
Sir, 'twas all one! My favour at her breast,
The dropping of the daylight in the West,
The bough of cherries some officious fool
Broke in the orchard for her, the white mule
She rode with round the terrace—all and each
Would draw from her alike the approving speech,
Or blush, at least. She thanked men,—good! but thanked
Somehow—I know not how—as if she ranked
My gift of a nine hundred years old name
With anybody's gift. Who'd stoop to blame
This sort of trifling? Even had you skill
In speech—(which I have not)—to make your will
Quite clear to such an one, and say "Just this
"Or that in you disgusts me; here you miss,
"Or there exceed the mark"—and if she let
Herself be lessoned so, nor plainly set
Her wits to yours, forsooth, and made excuse,
—E'en then would be some stooping, and I choose
Never to stoop. Oh, Sir, she smiled, no doubt,
Whene'er I passed her; but who passed without
Much the same smile? This grew; I gave commands;
Then all smiles stopped together. There she stands
As if alive. Will't please you rise? We'll meet
The company below, then. I repeat,
The Count your Master's known munificence
Is ample warrant that no just pretence
Of mine for dowry will be disallowed;
Though his fair daughter's self, as I avowed

At starting, is my object. Nay, we'll go
Together down, Sir! Notice Neptune, tho',
Taming a sea-horse, thought a rarity,
Which Claus of Innsbruck cast in bronze for me.

THE RED POPPY / Louise Glück (b. 1943)

The great thing
is not having
a mind. Feelings:
oh, I have those; they
govern me. I have
a lord in heaven
called the sun, and open
for him, showing him
the fire of my own heart, fire
like his presence.
What could such glory be
if not a heart? Oh my brothers and sisters,
were you like me once, long ago,
before you were human? Did you
permit yourselves
to open once, who would never
open again? Because in truth
I am speaking now
the way you do. I speak
because I am shattered.

DRAMATIC POETRY Poetry written for performance as a play. It is one of the three main genres of poetry (the others being *lyric poetry and *narrative poetry).

In ancient Greece, plays began as part of Dionysian festivals, during which poets entered their tragedies and comedies in contests and were awarded prizes (or not). Aristotle differentiates the two dramatic forms by saying that tragedy portrays men and women as better than they are, comedy as worse. Tragedy must present the story of a noble man's downfall because of a flaw in his character; it should evoke fear and pity in the audience and have a cathartic effect. Sophocles' *Oedipus the King* (the first part of a trilogy) serves as a model tragedy. Shakespeare's tragedies are looser, careless of the traditional "unities" (of time and space), and include explicit portrayals of violence on stage.

The comedies of Aristophanes are satiric, attacking warfare in *Lysistrata* and lampooning the tragic playwright Euripides and Dionysus himself. Comedy admits all sorts of buffoonery—slapstick, puns, mixups, malapropisms, and battles of wit. The title of Shakespeare's *All's Well That Ends Well* pretty much sums up the point of comedy.

Verse drama (and hence dramatic poetry) has had a hard time in the twentieth century, although William Butler Yeats, T.S. Eliot, and Federico Garcia Lorca have written serious plays in verse. Musical comedies have provided more room for poetry—but usually in the guise of comic verse and song, not dramatic poetry.

DRÓTTKVAETT (drote'-kwat, the *r* slightly rolled and the *ae* pronounced like the *a* in "at"; Old Norse, "court poem") Old Norse stanzaic form, consisting of eight lines with six syllables in each, three of them stressed, each line ending with a stressed syllable followed by an unstressed syllable. Every two lines are linked by *alliteration, which must occur twice in the first line and in the opening syllable of the second. Full *rhyme appears in even lines, slant rhyme in odd lines, and internal rhyme within lines. *Kennings appear frequently. The form was used by *skalds*, Old Norse court poets, but it survives in Iceland to the present day.

DUENDE (dwen'-day) Federico Garcia Lorca's term for "the roots that probe through the mire that we all know of and do not understand, but which furnishes us with whatever is sustaining in art." It is like "soul" in African-American music. In his essay "Duende: Theory and Divertissement," Lorca says that *duende* is what Goethe recognizes in the violin playing of Paganini: "A mysterious power that all may feel and no philosophy can explain."

ECHO VERSE A poem in which the last syllable or two of a line is repeated, perhaps with different spelling or meaning, as if an echo; usually this echo will be indented to a point under or beyond the syllable it mimics and will function as an independent line of one or two syllables.

Sometimes the word *Echo* will precede the repetition, like the indication of a speaker in a play. Aside from the sheer pleasure of repetition, echo verse often serves the purposes of *irony, the meaning of the echo conflicting with what the original sound means ("know" echoed by "no," for example). This incongruity can be especially powerful because the repetition is immediate yet skewed. On the other hand, doubt or uncertainty suggested in a line can be answered ringingly with an affirmation, a reversal appropriate not for cynical but for religious uses. Any poem in echo verse is bound to be a *dialogue, perhaps an exchange of questions and answers. This echo is really a kind of *rime riche, in which the rhyme words are pronounced or spelled the same. (James Cummins's "Echo," which appears in SESTINA, provides a different example of how repeated words or phrases can be used as echoes in a poem.)

HEAVEN / George Herbert (1593–1633)

O who will show me those delights on high!
                              Echo.   I.
Thou Echo, thou art mortall, all men know.
                              Echo.   No.
Wert thou not born among the trees and leaves?
                              Echo.   Leaves.
And are there any leaves, that still abide?
                              Echo.   Bide.
What leaves are they? impart the matter wholly.
                              Echo.   Holy.
Are holy leaves the Echo then of blisse?
                              Echo.   Yes.
Then tell me, what is that supreme delight?
                              Echo.   Light.
Light to the minde: what shall the will enjoy?
                              Echo.   Joy.
But are there cares and businesse with the pleasure?
                              Echo.   Leisure.
Light, joy, and leisure; but shall they persever?
                              Echo.   Ever.

ECLOGUE (ek´-log; Greek, "selection") A *pastoral poem, or one dealing with rural life, especially a *dialogue; a singing contest between two shepherds. In *Arcadia*, Sir Philip Sidney (1554–1586) includes an eclogue, "A Double Sestina" (beginning "Ye goat-herd gods, that love the grassy mountains"), which is spoken by two shepherds named Strephon and Klaius. *(See* GEORGIC *and* IDYLL.*)*

EKPHRASTIC POETRY (ek-fras'-tik; Greek, "speaking out"; also spelled *ecphrastic*) Poetry that imitates, describes, critiques, dramatizes, reflects upon, or otherwise responds to a work of nonliterary art, especially the visual. Although paintings may be the most common subjects of poems about visual art, there are also many poems about sculptures, drawings, prints, and architecture. Examples referring to sculpture include John Keats's "On Seeing the Elgin Marbles for the First Time" (in response to the friezes from the Parthenon that are housed in the British Museum) and Rainer Maria Rilke's "Archaic Torso of Apollo." *(See Richard Howard's "1801," a *dramatic monologue about the painter J.M.W. Turner, in* VERSE LETTER.*)

Photograph poems are somewhat different, since they are based upon pictures, perhaps snapshots from a family album, not ordinarily intended as works of art. Although they respond to images in a visual medium, photograph poems usually deal with artifacts of everyday life, as in Eric Pankey's "A Photograph of My Parents Ice Skating, 1954." Poems that focus on photographic art, such as the work of Walker Evans or Diane Arbus, are not very different from painting poems. Richard Howard has written two sequences based on portraits of famous artists, such as Charles Baudelaire, by the French photographer Felix Nadar. *(See Greg Williamson's double-exposure poem in* INVENTED FORMS AND STANZAS.*)

Nevertheless, all of these kinds of poems depend upon a second-hand image rather than the people or places themselves. Plato would call them imitations of imitations. The poem that merely replicates the painting (or other visual work) seems flat indeed. It should add something in its language that takes off from the picture, or talks back to it.

Many painting poems borrow the title of a picture. X.J. Kennedy takes "Nude Descending a Staircase" from Marcel Duchamp. W.D. Snodgrass gives the painter's name along with the title in "Matisse: 'The Red Studio,'" "Vuillard: 'The Mother and Sister of the Artist,'" "Monet: 'Les Nymphéas,'" "Manet: 'The Execution of the Emperor Maximilian,'" and "Van Gogh: 'The Starry Night.'"

Sometimes, of course, different poets will write about the same pictures—just as Renoir and Monet painted some of the same scenes. Anne Sexton wrote her own version of "The Starry Night." Both William Carlos Williams and W.H. Auden wrote poems based on *Landscape with the Fall of Icarus* by the Flemish painter Pieter Brueghel. (Auden's is called "Musée des Beaux Arts.") Williams wrote an entire sequence called *Pictures From Brueghel*, based on works such as *Children's Games* and *The Hunters in the Snow*.

E

The challenge of writing about a painting is to move beyond mere description. In "A Side of Beef," Jordan Smith speaks in the voice of the painter Chaim Soutine:

> What money there is
> goes for a side of beef delivered fresh each morning.
> By noon it will have lost those pigments ...

A poem that's based on a work of art will succeed insofar as it comes to terms with the recognition made by Rainer Maria Rilke as he contemplates a powerful fragment of Greek sculpture in "Archaic Torso of Apollo": "You must change your life." Anything much less than a revelation may sound like make-work, not the work of a "maker."

STARS WHICH SEE, STARS WHICH DO NOT SEE /
Marvin Bell (b. 1937)

> They sat by the water. The fine women
> had large breasts, tightly checked.
> At each point, at every moment,
> they seemed happy by the water.
> The women wore hats like umbrellas
> or carried umbrellas shaped like hats.
> The men wore no hats and the water,
> which wore no hats, had that well-known
> mirror finish which tempts sailors.
> Although the men and women seemed at rest
> they were looking toward the river
> and some way out into it but not beyond.
> The scene was one of hearts and flowers
> though this may be unfair. Nevertheless,
> it was probable that the Seine had hurt them,
> that they were "taken back" by its beauty
> to where a slight breeze broke the mirror
> and then its promise, but never the water.

NOTE: The painting is Georges Seurat's *A Sunday Afternoon on the Island of La Grande Jatte*. Bell says that the poem starts "from a scene like that pictured in the Seurat," except that he "removed the hats from the proper Victorian gentlemen."

THE HONGO STORE / Garrett Kaoru Hongo (b. 1951)

> 29 Miles Volcano
> Hilo, Hawaii
> *from a photograph*

My parents felt those rumblings
Coming deep from the earth's belly,
Thudding like the bell of the Buddhist Church.
Tremors in the ground swayed the bathinette
Where I lay squalling in soapy water.

My mother carried me around the house,
Back through the orchids, ferns, and plumeria
Of that greenhouse world behind the store,
And jumped between gas pumps into the car.

My father gave it the gun
And said, "Be quiet," as he searched
The frequencies, flipping for the right station
(The radio squalling more loudly than I could cry).

And then even the echoes stopped—
The only sound the Edsel's grinding
And the bark and crackle of radio news
Saying stay home or go to church.

"Dees time she no blow!"
My father said, driving back
Over the red ash covering the road.
"I worried she went go for broke already!"

So in this print the size of a matchbook,
The dark skinny man, shirtless and grinning,
A toothpick in the corner of his smile,
Lifts a naked baby above his head—
Behind him the plate glass of the store only cracked.

ELEGIAC DISTICH (el'-uh-jie'-uk or eh-lee'-jee-ak dis'-tik) A couplet with a line of *dactylic hexameter followed by a line of dactylic pentameter; used in Greek for *elegies and threnodies (laments for the dead) as well as *epigrams.

Some English poets, such as Edmund Spenser, Sir Philip Sidney, and A.C. Swinburne, have experimented with the form. Here is the first couplet from Sir Philip Sidney's "Musidorus's Elegiacs":

> Fortune, nature, love, long have contended about me,
> Which should most miseries cast on a worm that I am.

And here is the last of his elegiac distichs:

> Thus, thus, alas, woeful in nature, unhappy by fortune,
> But most wretched I am, now love awakes my desire.

Sidney is trying to imitate the quantities (long and short syllables) of the original Greek meter, but *accent is so powerful in English, what we may really hear is a pattern of six accents in the first line (hexameter) and five in the second (pentameter). *(See* DACTYL *and* EPITAPH.*)*

ELEGY (el'-uh-gee; Greek "mournful song") A poem for someone who has died; also called *lament* and *threnody*. Elegies are love poems for the dead, tributes and offerings to loss.

The person commemorated in an elegy can be a friend or family member (Ben Jonson's elegy for his son appears below) or a public figure (Walt Whitman's "When Lilacs Last in the Dooryard Bloom'd" mourns the death of Abraham Lincoln). Many poets have written elegies to other poets, such as W.H. Auden's "In Memory of W.B. Yeats."

John Milton's "Lycidas" is a *pastoral elegy*, a lament for his school friend, Edward King, as if in the voice of one shepherd mourning the death of another:

> Together both, ere the high Lawns appear'd
> Under the opening eye-lids of the morn,
> We drove a field, and both together heard
> What time the Gray-Fly winds her sultry horn,

Batt'ning our flocks with the fresh dews of night,
Oft till the Star that rose, at Ev'ning, bright
Toward Heav'ns descent had slop'd his westering wheel.
Mean while the Rural ditties were not mute,
Temper'd to th'Oaten Flute,
Rough *Satyrs* danc'd, and *Fauns* with clov'n heel,
From the glad sound would not be absent long,
And old *Damaetas* lov'd to hear our song.

(lines 25–36)

The *pastoral tradition goes back to antiquity and was from the start a matter of artifice, the specialty of academic poets, not of real shepherds. Nevertheless, the pose need not ruin the poetry; it might simply make it easier to speak of grief.

ON MY FIRST SON / Ben Jonson (1573–1637)

Farewell, thou child of my right hand, and joy;
My sin was too much hope of thee, loved boy:
Seven years thou'wert lent to me, and I thee pay,
Exacted by the fate, on the just day.
O could I lose all father now! for why
Will man lament the state he should envy,
To have so soon 'scaped world's and flesh's rage,
And, if no other misery, yet age?
Rest in soft peace, and asked, say, "Here doth lie
Ben Jonson his best piece of poetry."
For whose sake henceforth all his vows be such
As what he loves may never like too much.

ELISION (uh-lizh'-un; Latin, "to strike out") The slurring together of vowels in adjacent words, so that a syllable is effectively deleted. Elision may be marked with an apostrophe, as in John Donne's "Thou'art slave to fate, chance, kings, and desperate men" (from Holy Sonnet 10, "Death, Be Not Proud"). It is a way of squeezing two unstressed syllables into one in order to maintain the *meter.

ELLIPTICAL POETS A term coined by Stephen Burt in 1999 in *American Letters & Commentary*. In his essay "The Elliptical Poets," he classifies a group of poets who "are always hinting, punning, or swerving away from a never-quite-unfolded backstory," who "admire disjunction and confrontation," who "want to challenge their readers, violate decorum, surprise or explode assumptions about what belongs in a poem, or what matters in life, and to do so while meeting traditional lyric goals." The term *elliptical* (from *ellipsis*, the omission of an unnecessary connection within a sentence) suggests a predilection for quick shifts and inventive juxtapositions among these poets. As Burt says, they "delete transitions: one thought, one impression, tailgates another." Their poems are characterized by "Fragmentation, jumpiness, audacity; performance, grammatical oddity; rebellion, voice, some measure of closure."

Elliptical poets include Lucie Brock-Broido, Susan Wheeler, Thylias Moss, Forrest Gander, Claudia Rankine, Karen Volkman, Mary Jo Bang, and C.D. Wright (starting with her 1991 volume, *String Light*). Burt calls Liam Rector's *The Sorrow of Architecture*, published in 1984, the "first Elliptical book" and singles out Mark Levine's "Work Song" as the "ideal-typical Elliptical poem." *(See* FRAGMENTATION *and* MOVEMENTS AND SCHOOLS OF POETRY.*)*

WORK SONG / Mark Levine (b. 1965)

My name is Henri. Listen. It's morning.
I pull my head from my scissors, I pull
the light bulb from my mouth—Boss comes at me
while I'm still blinking.
Pastes the pink slip on my collarbone.
It's OK, I say, I was a lazy worker, and I stole.
I wipe my feet on his skullcap on the way out.

I am Henri, mouth full of soda crackers.
I live in Toulouse, which is a piece of cardboard.
Summers the Mayor paints it blue, we fish in it.
Winters we skate on it. Children are always

drowning or falling through cracks. Parents are distraught
but get over it. It's easy to replace a child.
Like my parents' child, Henri.

I stuff my hands in my shoes
and crawl through the snow on all fours.
Animals fear me. I smell so good.
I have two sets of footprints, I confuse the police.
When I reach the highway I unzip my head.

I am a zipper. A paper cut.
I fed myself so many times
through the shredder I am confetti,
I am a ticker-tape parade, I am an astronaut
waving from my convertible at Henri.

Henri from Toulouse, is that you?
Why the unhappy face? I should shoot you
for spoiling my parade. Come on, man,
put yourself together! You want so much to die
that you don't want to die.

My name is Henri. I am Toulouse. I am scraps
of bleached parchment, I am the standing militia,
a quill, the Red Cross, I am the feather
in my cap, the Hebrew Testament, I am the World Court.
An electric fan blows
beneath my black robe. I am dignity itself.

I am an ice machine.
I am an alp.
I stuff myself in the refrigerator
wrapped in newsprint. With salt in my heart
I stay good for days.

END-STOP A definite halt or strong pause at the end of a line.

Sometimes an end-stop is marked by punctuation such as a period (the "full stop" in British usage), question mark, colon, semi-

colon, or comma; sometimes there may be no punctuation even though the line is end-stopped, as long as a thought or a phrase is completed and doesn't run over to the next line (in which case the line would be *enjambed). End-stopping tends to slow down the movement of a poem because of the emphasis, pause, or hesitation at the end of the line.

The following sonnet by Shakespeare is entirely end-stopped, even though it contains just one period at the very end. But each line ends with a grammatical break and definite pause (reinforced by the list structure).

E

SONNET 66 / William Shakespeare (1564–1616)

Tir'd with all these, for restful death I cry:
As to behold desert a beggar born,
And needy nothing trimm'd in jollity,
And purest faith unhappily forsworn,
And gilded honour shamefully misplac'd,
And maiden virtue rudely strumpeted,
And right perfection wrongfully disgrac'd,
And strength by limping sway disabled,
And art made tongue-tied by authority,
And folly, doctor-like, controlling skill,
And simple truth miscall'd simplicity,
And captive good attending captain ill:
    Tir'd with all these, from these would I be gone,
    Save that to die, I leave my love alone.

NOTE: *desert*: one who is deserving; *nothing*: one who is undeserving; *strumpeted*: prostituted; *disgrac'd*: defaced; *simplicity*: stupidity.

ENJAMBMENT (en-jam'-ment; French, "stepping over") The use of a line whose sense and rhythmic movement continues to the next line. An enjambed line is also called a "run-on" line. It is the opposite of an *end-stop.

Enjambment is one of the essential techniques of *free verse (nonmetrical lined poetry). In lieu of *meter, the end of a line is an important way to mark the rhythmic flow of a poem (as are *cadence and the repetition of words and phrases, *anaphora, for example). Enjambment is like musical syncopation; instead of pausing, the musical phrase pushes ahead. Enjambment speeds up the movement and quickens the pace (because the sense, interrupted by a line break, demands that the reader rush ahead to complete the phrase or idea).

In the following poem, Mark Irwin uses enjambment to interrupt grammatical connections: "is / a form," "You knew / then," "all // in an apple," "paradise / was," "the present's // perfect drift," "to have / said," "shepherds / dying," "spaces / you would leave," "her awkward sister, // time," "we as humans / were meant to swerve." Some of this enjambment occurs between *stanzas (marked //); one enjambed line ends with a comma but forces the reader to push ahead to complete the sense. There are also some end-stops, for while a poet may choose to let enjambment predominate, it is usually desirable to let the cadences come to rest at line's end once in a while. Every poem that is not part of a sequence must necessarily end with an end-stop.

EVE / Mark Irwin (b. 1953)

Such perfect intuition is
a form to worship. You knew
then, the hell of unending, all

in an apple, so that paradise
was a kind of autumn;
yourselves, one with the present's

perfect drift. Better not to have
said a word to Adam
whose lips touched names upon the animals

while you dreamed of zoos, shepherds
dying. Not the green spaces
you would leave, but her awkward sister,

time. You knew that we as humans
were meant to swerve, to wake from sleep
and carry the knowledge of seasons on our tongues.

EPIC (ep'-ik; Greek, "song, narrative") A long *narrative poem that tells a story central to the myths and beliefs of a people.

Traditional epics belong to the oral tradition, in which poets or performers memorize, improvise, and add or delete lines to shape the story that may one day make its way into writing (and even then may be lost, like most of the cycle of Trojan War epics).

Ezra Pound described the epic as a "poem containing history." More specifically, that history belongs to a society or a nation, such as Homer's ancient Greeks or Nazim Hikmet's twentieth-century Turks.

Traditional epics, transmitted orally, include Homer's *The Iliad* and *The Odyssey* (ancient Greek), *Gilgamesh* (Sumerian), and *Mahabharata* (Sanskrit). Literary epics, imitating the subjects and methods of traditional epics, include Virgil's *The Aeneid* and John Milton's *Paradise Lost*. Modern and contemporary epics, exploring ways of magnifying and tying together twentieth-century postindustrial experience, include Nazim Hikmet's *Human Landscapes* (Turkish) and Pablo Neruda's *Canto General* (Spanish). Some twentieth-century American poets have searched especially hard for epic frameworks that could contain fragments and unite them in something whole: Ezra Pound's *The Cantos*, William Carlos Williams's *Paterson* (and perhaps his prose work, *In the American Grain*), H.D.'s *Trilogy* and *Helen in Egypt*, and Hart Crane's *The Bridge*. Charles Olson's *The Maximus Poems* and James Merrill's *The Changing Light at Sandover* may also count as epics. Perhaps Whitman's *Song of Myself* is an epic as well: the story of America through the perceptions of a "representative man" named Walt Whitman.

EPIC SIMILE (also called *Homeric simile*) An extended comparison used in epics such as Homer's *The Iliad*. For example, the poet may liken actions on the battlefield to natural phenomena (such as a star disappearing behind clouds) or scenes of country life (such as reapers cutting grain in a field), as in these lines from George Chapman's 1611 translation of *The Iliad* (Book XI, lines 55–66):

> And as amids the skie
> We sometimes see an ominous starre blaze cleare
>   and dreadfully,
> Then run his golden head in clouds and straight
>   appeare againe:
> So Hector otherwhiles did grace the vaunt-guard,
>   shining plaine,
> Then in the rere-guard hid himselfe and labour'd every where
> To order and encourage all: his armor was so cleare
> And he applide each place so fast that, like a
>   lightning throwne
> Out of the shield of Jupiter, in every eye he shone.
> And as upon a rich man's crop of barley or of wheate
> (Opposde for swiftnesse at their worke) a sort of
>   reapers sweate,
> Beare downe the furrowes speedily, and thicke their
>   handfuls fall:
> So at the joyning of the hoasts ran Slaughter through
>   them all.

The two epic similes in the lines above follow the pattern "And as …
So …" while the simile beginning "like a lightning" is not epic (because it is not extended and does not follow the rhetorical pattern—
which can, however, use different words to introduce the two halves
of a comparison).

EPIGRAM (ep'-ih-gram; Greek, "inscription") A short, pithy comic
or satirical poem.

In English, an epigram is usually in *rhyme and *meter, but in the
Greek Anthology some of the earliest epigrams are unrhymed and not
necessarily comic. Even prose can be described as epigrammatic, as in
Oscar Wilde's *The Importance of Being Earnest*. An epigram will often
contain, or embody, an aphorism: a memorable remark that encapsu-
lates an insight into some aspect of human nature or the world at large
(such as "If treason prosper, none dare call it treason"). (*See* META-
PHYSICAL POETS *for an epigram by Coleridge.*)

EPIGRAM / Alexander Pope (1688–1744)

When other Ladies to the Shades go down,
Still *Flavia, Chloris, Celia* stay in town;
Those Ghosts of Beauty ling'ring there abide,
And haunt the places where their Honour dy'd.

EPIGRAPH (ep'-ih-graf; Greek, "inscription") A note or quotation that precedes the body of some poems; also called a *headnote*. At worst, epigraphs can seem academic and stuffy, mere showing off, but they can also acknowledge sources of material, present something that the poem will respond to, or convey important background information for which the poem itself has no room. Wallace Stevens's "Nuances of a Theme by Williams" (which appears in RESPONSE) uses an epigraph from William Carlos Williams.

EPISTROPHE (uh-pis'-truh-fee; Greek, "upon a turning") The repetition of a word or phrase at the end of successive lines or clauses; the opposite of *anaphora. (See RHETORICAL DEVICES.)*

In Act V, Scene 1 of William Shakespeare's *The Merchant of Venice*, epistrophe appears in nine of the lines spoken by Bassanio and Portia:

BASSANIO. If you did know to whom I gave the ring,
　　　　　　If you did know for whom I gave the ring,
　　　　　　And would conceive for what I gave the ring,
　　　　　　And how unwillingly I left the ring,
　　　　　　When nought would be accepted but the ring,
　　　　　　You would abate the strength of your displeasure.

PORTIA. 　If you had known the virtue of the ring,
　　　　　　Or half her worthiness that gave the ring,
　　　　　　Or your own honor to contain the ring,
　　　　　　You would not then have parted with the ring.

EPITAPH (ep'-ih-taf; Greek, "upon a tomb") Verses that commemorate a person or group of people who have died.

Epitaphs are often inscribed upon tombs or gravestones. They are like elegies squeezed into the limited space of an *epigram. They must be brief and pithy. The following epitaph, an *elegiac distich, is spoken in the voice of Spartan soldiers who died fighting while defending the pass at Thermopylae:

EPITAPH / attributed to Simonides of Ceos (about 556–468 B.C.E.; tr. Richmond Lattimore)

> Traveler, take this word to the men of Lakedaímon:
>> We who lie buried here did what they told us to do.

EPITHALAMION, EPITHALAMIUM (ep'-ih-thuh-lame'-ee-un or -um; Greek, "upon a bridal chamber") Wedding poem; poem to celebrate a marriage; ode to a bride and groom.

E

"The Song of Solomon" in the Old Testament is an epithalamion:

> Behold, thou art fair, my beloved, yea, pleasant: also our
>> bed is green.
> The beams of our house are cedar, and our rafters of fir.

Edmund Spenser's "Epithalamion" and "Prothalamion" both use elaborately rhymed stanzas, each ending in a *refrain, to commemorate weddings. In the following epithalamion, which contains refrains that a chorus might sing, the Ancient Greek poet Sappho refers to Hymen (the god of marriage) and Ares (the god of war).

FRAGMENT 102 / Sappho (circa 620–550 B.C.E.; tr. Guy Davenport)

> I
> Raise the ridge-pole higher, higher,
> *O marriage night O binding god*
> Carpenters! Make the roof-tree taller,
> *O marriage night O binding god*
> He comes, the husband, and walks like Ares,
> *O marriage night O binding god*
> He's taller by far than a tall man,
> *O marriage night O binding god*

II

Pitch the roof-beam higher, builders.
O hymn Hymen, high men, O!
Joiners! The roof is far too low.
O hymn Hymen, high men, O!
He stands, the husband, as long as Ares,
O hymn Hymen, high men, O!
And he can't get it through the door.

EUGENE ONEGIN STANZA (also called *Pushkin's stanza*) A fourteen-line *stanza (sonnet-length), rhymed *ababccddeffegg* and written in *iambic tetrameter. Its *rhyme scheme consists of three kinds of *quatrain—alternating *(abab)*, *couplet *(ccdd)*, and envelope *(effe)*—before the final rhymed couplet *(gg)*.

Alexander Pushkin, a nineteenth-century Russian poet, used the form in a verse novel, *Eugene Onegin* (the first stanza of which appears below). The stanza works well for *narrative poetry and comic verse, somewhat like the *ottava rima stanza of Lord Byron's *Don Juan.* Vikram Seth's novel, *The Golden Gate*, is written entirely in Eugene Onegin stanzas—even the dedication and author's biographical note.

Chapter One, Stanza I from *EUGENE ONEGIN* /
Alexander Pushkin (1799–1837; tr. Walter Arndt)

"Now that he is in grave condition,
My uncle, principled old dunce,
Has won respectful recognition
And done the perfect thing for once.
His act should be a guide to others;
But what a bore, I ask you, brothers,
To tend a patient night and day
And venture not a step away!
Is there hypocrisy more glaring
Than to amuse one all-but-dead,
Fluff up the pillow for his head,
Dose him with melancholy bearing,
And think behind a public sigh:
Deuce take you, step on it and die!"

FABLE (Latin, "to speak") A story, in verse or prose, that uses animal characters to point out a moral.

Aesop's fables, from the Ancient Greek, tell stories such as the dog in the manger and the race between the tortoise and the hare. Jean de La Fontaine uses rhymed verse to tell his fables. The Br'er Rabbit stories, which derive from West Africa and were told originally by slaves in America, are also fables.

THE GRASSHOPPER AND THE ANT / Jean de La Fontaine
(1621–1695; tr. Richard Wilbur)

> Grasshopper, having sung her song
>   All summer long,
> Was sadly unprovided-for
> When the cold winds began to roar:
> Not one least bite of grub or fly
> Had she remembered to put by.
> Therefore she hastened to descant
> On famine, to her neighbor Ant,
> Begging the loan of a few grains
> Of wheat to ease her hunger-pains
> Until the winter should be gone.
> "You shall be paid," said she, "upon
> My honor as an animal,

Both interest and principal." •
The Ant was not disposed to lend;
That liberal vice was not for her.
"What did you do all summer, friend?"
She asked the would-be borrower.
"So please your worship," answered she,
"I sang and sang both night and day."
"You sang? Indeed, that pleases me.
Then dance the winter-time away."

FAIRY TALE A story immersed in a magic dream world in which frightening, marvelous things happen.

The Grimm brothers collected folk tales from the Black Forest in Germany, tales full of violence, difficult journeys, impossible odds, and the visits of supernatural creatures: witches, goblins, trolls, fairy godmothers. Today these stories are often reserved for children. They may be softened, presented in cartoons, and edited to remove the violence. But their true, inherent power is immense. Bruno Bettelheim, in *The Uses of Enchantment*, argues that real fairy tales, in all their terrifying glory, help children work their way through the thickets of the psyche, much like Hansel and Gretel. These stories exert their power like dreams or myths (except that Cinderella seems closer to us than Helen of Troy, more like an ordinary person confronting the extraordinary).

For the poet, fairy tales are close to the symbolic source of most true poetry, the dream state of clear but mysterious images and actions. Many poets, including Anne Sexton in the poem below, use fairy tales as source material, either explicitly or unconsciously, like the tunes upon which a composer might write variations.

CINDERELLA / Anne Sexton (1928–1974)

You always read about it:
the plumber with twelve children
who wins the Irish Sweepstakes.
From toilets to riches.
That story.

Or the nursemaid,
some luscious sweet from Denmark
who captures the oldest son's heart.
From diapers to Dior.
That story.

Or a milkman who serves the wealthy,
eggs, cream, butter, yogurt, milk,
the white truck like an ambulance
who goes into real estate
and makes a pile.
From homogenized to martinis at lunch.

Or the charwoman
who is on the bus when it cracks up
and collects enough from the insurance.
From mops to Bonwit Teller.
That story.

F

Once
the wife of a rich man was on her deathbed
and she said to her daughter Cinderella:
Be devout. Be good. Then I will smile
down from heaven in the seam of a cloud.
The man took another wife who had
two daughters, pretty enough
but with hearts like blackjacks.
Cinderella was their maid.
She slept on the sooty hearth each night
and walked around looking like Al Jolson.
Her father brought presents home from town,
jewels and gowns for the other women
but the twig of a tree for Cinderella.
She planted that twig on her mother's grave
and it grew to a tree where a white dove sat.
Whenever she wished for anything the dove

would drop it like an egg upon the ground.
The bird is important, my dears, so heed him.

Next came the ball, as you all know.
It was a marriage market.
The prince was looking for a wife.
All but Cinderella were preparing
and gussying up for the big event.
Cinderella begged to go too.
Her stepmother threw a dish of lentils
into the cinders and said: Pick them
up in an hour and you shall go.
The white dove brought all his friends;
all the warm wings of the fatherland came,
and picked up the lentils in a jiffy.
No, Cinderella, said the stepmother,
you have no clothes and cannot dance.
That's the way with stepmothers.

Cinderella went to the tree at the grave
and cried forth like a gospel singer:
Mama! Mama! My turtledove,
send me to the prince's ball!
The bird dropped down a golden dress
and delicate little gold slippers.
Rather a large package for a simple bird.
So she went. Which is no surprise.
Her stepmother and sisters didn't
recognize her without her cinder face
and the prince took her hand on the spot
and danced with no other the whole day.

As nightfall came she thought she'd better
get home. The prince walked her home
and she disappeared into the pigeon house
and although the prince took an axe and broke

it open she was gone. Back to her cinders.
These events repeated themselves for three days.
However on the third day the prince
covered the palace steps with cobbler's wax
and Cinderella's gold shoe stuck upon it.
Now he would find whom the shoe fit
and find his strange dancing girl for keeps.
He went to their house and the two sisters
were delighted because they had lovely feet.
The eldest went into a room to try the slipper on
but her big toe got in the way so she simply
sliced it off and put on the slipper.
The prince rode away with her until the white dove
told him to look at the blood pouring forth.
That is the way with amputations.
They don't just heal up like a wish.
The other sister cut off her heel
but the blood told as blood will.
The prince was getting tired.
He began to feel like a shoe salesman.
But he gave it one last try.
This time Cinderella fit into the shoe
like a love letter into its envelope.

At the wedding ceremony
the two sisters came to curry favor
and the white dove pecked their eyes out.
Two hollow spots were left
like soup spoons.

Cinderella and the prince
lived, they say, happily ever after,
like two dolls in a museum case
never bothered by diapers or dust,
never arguing over the timing of an egg,
never telling the same story twice,

> never getting a middle-aged spread,
> their darling smiles pasted on for eternity.
> Regular Bobbsey Twins.
> That story.

FEMININE ENDING (sometimes called *light* or *falling ending*) A line that ends with an unstressed syllable, such as "-ing" at the end of Percy Bysshe Shelley's "O wild West Wind, thou breath of Autumn's being."

The extra unstressed syllable is usually considered a metrical appendage, not part of the final *foot:

And, darkly bright, are bright in dark directed.

(Shakespeare, Sonnet 43)

The term derives from grammatical gender and is merely a poetic convention; a masculine line ends on a stressed syllable, as in Elizabeth Bishop's line "A blue-white sky, a simple web" (from "Brazil, January 1, 1502").

FIGURATIVE LANGUAGE Language that uses figures of speech, such as *metaphor and *simile, to present something in the guise of something else or compare one thing to another. It superimposes a "figure" upon the surface of what's really there, the literal.

Figurative language is a way of saying one thing and suggesting another, so the words have significance beyond the literal meaning. In Seamus Heaney's *sonnet "The Forge" (which follows), the literal scene is a blacksmith's shop in contemporary Ireland. The figurative scene is the mind or imagination of any craftsman or maker—such as a poet, who also knows "a door into the dark"— whose craft, like blacksmithing or poetry, seems like a vestige of the past.

Sylvia Plath wrote the following poem in January and February of 1960. On April 1st of the same year, she gave birth to her daughter Frieda Hughes (who is now herself a poet, the author of

Waxworks). In this poem, the speaker addresses a fetus in the womb. Almost every line contains a metaphor or simile. It is also an example of a *list poem and a poem using the *title as first line.

YOU'RE

> Clownlike, happiest on your hands,
> Feet to the stars, and moon-skulled,
> Gilled like a fish. A common-sense
> Thumbs-down on the dodo's mode.
> Wrapped up in yourself like a spool,
> Trawling your dark as owls do.
> Mute as a turnip from the Fourth
> Of July to All Fool's Day,
> O high-riser, my little loaf.
>
> Vague as fog and looked for like mail.
> Farther off than Australia.
> Bent-backed Atlas, our traveled prawn.
> Snug as a bud and at home
> Like a sprat in a pickle jug.
> A creel of eels, all ripples.
> Jumpy as a Mexican bean.
> Right, like a well-done sum.
> A clean slate, with your own face on.

—Sylvia Plath (1932–1963)

THE FORGE / Seamus Heaney (b. 1939)

> All I know is a door into the dark.
> Outside, old axles and iron hoops rusting;
> Inside, the hammered anvil's short-pitched ring,
> The unpredictable fantail of sparks
> Or hiss when a new shoe toughens in water.
> The anvil must be somewhere in the centre,
> Horned as a unicorn, at one end square,
> Set there immovable: an altar

> Where he expends himself in shape and music.
> Sometimes, leather-aproned, hairs in his nose,
> He leans out on the jamb, recalls a clatter
> Of hoofs where traffic is flashing in rows;
> Then grunts and goes in, with a slam and flick
> To beat real iron out, to work the bellows.

FOOT (plural, *feet*) A unit of measure in a metrical line, analogous to a measure in music, with syllables instead of notes.

In *accentual-syllabic verse, there are six common feet: the *iamb or iambic (˘ ´), the *trochee or trochaic (´ ˘), the *anapest or anapestic (˘ ˘ ´), the *dactyl or dactylic (´ ˘ ˘), the *pyrrhic (˘ ˘), and the *spondee or spondaic (´ ´). Most lines in English accentual-syllabic verse can be scanned (metrically analyzed) using just these feet, with the addition of the monosyllabic foot (a stressed syllable by itself: ´) and the feminine ending (an unstressed syllable by itself at the end of a line: ˘).

These terms come from Greek *prosody (which counts the length of syllables, not their accentuation) and fit uncomfortably into English metrics. However, they do work and are useful in investigating how the rhythm follows or diverges from the *meter (which is a metronomic pattern).

Greek *quantitative meter was based on the length of syllables (or quantities): long (−) and short (˘). Robert Graves suggests that the meter derived from dance steps, and that is certainly true in the Greek choral ode, as in the plays of Sophocles, in which the choruses were choreographed. For every group of three stanzas the members of the chorus would dance first left, then right, and then would stand still. *(See* ODE.*)*

Alexandrian scholars classified the feet (or metrical units, groups of rhythmically related syllables) by names we still use for English verse:

Two-syllable	Three-syllable	Four-syllable
⏑ — iamb	⏑ ⏑ — anapest	⏑ ⏑ ⏑ ⏑ proceleusmatic
— ⏑ trochee	— ⏑ ⏑ dactyl	— — — — dispondee
⏑ ⏑ pyrrhic	⏑ — ⏑ amphibrach	⏑ — — ⏑ antipast
— — spondee	— ⏑ — cretic or amphimac(er)	— ⏑ ⏑ — choriamb(us)
	⏑ ⏑ ⏑ tribrach	— ⏑ ⏑ ⏑ 1st paeon
	— — — molossus	⏑ — ⏑ ⏑ 2nd paeon
	⏑ — — bacchic	⏑ ⏑ — ⏑ 3rd paeon
	— — ⏑ antibacchic	⏑ ⏑ ⏑ — 4th paeon
		⏑ — — — 1st epitrite
		— ⏑ — — 2nd epitrite
		— — ⏑ — 3rd epitrite
		— — — ⏑ 4th epitrite
		— ⏑ — ⏑ ditrochee
		⏑ — ⏑ — di-iamb
		— — ⏑ ⏑ major ionic
		⏑ ⏑ — — minor ionic

F

For accentual-syllabic verse, change the long-short signs (– ˘) to stressed-unstressed (´ ˘). Four-syllable feet tend to break into two two-syllable feet. The *minor ionic is very common in English; it is called a *double foot (a pyrrhic and a spondee) and sometimes a double iamb. In accentual-syllabic verse, it is unusual to find three unstressed syllables in a row, unless one or more is elided. The middle of the three tends to assert itself slightly and become accented: a *relative stress. *(See* SCANSION.)

FORM (Latin, "shape") 1. An established pattern to which a poem conforms. The typical *sonnet, for example, consists of fourteen lines written to a set rhyme scheme. By this definition, the form is a receptacle which holds the words (or content) of a poem.

2. The shape made by the words of an individual poem, whether it follows a traditional pattern or not, whether it is metrical or not, whether it is in verse or in prose. Robert Creeley's remark that "form is just an extension of content" applies to this definition. The form arises from the words (content) of the poem.

Ezra Pound says, "I think there is a 'fluid' as well as a 'solid' content, that some poems may have form as a tree has form, some as water poured into a vase." Robert Hass has asserted that no two sonnets have the same form, obviously true given the second definition, obviously false given the first. It depends upon whether "form" is a physical shape or a platonic ideal. Is it like a mold into which a cook pours various ingredients? Or is it like the shape a person, tree, or mineral deposit might grow into? Generally, the first definition (form preceding content) applies more to *metrical verse, the second definition (form deriving from content) more to *free verse.

In any case, metrical poetry is often called formal, and poets who write in rhyme and meter are called formalist. Denise Levertov calls poetry that discovers its form as it proceeds organic. Perhaps the clearest way to distinguish these two definitions of form is to call the first "traditional form" and the second "organic form."

FOUND POEM Text discovered in some nonpoetic setting (an advertisement, for example), removed from its context and presented as a poem.

In the following example, Maxine Kumin apparently arranged the found passage into the first twelve lines, and then added her own comment in the concluding couplet of what turned out to be a *sonnet. (It rhymes *abbacddceffe gg*.)

POEM FOUND IN *THE NEW HAMPSHIRE DEPARTMENT OF AGRICULTURE WEEKLY MARKET BULLETIN* / Maxine Kumin (b. 1925)

> Ground saturated with water. Some
> thunderstorms and wind have lodged
> lots of hayland. Frost damage
> in isolated pockets. From
> Strafford, word of leaf miner
> on beets and swiss chard. Timothy
> just out of the boot and ready
> to cut. Corn planting 80 per-
> cent in, needs sun to green up well.
> Rose chafer sighted widely, but
> little sign of chewing yet.
> The next few days are critical.
>
> Thus heavily infested, June
> lurches harvestward again.

FOURTEENER A line consisting of seven *iambic *feet ($\smile$ $/$ | $\smile$ $/$ | $\smile$ $/$ | $\smile$ $/$ | $\smile$ $/$ | $\smile$ $/$ | $\smile$ $/$); iambic heptameter.

This *meter, typically in rhymed *couplets, was common in the sixteenth century. The greater flexibility of iambic pentameter led to the demise of the fourteener, which can sound singsong and monotonous. However, poets who translated from Greek and Latin, such as George Chapman and Arthur Golding, found in the fourteener a useful parallel for the classical hexameter line. There was room to swell and thunder and narrate in the long fourteeners. Here is Arthur Golding's translation of a passage about Daedalus, the designer of the labyrinth and of wings for himself and his son Icarus, from Ovid's *Metamorphoses* (Book VIII, 245–51):

> Now in this while gan *Daedalus* a wearinesse to take
> Of living like a banisht man and prisoner such a time
> In *Crete*, and longèd in his heart to see his native Clime.
> But Seas enclosèd him as if he had in prison be.
> Then thought he: though both Sea and land King *Minos*
>   stop fro me,
> I am assurde he cannot stop the Aire and open Skie:
> To make my passage that way then my cunning I will trie.

Fourteeners tend to roll on. In fact, the line is so long, it often seems to split into two halves, with a *caesura (pause) somewhere near the middle. Instead of seven stresses together, we often hear them broken into four-three, so a line might sound like:

> I am assurde he cannot stop
>   the Aire and open Skie

Rhymed fourteeners are in fact very similar to the *ballad stanza, as in these lines from "The Wife of Usher's Well":

> I wish the wind may never cease,
>   Nor fishes in the flood,
> Till my three sons come home to me
>   In earthly flesh and blood.

The chief difference is that a ballad stanza indicates exactly where the pause appears (a line break after the fourth stress in odd-numbered lines) while a fourteener may or may not have a pause in the middle. A ballad stanza also permits extra unstressed syllables. (Fourteeners from George Chapman's translation of Homer's *The Iliad* appear in EPIC SIMILE.)

FRAGMENT A piece or scrap from a larger whole that is either lost or unfinished.

Most of Sappho's poetry has been lost; what survives has come down to us either because ancient scholars quoted parts of it or bits turned up on strips of papyrus used to wrap mummies. A stray line or two may exist, or perhaps only a word here and there, utterances broken off abruptly. *(See* PALINODE *for a fragment by Stesichorus.)* Unfinished fragments might include Samuel Taylor Coleridge's "Kubla Khan" (although it may seem complete) and some of Ezra Pound's late *Cantos*.

Those kinds of fragments are unintentional, but poets also do it on purpose, writing fragments meant to suggest a brokenness in the world, shards that are meant to be expressive as wholes in themselves. William Carlos Williams uses fragments—scraps of imagery, quick glimpses that give way to other views—in some sections of his suite "January Morning." Here is part VI:

> —and a semicircle of dirt-colored men
> about a fire bursting from an old
> ash can,

The section ends with a comma, then part VII shifts to an image of trolley rails in cobblestones.

Another kind of fragment, found especially in contemporary poetry, is the *sentence fragment. Consisting of a word, phrase, or subordinate clause (which lacks a main verb), it is punctuated like a complete sentence, as in these lines from Weldon Kees's "Aspects of Robinson":

> Robinson afraid, drunk, sobbing Robinson
> In bed with a Mrs. Morse. Robinson at home;
> Decisions: Toynbee or luminol?

The lack of verbs here, and elsewhere in this poem, suggests a static, empty life cluttered with objects but heading nowhere.

FRAGMENT 123 / Sappho (circa 620–550 B.C.E.;
tr. Guy Davenport)

Black dreams of such virulence[
That sleep's sweetness[
And terrible grief[
The place is religious[
Happiness, no, and hope neither[
And I indeed am so[
Delightful the games[
And I[
This[

NOTE: The open bracket ([) indicates a gap in the remainder of the line.

NARROW FLAME / Linda Gregerson (b. 1950)

Dark still. Twelve degrees below freezing.
    Tremor along
  the elegant, injured right front

leg of the gelding on the cross-ties. Kneeling
    girl.
  The undersong of waters as she bathes

the leg in yet more cold. [tongue is broken]
    [god to me]
  Her hair the color of winter wheat.

NOTE: Gregerson writes, "The title and bracketed phrases are from Sappho, fragment 31."

FRAGMENTATION An experimental technique in which the poet breaks apart the logical structures and connective tissue of language and syntax in order to assemble the pieces into some fresh, surprising, jagged whole that does not necessarily represent things or events in traditionally realistic ways. Collage (literally a "gluing together") is the usual structure, dissonance the typical effect. The technique is parallel to movements in the other arts, such as serialism in music and cubism in painting, and coincides with the rapid technological advances and social upheavals of the early twentieth century. T.S.

Eliot's *The Waste Land*, published in 1922, juxtaposes unrelated passages and splices together fragments from different languages, asserting "These fragments I have shored against my ruins." The technique is central to the work of the *Language poets.

SOUL SAYS / Jorie Graham (b. 1950)

(AFTERWORD)

To be so held by brittleness, shapeliness.
By meaning. As where I *have to go where you go,*
I *have to touch what you must touch,*
in hunger, in boredom, the spindrift, the ticket ...
Distilled in you (can you hear me)
the idiom in you, the why—

The flash *of a voice.* The river *glints.*
The mother *opens the tablecloth up into the wind.*
There as the fabric descends—the alphabet of ripenesses,
what is, what could have been.
The bread on the tablecloth. Crickets shrill in the grass.

O pluck my magic garment from me. So.

                        [lays down his robe]

Lie there, my art—

(This is a form of matter of matter she sang)

(Where the hurry is stopped) (and held) (but not extinguished) (no)

(So listen, listen, this will soothe you) (if that is what you want)

Now then, I said, I go to meet that which I liken to
(even though the wave break and drown me in laughter)
the wave breaking, the wave drowning me in laughter—

NOTE: In the notes at the end of *Region of Unlikeness*, Jorie Graham writes: "Prospero speaks throughout the poem." Prospero is the magician and main character of William Shakespeare's *The Tempest*. Starting with "O pluck my magic garment," Graham quotes two of his lines (and a stage direction) from Act I, Scene II, when he's speaking to his daughter Miranda—although he actually says "Lend thy hand / And pluck my magic garment ..." *(See* BLANK VERSE *for a passage spoken by Prospero in the play.)*

FREE VERSE Nonmetrical verse; lines that are not measured or counted for number of *accents, number of *syllables, or length of syllables; lines that are free of *meter; also called *vers libre*.

Free verse is as old as the Bible, whose long verses are not metrical, although they are structured according to repetition and variation of words and phrases. Despite the use of occasional free verse by otherwise metrical poets like the eighteenth century's Christopher Smart ("For I will consider my Cat Jeoffry" from *Jubilate Agno*) and Johann Wolfgang von Goethe ("Prometheus"), modern free verse begins in English with Walt Whitman (who modeled his long lines on the Bible and grand opera) and in French with Arthur Rimbaud (who did not). Rimbaud simply rebelled against everything, both social and poetic conventions.

There are no particular rules for free verse, but there are many precedents. And although free verse cannot be classified numerically, like iambic pentameter, it can nevertheless be described in a general way. There are several distinct types of free verse, dependent on the relative length of the lines, the preponderance of *end-stopping or *enjambment (run-on lines), the preservation or breaking of phrase units, and the visual or typographical arrangement on the page. A free verse poet can, of course, combine any or all of these if a poem is long enough (as Ezra Pound does in *The Cantos* and William Carlos Williams in *Paterson*).

Several kinds of free verse are listed here. Model poems follow at the end of the entry.

• Short-lined free verse: The lines might range between one syllable and several words, about an inch or two of type, between one and three stresses, but these are just estimates—after all, if the lines begin to look and sound like each other, their freedom from meter might be in jeopardy. Early twentieth-century free verse, by the *Imagists, for example, tended to retain phrase units as distinct lines; later

poetic descendents, such as the *Black Mountain poets, began to enjamb more, breaking phrase units between lines, ending lines with
minor words such as prepositions or articles.

• Long-lined free verse: The lines might stretch between left and right
margins, or they might tumble over the right-hand edge; if they do,
they are "tucked under," indented a few letters to indicate that they
belong to the line above, the two (or three or more) constituting a
single, discrete line. The Bible's long lines inspired Walt Whitman,
who inspired Robinson Jeffers, Allen Ginsberg, and many others.
Shorter lines can occasionally be interspersed among the long ones
for rhythmic variation or emphasis, as they are in Walt Whitman's
"A Noiseless Patient Spider." (Short-lined free verse is not so toler-
ant of long lines, although medium lengths are okay; generally long-
lined free verse seems more raggedy, while short-lined seems neater.)
Whitman's poem also shows how free verse can mimic metrical verse
in an approximate way. The poem consists of two stanzas equal in
lines (five each), and the first lines of both stanzas are relatively short;
the poem, however, does not scan according to either number of
syllables or number of accents (although it comes fairly close). Long-
lined free verse is more often end-stopped than enjambed.

• Variable-length free verse: Much free verse mixes short lines with
medium-length and long lines. The constant variety can be pleasing
in itself, an almost regular irregularity, a nimble shifting, a closing
and opening, as in Galway Kinnell's poems in *Body Rags* and *The
Book of Nightmares*. This kind of free verse can also be based on an
average line that is medium in length, shortening or lengthening for
rhythmic or expressive purposes. As such, it is probably the most
common kind of free verse.

• Spatial or typographical arrangement: The typewriter or computer
keyboard is often used to "score" the music of poetry visually upon
the page. Although poets have written *pattern poems (words
arranged into an actual picture, such as a pillar or an altar) since
antiquity, technology and the rise of the avant-garde led to experi-

F

ments by Stéphane Mallarmé, Ezra Pound, William Carlos Williams, e e cummings, and others, using the page as a kind of canvas for the spatial arrangement of words, phrases, and lines, which can be scattered widely or blocked together, using white space for mental pauses.

T.S. Eliot writes, "No *vers* is *libre* for the man who wants to do a good job." At its best, free verse can surge in waves or retract, inventing itself as it goes. At its worst, it can be, as Ezra Pound points out, prose chopped up "into line lengths."

Novices often imagine that short-lined free verse must be speedier than long lines, but that's not usually the case. Short lines invite pauses at the ends of the lines, and the fewer words in each line necessarily receive more prominence than the many words in long lines. Enjambment may quicken the pace over end-stopping—but not always. Robert Creeley's poems often have lines broken after an article, which imposes at least a slight pause, a musical effect that slows down the movement. Poets who write long-lined free verse, such as Allen Ginsberg and Gerald Stern, tend to read aloud quickly; poets such as Gary Snyder and Creeley read short lines slowly, carefully, punctuating almost every word. It is like the difference between flow and trickle, express and local. At root, there may be a kind of equivalence in lines, so long lines have to move quickly in the given space while short lines can prolong the moment.

In the twentieth century, theories have propelled the spread of free verse. The Imagists generally isolated their images in short-lined, phrasal free verse. Ezra Pound, the movement's founder, writes, "To break the pentameter, that was the first heave." He also speaks of composing according to "the musical phrase" instead of the metronome. Following directly upon the theory and the practice of Pound, Charles Olson's projective verse calls for open, organic, inclusive form and flexible rhythms based upon breath units. Robert Duncan's open field composition also seeks open form, deriving "melody and story from impulse not from plan." (*See* BEAT POETRY, BIBLICAL VERSE, BLACK MOUNTAIN SCHOOL, DEEP IMAGE POETRY, IMAGISM, POETRY, PSALM, *and* TRIADIC LINE.)

Short-Lined Free Verse

GIRAFFE / Stanley Plumly (b. 1939)

The only head in the sky.
Buoyed like a bird's,
on bird legs too.
Moves in the slowmotion
of a ride
across the longlegged miles
of the same place.
Grazes in trees.
Bends like a bow
over water
in a shy sort of
spreadeagle.
Embarrassed by
such vulnerability,
often trembles, gathering
together
in a single moment
the whole loose
fragment of body
before the run downwind.
Will stand still
in a camouflage of kind
in a rare daylight
for hours,
the leaves spilling
one break of sun
into another,
listening to the lions.
Will, when dark comes
and the fields open
until there are
no fields,

F

117

turn in the length
of light
toward some calm
still part of a tree's
new shadow, part of the moon.
Will stand all night
so tall
the sun will rise.

Long-Lined Free Verse

THE NECKTIES / Rodney Jones (b. 1950)

Let me hang around the driftwood long enough and I forget what it means to wear shirts and long pants,
to wait in line in the back of the department store while
the alterations are being done.
I forget the pleats, the pressed creases, and the lapels of
jackets,
the French cuffs hiding their ashes, their laundered balls
of paper like spitwads from elementary school.
Let me sit down each morning at Sonny's, eating my
poached eggs and bacon with the fishermen
whose faces have taken cancer from the sun, whose arms
are stenciled with the names
of girls they met far from here, the strange anchors lifted
from other seas.

After the first week the whiteness leaves, and the pale
wishes of our city.
I walk all day through the bevies of sunbathers, and, because I'm old enough,
not every oiled thigh is leading up to a rendezvous out
there in the dunes where the sea thistles itch
and misplaced spectacles burrow down among the roots of
sawgrass.
By the third week I avoid company and don't wash except
in seawater.

I welcome the old onion of my animal struggling up from
    the armpits.
I think I am becoming that ocean, defenseless as far as I
    am unbounded,
my shores polluted, my laughter coming in waves, my tears
    rising with my gall.

The charm is to approach nakedness, the hand almost
    touching the wild bird, almost the song
coming apart in the hand—but our smallest fashion is like
    the neon sign under the palm branch,
advertising our dominion and holy separateness, and I
    must remember again my father's neckties
slipping through my hands in the cool closet, the synthetic
    and silk tentacles
of a respectability he married in his mind to clean nails
    and chandeliers.
Tying them scrupulously, the way a winter fisherman ties
    the perfect fly, he went out to his job
with his words cramped and his breath hobbled to the
    logos of his good life.

In memory I hoard each tie, fashioning the serpent and
    the hangman's noose, as I have lingered
over the pebbles of his alligator shoes and watched his
    suits above me fill with years of duplicate Sundays.
His secret ritual, to keep the world always at his throat, I
    have buried among the susurrations of his disapproval.
Naked tonight, I swim halfway to my father, the yokes of
    his dead gods fallen around me.
In my exhaustion I lie in the welts of moonlight on the
    sand, relying this time on the nose,
the forgotten sense of the twentieth century, to show me
    again the rancor and the lost essences,
to separate the odor of sex from the odor of death in the
    odor of the sea.

Variable-Length Free Verse

GOING HOME BY LAST LIGHT / Galway Kinnell (b. 1927)

1

Redheaded by last light,
with high-stepped, illusionist amble
I walk toward the white room
where she is waiting,
past
pimentos,
red cabbages,
tomatoes flickering in their bins,
past melons, past mushrooms and onions.

2

Those swarms
of Mayflies that used to rise
at the Vermont threshold, "imagos"
thrown up for a day,
their mouths shriveling closed,
their wings,
their sexual parts, newborn and perfect...

3

For several minutes
two mosquitoes have been making love
on top of this poem,
changing positions, swooning, even they,
their thighs
fragile as a baby's hairs, knowing
the ecstasy.

4

A day!
The wings of the earth
lift and fall
to the groans, the cold, savage thumpings of a heart.

Spatial or Typographical Arrangement of Free-Verse Lines

EVERYBODY LYING ON THEIR STOMACHS,
HEAD TOWARD THE CANDLE, READING,
SLEEPING, DRAWING / Gary Snyder (b. 1930)

The corrugated roof
Booms and fades night-long to

million-darted rain
squalls   and

outside

lightning

Photographs in the brain
Wind-bent bamboo.

through

the plank shutter
set

Half-open   on eternity

FUGITIVES A poetic group whose members met at Vanderbilt University in Nashville, Tennessee, in the 1920s and founded a literary periodical, *The Fugitive*, devoted to verse that was generally formalist, ironic, and regional (meaning Southern). They considered themselves fugitives from the disorder of contemporary poetry, from Victorian sentimentality, and from "the high-caste Brahmins of the Old South." The magazine ran from 1922 to 1925 and was summed up in a 1928 anthology. Some of the most prominent Fugitives were John Crowe Ransom, Allen Tate, and Robert Penn Warren. The social, cultural, and political views of the group developed into Agrarianism, presented in *I'll Take My Stand* (1930), which championed the traditional values of the rural South as a corrective to

F

industrialization. The critical views of the Fugitives developed into an important part of the New Criticism (a term coined by Ransom in a book about the criticism of William Empson, T.S. Eliot, I.A. Richards, and Yvor Winters), which championed the close reading of poems, a minute attention to the actual words, and a shunning of what might be behind the words—biographical facts or the poet's intentions.

The following poem by John Crowe Ransom is a *dialogue in *sonnet form. Each *stanza begins and ends with a *refrain. There is an intentionally old-fashioned—and ironic—sound to what the two figures (Death and the Maiden) say. "Dustcoat" is an especially apt word here; it denotes the long coat worn by a motorist in the early days of automobiles, but it also suggests "dust to dust," an image of death.

F

PIAZZA PIECE / John Crowe Ransom (1888–1974)

—I am a gentleman in a dustcoat trying
To make you hear. Your ears are soft and small
And listen to an old man not at all,
They want the young men's whispering and sighing.
But see the roses on your trellis dying
And hear the spectral singing of the moon;
For I must have my lovely lady soon,
I am a gentleman in a dustcoat trying.

—I am a lady young in beauty waiting
Until my truelove comes, and then we kiss.
But what grey man among the vines is this
Whose words are dry and faint as in a dream?
Back from my trellis, Sir, before I scream!
I am a lady young in beauty waiting.

G

GEORGIC (Greek, "farmer," from "earth" + "work") A poem about life in the country, in particular the work of farmers.

The earliest known georgic is Hesiod's *Works and Days*, written around 750 B.C.E. Virgil (70–19 B.C.E.) wrote his *Georgics*, or poems about farm life, between 37 and 30 B.C.E. while he was living on the estate of Maecenas, a Roman statesman and patron of the arts. These poems are *didactic, offering instruction and advice on cultivating fields, planting groves, raising livestock, and keeping bees:

> What makes the valleys laugh and sing, what star
> Should speed the plough and marry vine to elm,
> The care of kine and how to rear a flock,
> What skill shall keep the parsimonious bee,
> Hence is my song ...
>
> (tr. T.F. Royds)

More recently, the Kentucky poet Wendell Berry has written many poems about the work and life of farming. *(See* IDYLL *and* PASTORAL.*)*

ENRICHING THE EARTH / Wendell Berry (b. 1934)

> To enrich the earth I have sowed clover and grass
> to grow and die. I have plowed in the seeds
> of winter grains and of various legumes,
> their growth to be plowed in to enrich the earth.

I have stirred into the ground the offal
and the decay of the growth of past seasons
and so mended the earth and made its yield increase.
All this serves the dark. I am slowly falling
into the fund of things. And yet to serve the earth,
not knowing what I serve, gives a wideness
and a delight to the air, and my days
do not wholly pass. It is the mind's service,
for when the will fails so do the hands
and one lives at the expense of life.
After death, willing or not, the body serves,
entering the earth. And so what was heaviest
and most mute is at last raised up into song.

GHAZAL (guz´-ul; Arabic, "talk about love" or "the cry of a gazelle when it is hunted down and trapped") A *lyric poem of at least five and up to roughly fifteen *couplets, originally written in Persian, Arabic, Urdu, and other Middle Eastern languages. The form probably originated in Arabia in the seventh century. The couplets are not connected but stand as independent units within the poem. The poet is free to make associative jumps from one couplet to the next but not to *enjamb between them. Only the first couplet (*matla*) rhymes (*aa*), but the second line of every succeeding couplet rhymes with it (*Xa*). In the last couplet, the poet may insert his name, although this is sometimes omitted.

In traditional ghazals, the rhyme word (*qafia*) is usually followed by a *refrain (*radif*) made up of a single word or a phrase. This rhyme-and-refrain combination also occurs at the end of the first line of the opening couplet. Sometimes the poet omits the rhyme or the refrain but must do so consistently through any given set of couplets. In the ghazal below by the Persian poet Hafiz, the rhyme words (including a slant rhyme in line one) are "desire," "snare," "where," "air," "there," "share," "air," and "everywhere," while the refrain is "I rise."

The ghazal may have originated in the erotic prologue of an earlier form, the *qasida*, which is also written in couplets and rhymed *aa Xa Xa Xa*, etc. But it consists of more than fifteen couplets, up to about a hundred, and is used for occasional verse and public declamation. Ghazals are traditionally sung (up to the present day in places where Urdu is spoken) and usually deal with erotic or mystical love, often connected with Sufi mysticism.

Federico Garcia Lorca (1898–1936) wrote a number of ghazals, including "Ghazal of the Terrifying Presence." Some contemporary poets have dispensed with rhyme in their ghazals, emphasizing the imaginative shifts between couplets. Adrienne Rich has written two sequences: *Ghazals: Homage to Ghalib* (in honor of the great nineteenth-century master of ghazals in Urdu) and *The Blue Ghazals*. Jim Harrison has written a sequence called *Ghazals*. In "Sheffield Ghazals," Galway Kinnell imitates the form by using long lines ending in periods instead of couplets. But many American poets now use the rhymes and refrains of the traditional ghazal. The poet Agha Shahid Ali edited an anthology of them, *Ravishing DisUnities: Real Ghazals in English*.

WHERE CAN I HEAR THE NEWS / Hafiz of Shiraz
(1325–1389; tr. John Drury)

> (inscribed on the poet's tomb in Shiraz, Iran)

Where can I hear the news, so that out of desire I rise?
So that, like a homing pigeon from a snare, I rise?

If you command me to your service, I'll renounce
the world and its worldliness, though it's where I rise.

O Lord, loosen the rain from your thunderhead of mercy—
as long as, like dust that floats in the air, I rise.

Bring a singer and some excellent wine to my tomb,
wafting your fragrance, dancing, so that out of there I rise.

Climb to your full height and sway like a cypress to raise me.
Clapping my hands, applauding the world we share, I rise.

Although I'm old, embrace me for a solitary night,
so that with the dawn, aroused in the fresh air, I rise.

On the day I die, bless Hafiz with one last look at you
before, leaving desire behind me everywhere, I rise.

THE BLUE GHAZALS (9/21/68) / Adrienne Rich (b. 1929)

Violently asleep in the old house.
A clock stays awake all night ticking.

Turning, turning their bruised leaves
the trees stay awake all night in the wood.

Talk to me with your body through my dreams.
Tell me what we are going through.

The walls of the room are muttering,
old trees, old Utopians, arguing with the wind.

To float like a dead man in a sea of dreams
and half those dreams being dreamed by someone else.

Fifteen years of sleepwalking with you,
wading against the tide, and with the tide.

MY WORD / Agha Shahid Ali (1949–2001)

I am lying even now—I give you my word.
Kind of a picnic, an occupied shoe. My word!

My telegram arrives, no one's there to read it—
not even he who on tombs will bedew my word.

Danger invites rescue, we have a good thing going.
So let's break everything, please rescue my word.

The ghost said nothing that added to our knowledge.
Upon the candle—which lit itself—who blew my word?

I'm at home, betrothed to blue, with her refracted light.
The light is home, this blue is blue all through my word.

Hard to say who's winning. Nobody is winning.
Kansas City! Oriental art! Big Zoo! My word!

I took the shortest route through Belief's sad country
when archangels, on the Word's command, slew my word.

This erasure tilts words toward memory or tilts
against your word—at the tiny hour of two—my word.

Forgive me, please, could we be alone forever?
I have never been alone; I'll live to rue my word.

Our silence, Beloved Enemy, is not beyond
whatever love has done to your word, to my word.

Now don't put on, please, that face, just wait for me here.
I stand no one up. See you in a few. My word.

Will the barbarians bring again their invisible language?
They were the solution, they foreknew my word.

Yours too, Shahid, will be a radical departure.
You'll go out of yourself and then into my word.

(FOR JAMES TATE)

G

GLOSA, GLOSE (gloe´-sa; Spanish, "gloss") A Spanish verse form, introduced by court poets around the turn of the fifteenth century, beginning with a short *stanza or *texte* that states the theme of the poem; succeeding stanzas explain or gloss each of those lines, repeating them freely as *refrains. Lewis Turco's "Simon Judson," from *Bordello*, is an example in English.

H

HAIBUN (hie'-bun, the "u" pronounced as in "put") A Japanese form in which a prose text is interspersed with verse, specifically *haiku (three lines containing a total of seventeen syllables). A haiku typically appears at the end of a haibun, but other haiku may appear earlier, even at the beginning. Haibun often takes the form of a diary or travel journal. (*See* VERSE MIXED WITH PROSE.)

ARRIVAL IN TOKYO / James Merrill (1926–1995)

Our section of town is Roppongi, where thirty years ago I dined in W's gloomy wooden farmhouse. The lanes and gardens of his neighborhood have given way to glitzy skyscrapers like this hotel—all crystal and brass, a piano and life-size ceramic Saint Bernard in the carpeted lobby. It is late when the revolving door whisks us forth, later yet when our two lengthening shadows leave the noodle shop to wander before bed through the Aoyama cemetery. Mishima is buried down one of its paths bordered by cherry trees in full, amazing bloom. Underneath, sitting on the ground—no, on outspread plastic or paper, shoes left in pairs alongside these instant "rooms"—a few ghostly parties are still eating and drinking, lit by small flames. One group has a transistor, another makes its own music, clapping hands and singing. Their lantern faces glow in the half-dark's black-beamed, blossom-tented

dusk within the night.
The high street lamp through snowy
branches burns moon-bright.

HAIKU (hie'-koo; Japanese, "amusement" + "sentence"; plural, *haiku*; also called *hokku*) A Japanese poetic form made up of three lines with a total of seventeen syllables, usually arranged 5-7-5.

In English and American poetry, many haiku simply follow that syllabic pattern. Sometimes a poet will rhyme lines one and three, perhaps even using the form as a haiku *stanza in a longer poem, as in Richard Wilbur's "Alatus" and "Thyme Flowering among Rocks." *(See James Merrill's haiku in* HAIBUN *and Paul Muldoon's "News Headlines from the Homer Noble Farm" in* TERZA RIMA.*)* But a poem could also consist of a different number of lines and syllables and still be considered a haiku. The spirit of haiku often identifies it more than the *meter. The essential elements are brevity, immediacy, spontaneity, imagery (often the juxtaposition of contrasting images), a reference to one of the four seasons, and sudden illumination. That flash of awareness is crucial. Haiku is, after all, an important path to insight in Zen Buddhism.

R.H. Blyth calls haiku "the poetry of the seasons." If a poem follows the three-line form but lacks any suggestion of a season, it is technically a *senryu (sen'-ree-yoo)*.

Haiku grew out of two earlier Japanese forms, *tanka (or waka)*, a five-line stanza arranged 5-7-5-7-7, and *renga ("linked verse")*, a collaborative form in which two or more poets would take turns, the first using the first three lines of a tanka, the second using the last two lines, and then continuing for some time. That opening was called a *hokku*, or "starting verse." Matsuo Basho is credited with pioneering the haiku as an independent form.

In English, poets sometimes dispense with the seventeen-syllable count and may use fewer or more lines for their haiku. Allen Ginsberg translates Basho's *Furuike ya*, the best known of all haiku, in a single line:

Old pond—frog jumps in—kerplunk!

H

In "A Month in Summer," her version of a Japanese poetic diary (or *utanikki*), Carolyn Kizer follows the four-line form that Nobuyuki Yuasa uses for his translations of Issa.

FOUR HAIKU / Matsuo Basho (1644–1694)

sweeping the garden
but letting the temple keep
the willows' droppings

(tr. Cid Corman)

the autumn coolness
hand and hand paring away
eggplants cucumbers

(tr. Cid Corman)

what with fleas and lice
the horse having a good piss
right at the pillow

(tr. Cid Corman)

The temple bell stops—
but the sound keeps coming
out of the flowers.

(tr. Robert Bly)

FOUR HAIKU / Kobayashi Issa (1763–1827; tr. Robert Bly)

This line of black ants—
maybe it goes all the way back
to that white cloud!

I look into a dragonfly's eye
and see
the mountains over my shoulder.

Cricket, be
careful! I'm rolling
over!

Now listen, you watermelons—
if any thieves come—
turn into frogs!

HAIKU / Etheridge Knight (1931–1991)

1

Eastern guard tower
glints in sunset; convicts rest
like lizards on rocks.

2

The piano man
is stingy at 3 A.M.
his songs drop like plum.

3

Morning sun slants cell.
Drunks stagger like cripple flies
On jailhouse floor.

4

To write a blues song
is to regiment riots
and pluck gems from graves.

5

A bare pecan tree
slips a pencil shadow down
a moonlit snow slope.

6

The falling snow flakes
Cannot blunt the hard aches nor
Match the steel stillness.

7

Under moon shadows
A tall boy flashes knife and
Slices star bright ice.

8

In the August grass
Struck by the last rays of sun
The cracked teacup screams.

9

Making jazz swing in
Seventeen syllables AIN'T
No square poet's job.

HARLEM RENAISSANCE An African-American literary movement centered in Harlem in the 1920s.

Influenced by jazz and blues, continuing the poetic tradition
that was presented in James Weldon Johnson's *The Book of American
Negro Poetry* (1922), the poets of the Harlem Renaissance celebrated
black culture, contemplated the movement of blacks from the rural
South to the urban North, and attacked the forces that oppressed
blacks in America.

Poets of the Harlem Renaissance include Langston Hughes, Jean
Toomer, Claude McKay, and Countee Cullen. In the following poem,
Langston Hughes replies to Walt Whitman's "I Hear America Singing."

I, TOO / Langston Hughes (1902–1967)

I, too, sing America.

I am the darker brother.
They send me to eat in the kitchen
When company comes,
But I laugh,
And eat well,
And grow strong.

Tomorrow,
I'll sit at the table
When company comes.
Nobody'll dare

Say to me,
"Eat in the kitchen,"
Then.

Besides,
They'll see how beautiful I am
And be ashamed,—

I, too, am America.

HEROIC COUPLET Two adjacent lines of *iambic pentameter that rhyme together. Defined more strictly, the lines in a heroic couplet form a discrete unit, a complete sentence, and often use phrases that are parallel, antithetical, or otherwise balanced, as in John Dryden's *Absalom and Achitophel*:

> In Friendship false, implacable in Hate:
> Resolv'd to Ruine or to Rule the State.

Iambic pentameter couplets first appeared in English in *The Canterbury Tales* of Geoffrey Chaucer and later in early plays of Shakespeare such as *Romeo and Juliet*. It was codified into a strict, mostly *end-stopped, highly rhetorical instrument by poets of the Restoration and the Enlightenment such as John Dryden and Alexander Pope. The heroic couplet dominated English poetry from 1688 to 1776. The direct influence was both French (whose standard line has long been the rhymed couplet—in *alexandrines rather than in iambic pentameter) and Greco-Roman (whose classical meter, the *hexameter, could be approximated by heroic couplets). French classical drama (especially the tragedies of Jean Racine and the comedies of Jean-Baptiste Poquelin de Molière) preceded the English classicists somewhat and wielded great influence in the realm of metrical proprieties.

During its heyday, the heroic couplet was used for satirical verse (such as Pope's *The Dunciad*), mock-epic (such as Pope's *The Rape of the Lock*, a passage of which appears below), and verse essay (such as Pope's *Essay on Man*). Used strictly, however, the heroic couplet

H

tends toward the strait-laced and stiff (despite Pope's venom); the rules, as well as the elegant dance-steps of syntax that adhere to them, keep its rhythmic bounds narrow. Chaucer's looser treatment allows for a more easygoing narrative.

from *THE RAPE OF THE LOCK* (Canto II, 19–46) /
Alexander Pope (1688–1744)

> This nymph, to the destruction of mankind,
> Nourish'd two locks which graceful hung behind
> In equal curls, and well conspir'd to deck
> With shining ringlets the smooth iv'ry neck.
> Love in these labyrinths his slaves detains,
> And mighty hearts are held in slender chains.
> With hairy springes we the birds betray,
> Slight lines of hair surprise the finny prey,
> Fair tresses man's imperial race ensnare,
> And beauty draws us with a single hair.
>
> Th' advent'rous Baron the bright locks admir'd,
> He saw, he wish'd, and to the prize aspir'd.
> Resolv'd to win, he meditates the way,
> By force to ravish, or by fraud betray;
> For when success a lover's toil attends,
> Few ask if fraud or force attain'd his ends.
>
> For this, ere Phoebus rose, he had implor'd
> Propitious Heav'n, and ev'ry pow'r ador'd,
> But chiefly Love—Love an altar built,
> Of twelve vast French romances, neatly gilt.
> There lay three garters, half a pair of gloves,
> And all the trophies of his former loves.
> With tender billet-doux he lights the pyre,
> And breathes three am'rous sighs to raise the fire.
> Then prostrate falls, and begs with ardent eyes
> Soon to obtain, and long possess the prize:
> The pow'rs gave ear, and granted half his pray'r,
> The rest the winds dispers'd in empty air.

H

HOW-TO POEM A poem in the form of a set of instructions, usually in the imperative: Do this, do that.

The how-to poem tells the reader how to do something. It needs to be as clear as a good instruction manual and as rich as good poetry in its imagery, rhythms, and imagination. In "What You Should Know to Be a Poet," for example, Gary Snyder advises the novice to learn the names of things, as well as a kind of magic, and goes on to list ordinary, fantastic, and erotic kinds of knowledge. In the how-to poem below, Ted Kooser offers both a recipe and a way of experiencing the details and spaces of one's life.

HOW TO MAKE RHUBARB WINE / Ted Kooser (b. 1939)

> Go to the patch some afternoon
> in early summer, fuzzy with beer
> and sunlight, and pick a sack
> of rhubarb (red or green will do)
> and God knows watch for rattlesnakes
> or better, listen; they make a sound
> like an old lawn mower rolled downhill.
> Wear a hat. A straw hat's best
> for the heat but lets the gnats in.
> Bunch up the stalks and chop the leaves off
> with a buck knife and be careful.
> You need ten pounds; a grocery bag
> packed full will do it. Then go home
> and sit barefooted in the shade
> behind the house with a can of beer.
> Spread out the rhubarb in the grass
> and wash it with cold water
> from the garden hose, washing
> your feet as well. Then take a nap.
> That evening, dice the rhubarb up
> and put it in a crock. Then pour
> eight quarts of boiling water in,

H

cover it up with a checkered cloth
to keep the fruit flies out of it,
and let it stand five days or so.
Take time each day to think of it.

Ferment ten days, under the cloth,
sniffing of it from time to time,
then siphon it off, swallowing some,
and bottle it. Sit back and watch
the liquid clear to honey yellow,
bottled and ready for the years,
and smile. You've done it awfully well.

HUDIBRASTICS (hyoo-dih-bras'-tix) Comic, narrative verse written in rhymed *iambic tetrameter *couplets, as in Samuel Butler's
mock-heroic poem *Hudibras*, published from 1663 to 1678.

The effect is close to doggerel but permitted (even welcomed) because of the satiric nature of Hudibrastics. Rhyme is crucial to the
form, and the best rhymes are the most outrageous and farfetched.
Butler remarks parenthetically,

(For rhyme the rudder is of verses,
With which like ships they steer their courses).

Hudibras, who is caricatured as a knight errant, takes his name from
Edmund Spenser's *The Faerie Queen* and his nature from Miguel de
Cervantes' *Don Quixote*.

John Barth's novel *The Sot-Weed Factor*, set in colonial Maryland,
is based on a poem written in Hudibrastics by Ebenezer Cooke (c.
1672–1732):

The Indians call their wat'ry Wagon
Canoe: a Vessel none can brag on.

In his essay "The Prose and Poetry of It All, or, Dippy Verses," Barth
remarks, "The Hudibrastic couplet, like Herpes simplex, is a conta-
gion more easily caught than cured."

from *HUDIBRAS* (Canto I, 1–14) / Samuel Butler (1612–1680)

When civil fury first grew high,
And men fell out, they knew not why;
When hard words, jealousies, and fears,
Set folks together by the ears,
And made them fight, like mad or drunk,
For Dame Religion, as for punk;
Whose honesty they all durst swear for,
Though not a man of them knew wherefore:
When Gospel-Trumpeter, surrounded
With long-ear'd rout, to battle sounded,
And pulpit, drum ecclesiastick,
Was beat with fist, instead of a stick;
Then did Sir Knight abandon dwelling,
And out he rode a colonelling.

NOTE: Butler is satirizing the Puritans, the "Roundheads" who kept their hair cut short (hence "long-ear'd," since their ears showed, unlike those of the long-haired Cavaliers). In the first line of the first edition, "fury" was "dudgeon." *punk*: prostitute; *a colonelling*: soldiering.

H

I

IAMB or **IAMBUS, IAMBIC** (eye'-am, eye-am'-bic; Greek, "to attack in words"; but Robert Graves says it was "traditionally named in honour of the lasciviously hobbling Iambe" and "may have begun with ... totem dances which imitated the hobbling of partridge or quail") A *foot consisting of an unstressed syllable followed by a stress (˘ ´). Iambic words include *arrange, complain,* and *revenge.*

Iambic meter is called duple meter because each foot contains two syllables. In Ancient Greek, the first iambic verse was composed by Archilochos; originally this measure was used for *satire. Thomas Gray's opening of "Elegy Written in a Country Churchyard" is an iambic line:

The cúr-| few tólls | the knéll | of párt-| ing dáy.

The line is iambic pentameter (pen-tam´-uh-ter; Greek, "five measures"), meaning that it contains five iambic feet (˘ ´ | ˘ ´ | ˘ ´ | ˘ ´ | ˘ ´).

Iambic pentameter is the single most important meter in English, used in Chaucer's *The Canterbury Tales,* Shakespeare's plays and sonnets, Milton's *Paradise Lost,* and in much of the poetry of Alexander Pope, William Wordsworth, John Keats, Robert Browning, Robert Frost, W.B. Yeats, Wallace Stevens, and innumerable other poets. It is flexible in its rhythm, long enough so at least one pause (or *caesura) appears in most lines. But this caesura can turn up in different spots within the lines, allowing the poet much melodic freedom. Iambic pentameter's chief use, however, is not in providing music but in permitting speech, the sound of people talking. It dominates the speech of Shakespeare's plays. At the same time, it is an effective measure for giving musical form to thought so ideas become more real through the inflections and pauses and diction of a human voice, one whose talk verges on song.

Iambic tetrameter *(teh-tram´-uh-ter; Greek, "four measures")* consists of four iambs ($\smile$ ´ | $\smile$ ´ | $\smile$ ´ | $\smile$ ´). Not as weighty or rhythmically flexible as iambic pentameter, tetrameter sounds more songlike, tighter yet airier, compact and capable of both grace and power.

Here are some examples of iambic meter:

Iambic	Number of Feet	Example
monometer	1	Thus I Passe by And die: —Robert Herrick, "Upon His Departure Hence"
dimeter	2	While Angels sing And Mortals ring —Thomas Traherne, "On Christmas-Day"
trimeter	3	With sweetnesse of thy breath; O smother me to death: —Michael Drayton, "To His Valentine"
tetrameter	4	The grave's a fine and private place, But none, I think, do there embrace. —Andrew Marvell, "To His Coy Mistress"

pentameter	5	Yet come to me in dreams, that I
		    may live
		My very life again though cold
		    in death:
		—Christina Rossetti, "Echo"

hexameter	6	Invention, nature's child, fled
		    step-dame study's blows;
		And others' feet still seemed but
		    strangers in my way.
		—Sir Philip Sidney, *Astrophil and Stella*, I

Idyll

An iambic poem, however, is not required to stick to the same line length throughout, although most poems do. Sometimes a poet inserts occasional lines of iambic trimeter in an otherwise pentameter poem, as in John Milton's "Lycidas." The following poem by Ben Jonson achieves the effects of music, spontaneity, and wit by altering its line lengths as it proceeds. *(See* ACCENTUAL-SYLLABIC METER.*)*

MY PICTURE LEFT IN SCOTLAND / Ben Jonson (1572–1637)

I now thinke, LOVE is rather deafe, then blind,
For else it could not be,
That she,
Whom I adore so much, should so slight me,
And cast my love behind:
I'm sure my language to her, was as sweet
And every close did meet
In sentence, of as subtile feet,
As hath the youngest Hee,
That sits in shadow of Apollo's tree.
Oh, but my conscious feares,
That flie my thoughts betweene,
Tell me that she hath seene
My hundreds of gray haires,
Told seven and fortie yeares.
Read so much wast, as she cannot imbrace
My mountaine belly, and my rockie face,
And all these through her eyes, have stopt her eares.

IDYLL, IDYL (eye'-dul or eye'-dil; Greek, "short descriptive poem" or "little picture") 1. Short poem depicting rural life or a country scene. The adjective *idyllic* refers to something that is natural, simple, peaceful, and picturesque.

2. Specifically, the name given to *pastorals written by Theocritus (third century B.C.E.), the apparent originator of the genre. Although his poems deal with the lives and loves of shepherds, Theocritus was

in fact an academic poet, associated with the critics of Alexandria, Egypt. Here is the beginning of John Dryden's translation of the third idyll of Theocritus (whose original is unrhymed):

> To Amaryllis love compels my way;
> My browzing goats upon the mountains stray:
> O Tityrus, tend them well, and see them fed
> In pastures fresh, and to their wat'ring led;
> And 'ware the ridgeling with his butting head.
> Ah, beauteous nymph, can you forget your love,
> The conscious grottos, and the shady grove;
> Where stretch'd at ease your tender limbs were laid,
> Your nameless beauties nakedly display'd?

Idylls and other pastoral poems tend to sound artificial, the landscape idealized into a countryside called Arcadia. Daryl Hine asserts that *bucolic* (or "cowboy song") is a more appropriate term for the poems of Theocritus, but they are traditionally called idylls.

3. A longer narrative piece, such as Alfred, Lord Tennyson's *Idylls of the King* (which relates various legends about King Arthur, mostly in *blank verse):

> And Arthur and his knighthood for a space
> Were all one will, and thro' that strength the king
> Drew in the petty princedoms under him,
> Fought, and in twelve great battles overcame
> The heathen hordes, and made a realm and reign'd.

Tennyson explains his use of the term *idyll*: "Regarding the Greek derivation, I spelt my Idylls with two *l*'s mainly to divide them from the ordinary pastoral idyls usually spelt with one *l*. These idylls group themselves round one central figure."

IMAGE, IMAGERY (im'-idge; Latin, "likeness, semblance, picture, concept, imitation or copy") A mental picture; a concrete representation of something; a likeness the senses can perceive.

Imagism

Ezra Pound says that an image "presents an intellectual and emotional complex in an instant of time." A poetic image transfers itself to our minds with a flash, as if projected upon a movie screen. Many images, such as "a bracelet in a wheel barrow," appeal primarily to the sense of sight. But an image can invoke the other senses too, as in a "sniff of perfume," a "jangling of banjoes," a "scratchy blanket," or a "tart cherry." Images serve as a poem's evidence, its proof that the experience depicted is authentic.

Poetry without images, or with too few, seems vacant, generalized, and uncompelling. But stale images are no substitute for the real thing, which must hit us as a discovery, however small. Images can be simple descriptions of real life, as in these lines from Geoffrey Chaucer's "General Prologue" to *The Canterbury Tales*:

> A Marchant was ther with a forked beerd,
> In motelee, and hye on hors he sat,
> Upon his heed a Flandrissh bevere hat,
> His bootes clasped faire and fetisly.

NOTE: *fetisly*: elegantly

Images can also be metaphorical, as in these lines from Elizabeth Bishop's "The Burglar of Babylon":

> And the heads of those in swimming
>   Were floating coconuts.

Images can also be strange and visionary, as in these lines from Charles Simic's "Concerning My Neighbors, the Hittites":

> Their dogs bury themselves and leave the bones
> To guard the house. A single weed holds all their storms
> Until the spiderwebs spread over the heavens.

IMAGISM A poetic movement invented by Ezra Pound around 1909 and intended as an antidote to the rhetorical excesses of Victorian poetry and the pastoral complacency of Georgian verse.

Pound, along with H.D. (Hilda Doolittle) and Richard Aldington, announced three principles:

1. Direct treatment of the "thing" whether subjective or objective.
2. To use absolutely no word that does not contribute to the presentation.
3. As regarding rhythm: to compose in the sequence of the musical phrase, not in sequence of a metronome.

Imagist poems, strongly influenced by *haiku and other eastern verse, were short, written in *free verse, and presented images without comment or explanation. Amy Lowell later led the movement, which expired near the end of World War I. Vorticism, an offshoot from Imagism masterminded by Ezra Pound, survived through a couple of issues of the magazine *Blast!* and was intended primarily to publicize the paintings, fiction, and poetry of Wyndham Lewis.

OREAD / H.D. (Hilda Doolittle, 1884–1961)

> Whirl up, sea—
> whirl your pointed pines,
> splash your great pines
> on our rocks,
> hurl your green over us,
> cover us with your pools of fir.

NOTE: *Oread*: a mountain nymph in Greek mythology.

I

IMITATION (Latin, "copy") 1. Translation, especially a free translation or loose adaptation of the original, as in Robert Lowell's *Imitations*, which includes poems based on the work of Charles Baudelaire, Arthur Rimbaud, Eugenio Montale, and others. *(See* TRANSLATION.*)*

2. Method of learning an art, such as poetry, by copying the work of other artists. According to Ben Jonson, the poet must "be able to convert the substance or riches of another poet to his own use." W.H. Auden discusses how a young poet chooses a "master." (His choice was Thomas Hardy.) The apprentice tries to mimic the master poet's work, copying the *forms and *meters and tricks of breaking lines, attempting to catch the characteristic *tone, choosing similar sub-

jects, or even substituting his own words for the poet's words, noun for noun, verb for verb, in a word-substitution poem.

3. In some critical views, the purpose or means of an art, as in holding a mirror up to nature. The poet thus copies or mimics what he perceives in the world, like a camera that reacts chemically to light.

IN MEMORIAM STANZA An *iambic tetrameter *quatrain rhymed *abba*, used by Alfred, Lord Tennyson in his long elegy *In Memoriam A.H.H.*

from *IN MEMORIAM A.H.H.* (VII) / Alfred, Lord Tennyson (1809–1892)

> Dark house, by which once more I stand
> Here in the long unlovely street,
> Doors, where my heart was used to beat
> So quickly, waiting for a hand,
>
> A hand that can be clasp'd no more—
> Behold me, for I cannot sleep,
> And like a guilty thing I creep
> At earliest morning to the door.
>
> He is not here; but far away
> The noise of life begins again,
> And ghastly thro' the drizzling rain
> On the bald street breaks the blank day.

INTERNAL RHYME A *rhyme in which at least one rhyme sound occurs within a line, not just at the end, as in Samuel Taylor Coleridge's "The fair breeze blew, the white foam flew" (from "The Rime of the Ancient Mariner"). When it occurs at the midpoint of the line (as in that example), the rhyme is called *leonine*. (*See* BALLAD.)

INVENTED FORMS AND STANZAS Every poetic form, such as the *sonnet, *sestina, and *villanelle, had to be invented at some point and then become traditional and fixed through its use by poets other than its inventor. However, some poets continue to make up their own formal arrangements and stanzaic patterns, either for the nonce in an individual poem (such as Marianne Moore's "The Fish," which appears in SYLLABIC VERSE) or for a longer work (such as John Berryman's *Homage to Mistress Bradstreet* and *The Dream Songs*), and those forms and stanzas may or may not catch on with other poets. Gerard Manley Hopkins's *curtal sonnet has found relatively few followers. However, when Billy Collins invented the paradelle and publicized it as a rediscovered Troubadour form, it was taken up by many poets. Similarly, Lewis Turco introduced the terzanelle in *The Book of Forms*; its provenance apparently cannot be traced back any farther. The impulse is both playful and generative. It is perhaps the opposite of the architect Louis Sullivan's dictum, "Form follows function." In the case of invented poetic structures, form often precedes the actual composition, although it could certainly develop simultaneously with the drafting of a prototype stanza. *(See* CORRUPTED FORM, FORM, NONCE FORM, *and* STANZA, *as well as* FRAGMENT, *in which "Narrow Flame" demonstrates the three-lined stanza invented by Linda Gregerson and used in much of her work.)*

Double Exposure A twelve- or sixteen-line poem in iambic pentameter, rhymed *ababcdcdefef(ghgh)*, in which the odd-numbered lines are boldfaced and justified along the right margin but ragged on the left (making them indented), while the even-numbered lines are in standard type, flush left. The different typefaces indicate alternating strains of speech, dealing with different subjects and images, superimposed on each other like a photographic double exposure. They can be read separately, boldfaced lines together, standardized lines together, but much of the energy and wit emerges when the lines are read continuously, boldface merging into standard and then back again. The titles, many of which are broken into separate lines, suggest the contrasting subjects of these double exposures:

> PLUMBER IN CRAWL SPACE
> UNDER NEW YORK CITY SKYLINE

The blend of flush-left and flush-right lines gives each poem a rectangular shape that suggests a photograph. Greg Williamson introduced this form in the second section of *Errors in the Script*. (*See* EKPHRASTIC POETRY.)

CAMERA SHAKE WITH WIDE ANGLE FIELD OF SNOW /
Greg Williamson (b. 1964)

> **Just got these photos back. Let's have a look.**
> Now what the—? Tell me it's not an overprint.
> **I thought, you know, I'd stick 'em in a book,**
> But look at those warped trees, the aqua tint,
> **"My Life in Pictures." Now I'm not so sure.**
> Its long horizon's tipping off the page.
> **I mean, what *is* that red-eyed, furry blur?**
> Since "photos capture life," then by my gauge,
> **It's either my own Henry Pussycat,**
> Turning upon the blue, inclining snow,
> **Or Yeti. Hmm. You'd think I'd remember that.**
> The world's a whole lot weirder than we know.

Dream Song In "One Answer to a Question: Changes," John Berryman writes that the form of the dream song "comprises eighteen-line sections, three six-line stanzas, each normally (for feet) 5-5-3-5-5-3, variously rhymed and not but mostly rhymed with great strictness." Some of the rhyme schemes Berryman uses include *abcabc*, *abbacc*, *abccba*, *aabccb*, and *abacbc*, but he rhymes freely and erratically, improvising as he goes. Some lines in a particular dream song may lack a rhyming counterpart or may rhyme with a line in a neighboring stanza. Berryman began working on his dream songs in 1955; the first installment, *77 Dream Songs*, appeared in 1964.

OF 1826 (*DREAM SONG* 22) / John Berryman (1914–1972)

> I am the little man who smokes & smokes.
> I am the girl who does know better but.
> I am the king of the pool.

I am so wise I had my mouth sewn shut.
I am a government official & a goddamned fool.
I am a lady who takes jokes.

I am the enemy of the mind.
I am the auto salesman and lóve you.
I am a teenage cancer, with a plan.
I am the blackt-out man.
I am the woman powerful as a zoo.
I am two eyes screwed to my set, whose blind—

It is the Fourth of July.
Collect: while the dying man,
forgone by you creator, who forgives,
is gasping 'Thomas Jefferson still lives'
in vain, in vain, in vain.
I am Henry Pussy-cat! My whiskers fly.

NOTE: Before John Adams died on July 4, 1826, he reportedly said, "Thomas Jefferson still lives." Jefferson died earlier the same day.

Fibonacci A poem that uses the mathematical Fibonacci sequence (1, 1, 2, 3, 5, 8, 13, etc.) in which each number is the sum of the previous two numbers. Judith Baumel's "Speaking in Blizzards" and "Fibonacci" (from *The Weight of Numbers*) use the sequence to determine the number of lines in each stanza as the poem progresses. Inger Christensen's *alphabet* also uses the Fibonacci sequence from section to section and within some of the sections.

Mistress Bradstreet Stanza An eight-line stanza with a beat count of 5-5-3-4-5-5-3-6, usually rhymed *abcbddba*, with the *a* and *d* rhymes maintained with the most fidelity. Sometimes the third and seventh lines rhyme. Often, one or more rhymes in a given stanza will vanish. John Berryman writes that he invented this eight-line stanza "after a lifetime's study, especially of Yeats's, and in particular the one he adopted from Abraham Cowley for his elegy 'In Memory of Major Robert Gregory.' Mine breaks not at midpoint but after the short third line; a strange four-beat line leads to the balancing heroic couplet of lines five and six, after which seven is again short (three feet, like line three) and then the stanza widens into an alexandrine rhyming all the way back to one. I wanted something at once flexible and grave, intense and quiet, able to deal with matter both high and low." Berryman's poem first appeared in 1953 in *The Partisan Review*. John Drury's "The Stunt Man" also uses the Mistress Bradstreet stanza.

Paradelle This form, originally introduced by Billy Collins with his "Paradelle for Susan" (from *Picnic, Lightning*, published in 1998), consists of four six-line stanzas. In each of the first three stanzas, line one is repeated as line two and line three is repeated as line four (giving the form a hint of the *blues); lines five and six must use each of the words that appear in lines one and three (repeating and adding none). The fourth stanza uses all of the words (and only those words) used in the first three stanzas. The name of the form is a portmanteau word combining "parody" and "villanelle." Collins claimed that the paradelle was "one of the more demanding French fixed forms." What started as a gleeful hoax has, amazingly, developed into a popular form.

Terzanelle A combination of the *villanelle and *terza rima, this form uses the following pattern of rhymes, *refrains (*A1* and *A2*), and *repetons (*B, C, D, E, F*) in its six stanzas: (1) *A1 B A2*, (2) *b C B*, (3) *c D C*, (4) *d E D*, (5) *e F E*, (6) *f A1 F A2* or *f F A1 A2*. The lines indicated by capital letters are repeated. *A1* and *A2* rhyme but are otherwise different; both are repeated. The lowercase letters indicate lines that rhyme with repeated lines but are not, themselves, repeated. Lewis Turco's "Terzanelle in Thunderweather" appears in *The New Book of Forms*.

INVERSION 1. The reversal of an expected metrical *foot, as when a *trochee is substituted for one or more of the feet in an *iambic line (called a trochaic inversion). Robert Lowell's "The Drunken Fisherman" begins with a trochaic inversion ("Wallow"):

Wallowing in this bloody sty,
I cast for fish that pleased my eye

2. A wrenching or disruption of the usual word order in a sentence, as when Alfred, Lord Tennyson writes "Heavily hangs the tiger-lily" (instead of "The tiger-lily hangs heavily"). Inversion makes this line more musical, but also more artificial, less conversational. Since Ezra Pound railed against inversion in the early twentieth century, it has fallen from favor, although it recurs in a number of intentionally wrenched phrases in John Berryman's *Dream Songs*.

IRONY (eye'-run-ee; Greek, "dissimulation, pretended ignorance"; the adjective, *ironic*, is pronounced eye-ron'-ik) The recognition or use of some discrepancy between appearance and reality. Irony is a *rhetorical device by which a writer may put a "spin" on his words, like a pitcher delivering a breaking ball, something that doesn't follow a straight path.

In *verbal irony*, what a speaker says differs from what he actually means or intends. Tongue-in-cheek humor is a subtle example of this kind of irony; sarcasm is the coarse, vulgar version.

Situational irony involves a mismatch between what seems to be and what actually is, as in 1948 when *The Chicago Tribune* printed a headline that read "Dewey Defeats Truman."

In Greek comedy, a trickster named Eiron (whose name embodies the term *irony*) outwits a braggart named Alazon by feigning ignorance of something and leading him on until he is trapped. Socrates uses this manipulative, argumentative tactic (called *Socratic irony*) as he asks a string of innocent-seeming questions of his pupils and adversaries in Plato's dialogues.

In *dramatic irony*, a character in a poem or play or story is not aware of the import of what he utters. The duke who speaks in Robert Browning's "My Last Duchess" (which appears in DRAMATIC MONOLOGUE) has no idea how much he is revealing to his guest and the reader.

Irony

In his essay "Pure and Impure Poetry," Robert Penn Warren argues for the importance of irony in poems, asserting that "poetry wants to be pure, but poems do not." The poet, he says, "proves his vision by submitting it to the fires of irony—to the drama of his structure—in the hope that the fires will refine it." Irony is a means of increasing the tension and intensity in a poem.

I

JUXTAPOSITION (jux´-tuh-puh-zih´-shun; French, "placed close by")
The placement of contrasting things (such as different *images) side by
side. The effect can be startling, amusing, or illuminating. Sometimes a
*metaphorical connection is implicit, as in the last line of Guillaume
Apollinaire's "Zone," which juxtaposes images of the *sun* and a *throat*
that has been *slit*: "*Soleil cou coupé.*" In section fifteen of "Song of Myself,"
Walt Whitman juxtaposes images of different people in adjacent lines:

> The pure contralto sings in the organ loft,
> The carpenter dresses his plank, the tongue of his fore-
> plane whistles its wild ascending lisp,
> The married and unmarried children ride home to their
> Thanksgiving dinner,
> The pilot seizes the king-pin, he heaves down with a strong arm,
> The mate stands braced in the whale-boat, lance and har-
> poon are ready,
> The duck-shooter walks by silent and cautious stretches,
> The deacons are ordain'd with cross'd hands at the altar,
> The spinning-girl retreats and advances to the hum of the
> big wheel,
> The farmer stops by the bars as he walks on a First-day
> loafe and looks at the oats and rye ...

Later on, Whitman places a prostitute who "draggles her shawl" next
to the President "holding a cabinet council." (*See* HAIKU.)

KENNING (Old Icelandic, "to name after") A multi-word substitute for a noun, such as "whale-road" for "sea."

Kennings appear frequently in Old English poems, such as *Beowulf*, and in related Germanic languages, especially Norse and Icelandic. A kenning is a kind of periphrasis, or roundabout way of using several words instead of one. Instead of "feather," for example, the poet might refer to "joy of a bird." Generally kennings use figures of speech. "Battle," for example, turns into "storm of swords," a phrase which exemplifies both *metaphor (the storm representing a violent clash) and *metonymy (the swords representing men with weapons). This grammatical structure (noun + prepositional phrase) is very common, as in "flame of battle" for "sword." But hyphenated nouns, such as "oar-steed" for "ship," also appear frequently.

A kenning resembles the *epithet*, such as "loud-roaring" for "sea," which appears in Greek epic poetry. The main difference is that in Greek verse the epithet serves primarily as a formula to plug into a particular metrical pattern, so the epic poet can say "Grey eyes" instead of "Athena" if he needs two syllables instead of three. (*See* ALLITERATIVE METER, EPIC, *and* RHETORICAL DEVICES.)

KYRIELLE (keer-ee-el´) French four-line *stanza form in which each line contains eight syllables and the fourth line is a *refrain.

If the refrain rhymes with other lines, the usual *rhyme schemes are *aabB ccbB* (etc.) and *abaB cbcB* (etc.). If the refrain is not rhymed, the rhyme scheme is usually *aaaR bbbR* (etc.). In either case, the capital letter indicates a refrain, either rhymed *(B)* or unrhymed *(R)*. Theodore Roethke uses the kyrielle, with an unrhymed refrain, for some of his light verse and nonsense poems, such as "Dinky."

W.B. Yeats's "The Ragged Wood" rhymes *abaB*, although the refrain differs slightly from stanza to stanza and the lines are in *iambic pentameter instead of octosyllabics:

> O hurry where by water among the trees
> The delicate-stepping stag and his lady sigh,
> When they have but looked upon their images—
> Would none had ever loved but you and I!
>
> Or have you heard that sliding silver-shoed
> Pale silver-proud queen-woman of the sky,
> When the sun looked out of his golden hood?—
> O that none ever loved but you and I!
>
> O hurry to the ragged wood, for there
> I will drive all those lovers out and cry—
> O my share of the world, O yellow hair!
> No one has ever loved but you and I.

The following kyrielle rhymes *aabB*.

KYRIELLE / John Payne (1842–1916)

> A lark in the mesh of the tangled vine,
> A bee that drowns in the flower-cup's wine,
> A fly in the sunshine,—such is man.
> All things must end, as all began.
>
> A little pain, a little pleasure,
> A little heaping up of treasure;
> Then no more gazing upon the sun.
> All things must end that have begun.

K

Kyrielle

Where is the time for hope or doubt?
A puff of the wind, and life is out;
A turn of the wheel, and rest is won.
All things must end that have begun.

Golden morning and purple night,
Life that fails with the failing light;
Death is the only deathless one.
All things must end that have begun.

Ending waits on the brief beginning;
Is the prize worth the stress of winning?
E'en in the dawning the day is done.
All things must end that have begun.

Weary waiting and weary striving,
Glad outsetting and sad arriving;
What is it worth when the goal is won?
All things must end that have begun.

Speedily fades the morning glitter;
Love grows irksome and wine grows bitter.
Two are parted from what was one.
All things must end that have begun.

Toil and pain and the evening rest;
Joy is weary and sleep is best;
Fair and softly the day is done.
All things must end that have begun.

L

LAI, LAY (lay; French, "song, tune") 1. A brief *narrative or *lyric poem intended to be sung. The lines rhyme in *couplets and are octosyllabic (containing eight syllables each). This form, called the *French lai*, was popular in the Middle Ages. Marie de France wrote the earliest existing narrative lai, and Gautier de Dargies wrote the earliest existing lyric lai. Guillaume de Machaut (1300?–1377) is the great master of the Medieval lai, as well as the *ballade, *chant royal, and *rondel.

2. French nine-line *stanza, rhymed *aabaabaab*, the *a* lines having five syllables each, the *b* lines having two syllables each. If there is more than one stanza in the poem, the rhyme sounds will change from stanza to stanza (so that stanza two uses *c* and *d*, stanza three uses *e* and *f*, and so on). Different syllable counts are acceptable, but the *a* lines should be uniformly longer than the *b* lines. The nineteenth-century French poet Théodore de Banville codified this form, which he termed the *lai ancien* (old lai), as well as the variations that follow.

In a *lai nouveau* (new lai), the first two lines become *refrains one and two, and the poem becomes a variation of the *villanelle. Only two rhymes (*a* and *b*) are used throughout the poem, refrain one recurring as an extra line at the end of stanza two, refrain two at the end of stanza three, and so on, until the final stanza, whose last two lines are refrains two and one (reversing the original order).

If each stanza's five-syllable lines rhyme with the two-syllable lines from the previous stanza, the lai becomes a *virelai* (or *virelay*), an interlocking form like *terza rima. When the virelai reaches its last stanza, the two-syllable lines will rhyme with the opening stanza's five-syllable lines, making the *rhyme scheme circular.

3. In current usage, *lay* is used synonymously, though poetically, with *song. It can also denote a historical *ballad such as Sir Walter Scott's "The Lay of the Last Minstrel."

LANGUAGE POETRY Poetry that seeks to detach words from their conventional moorings so something new and unprecedented emerges, not an imitation of life or the world.

The Language movement owes much to predecessors such as Gertrude Stein, whose *Tender Buttons* experimented with language used abstractly and nonsensically, freed of its servitude to content and meaning. Other influences include Tristan Tzara, Louis Zukofsky, Charles Olson, and John Ashbery. As a movement, its name was launched by Bruce Andrews and Charles Bernstein, the editors who founded the magazine $L=A=N=G=U=A=G=E$ in 1971. Eventually the equal signs disappeared, a network of periodicals and presses (such as *The Figures*) sprang up, and Language poetry became a major strain of late-twentieth-century American poetry. Writers associated with the Language movement include Charles Bernstein, Clark Coolidge, Lyn Hejinian, Leslie Scalapino, and Ron Silliman.

Language poets aim to break away from what we know already, experimenting with what poems can be, mixing the genres of verse and prose, coming up with constructs that push beyond the limits of memory, emotion, and tradition that confine and diminish conventional verse. Detractors might argue that much of this so-called Language poetry drones and babbles, a mass of pretentious gibberish, a dead-end of *nonsense verse that is not even funny. But experimental writing necessarily runs many risks, such as pursuing novelty for its own sake, alienating the reader, and courting obscurity. Language poetry rejects conformity and comfortableness. It means to be subversive. Charles Bernstein declares in *A Poetics*, "I care most about poetry that disrupts business as usual, including literary business: I care most for poetry as dissent, including formal dissent; poetry that makes sounds possible to be heard that are not otherwise articulated."

LIFT PLOW PLATES / Charles Bernstein (b. 1950)

For brief scratches, omits,
lays away the oars (hours).
Flagrant immersion besets all
the best boats. Hands, hearts
don't slip, solidly
(sadly) departs.
Empire of sudden letting, soaks
up flaps of fumes, these (his)
fumes. When in the midst
of—days, chartered
whether or not. And suits.
Simple things (thugs)
poisoned with inception.
Such tools as
amount to ill-bred
orientation. Mrs. X
urging Mr. Z to amortize Miss
O. The snowperson snowed
under. On beam, off target.

from THE CELL / Lyn Hejinian (b. 1942)

Lighting by trees
Flattening by depictions of an
        industrialist in a cauldron
A fiction of factors on
        a film
The animals (not dogs) stampeding
        backwards to laughter

It's not in their eyes
Writing by putting a leg
    over a knee is animal
And again it is also
    mineral
It is anatomical to repeat
    but the time isn't right
The times aren't the same
So poetry isn't a reminder

December 10, 1986

LIGHT VERSE Humorous verse, usually rhymed; verse in the service of amusement; rhymed lines whose subject matter and attitudes are light as opposed to weighty, dark, and serious.

Poets have used several poetic forms, including *double dactyls, *clerihews, *limericks, and *nashers, exclusively for light verse. But other forms, such as *epigrams, *heroic couplets, *rondeaux, *skeltonics, *sonnets, and *villanelles, have also served admirably for both light verse and more serious poems. Verse that is comic, humorous, or witty need not be light verse, however, as long as it has a certain depth of emotion or range of imagination.

Much light verse is simply doggerel: singsong, jingling verses, roughly and often ineptly measured (although Goethe's *Faust* contains a number of passages in doggerel—and is hardly inept).

Light verse that pokes fun at upper-class manners and mores is called *vers de société* (*var´-deh-so-see-ay-tay´; French for "society verse"*).

LIMERICK A light verse form, often bawdy or scatological, consisting of a five-line *stanza rhymed *aabba*.

The pattern of feet (or stresses) in the lines is 3-3-2-2-3, usually in *anapestic ($\smile \smile \,´$) or *amphibrachic ($\smile \,´\, \smile$) meter. The rhythms, however, can be very loose (befitting a comic form), as in the lines attributed to President Woodrow Wilson (1856–1924):

> I sat next to the Duchess at tea;
> It was just as I feared it would be:
>   Her rumblings abdominal
>   Were truly phenomenal,
> And everyone thought it was me!

The stanzaic arrangement of the limerick goes back at least to the sixteenth century and the *mad-song stanza.

LINE (also called *verse, stich*) An aural and visual stretch of words; the basic compositional unit of a poem written in *verse.

Aloud, in a song or a recited poem, a line is like a melodic phrase, lasting a certain length before the piece "turns" to the next line or ends. On the page, a line is a typographical unit, a horizontal row of words. If it ends arbitrarily when it reaches the right margin, the text is prose. If, however, it ends where the writer requires it to end, the text is verse (meaning written in discrete lines—or verses—determined by the poet, not a typesetter). In poetry, a line can (and often will) continue beyond the right margin, as in the long-lined poems of Walt Whitman; in this case the continuation is indented beneath the first part of the line.

The poet can determine a line's length in several ways: (1) by using a regular *meter, such as *iambic pentameter, which requires that a set number of syllables (ten) and stresses (five) must accumulate before the line ends; (2) by ending a line on a rhyme word, whether or not the poem is in meter; (3) by following a *cadence, an unmeasured surge of rhythm; (4) by choosing a line's length visually, making it either similar to the nearby lines or different; (5) by imposing a *line break, either where a pause occurs or between words usually grouped together (such as a prepositional phrase).

LINE BREAK The place where a line ends, where it is broken off.

This term applies especially to *free verse, because the poet (and not a metrical imperative) determines when and where to turn from one line to the next. "Break" suggests a sundering, a snapping off of the line, which may come right in the middle of a phrase. One exercise useful in experimenting with free verse is to take a passage of prose (or someone's poem written out as prose) and break it (or re-break it) into lines. As Louis Simpson remarks, the poet's "impulse" determines each line break.

Denise Levertov regards the line break as "roughly a half-comma in duration." She considers it a "crucial precision tool" that "can record the slight (but meaningful) hesitations between word and word that are characteristic of the mind's dance among perceptions but which are not noted by grammatical punctuation." Where and how a line is broken, that "fractional pause," affects the pitch pattern of a poem and its *"significant, expressive melody."* To demonstrate variations in lineation, she cites a passage about eating plums in William Carlos Williams's "To a Poor Old Woman":

> They taste good to her.
> They taste good
> to her. They taste
> good to her.

The following poem by Adrienne Rich shows some of the ways a poet can break free-verse lines. She can, of course, break where natural pauses occur ("with chords of Joy / where everything is silence"), although this poem rushes on and omits most punctuation. She can separate phrases or grammatical units between the halves of a conjunction ("impotence / or infertility"), adjective and noun ("climacteric / music"), adverb and adjective ("entirely / isolated"), noun and verb ("the man / does not want out"), article and noun ("the / beating"), or a preposition and its object ("upon / a splintered table"). She can gradually pull in the lines and let them out, giving a visual shape like the ebb and flow of tides and a cadence like the lulls and swells of symphonic music.

THE NINTH SYMPHONY OF BEETHOVEN UNDERSTOOD AT LAST AS A SEXUAL MESSAGE / Adrienne Rich (b. 1929)

A man in terror of impotence
or infertility, not knowing the difference
a man trying to tell something
howling from the climacteric
music of the entirely
isolated soul
yelling at Joy from the tunnel of the ego
music without the ghost
of another person in it, music
trying to tell something the man
does not want out, would keep if he could
gagged and bound and flogged with chords of Joy
where everything is silence and the
beating of a bloody fist upon
a splintered table

NOTE: The fourth movement of Ludwig van Beethoven's "Ninth Symphony" sets Friedrich von Schiller's "Ode to Joy" to music.

LIST POEM A poem that names or enumerates a series of things; a catalogue, as in many of Walt Whitman's poems (such as the excerpt from "Song of Myself" that appears in JUXTAPOSITION).

The genealogies of the Old Testament and the catalogue of ships in Homer's *The Iliad* are examples of lists. But, although they may record a roster of names, the lists in contemporary poems more often consist of images and specific details, as in the poem below. Sylvia Plath's "You're" (which appears in FIGURATIVE LANGUAGE) is a list poem.

THE FAMILY IS ALL THERE IS / Pattiann Rogers (b. 1940)

Think of those old, enduring connections
found in all flesh—the channeling
wires and threads, vacuoles, granules,

List Poem

plasma and pods, purple veins, ascending
boles and coral sapwood (sugar-
and light-filled), those common ligaments,
filaments, fibers and canals.

Seminal to all kin also is the open
mouth—in heart urchin and octopus belly,
in catfish, moonfish, forest lily,
and rugosa rose, in thirsty magpie,
wailing cat cub, barker, yodeler,
yawning coati.

And there is a pervasive clasping
common to the clan—the hard nails
of lichen and ivy sucker
on the church wall, the bean tendril
and the taproot, the bolted coupling
of crane flies, the hold of the shearwater
on its morning squid, guanine
to cytosine, adenine to thymine,
fingers around fingers, the grip
of the voice on presence, the grasp
of the self on place.

Remember the same hair on pygmy
dormouse and yellow-necked caterpillar,
covering red baboon, thistle seed
and willow herb? Remember the similar
snorts of warthog, walrus, male moose
and sumo wrestler? Remember the familiar
whinny and shimmer found in river birches,
bay mares and bullfrog tadpoles,
in children playing at shoulder tag
on a summer lawn?

The family—weavers, reachers, winders
and connivers, pumpers, runners, air

and bubble riders, rock-sitters, wave-gliders,
wire wobblers, soothers, flagellators—all
brothers, sisters, all there is.

Name something else.

LOGOPOEIA (log'-oh-pee'-uh) Ezra Pound's term for the use of mental associations in poetry, "stimulating the associations (intellectual or emotional) that have remained in the receiver's consciousness in relation to the actual words or word groups employed," one of the three means by which a poet can "charge language with meaning." *(See* MELOPOEIA *and* PHANOPOEIA.*)*

LONG POEM A poem whose length and scope exceed those of the short *lyric or *narrative poem.

   *Epics, romances, and verse novels obviously qualify as long poems, but so do poems of several pages, such as T.S. Eliot's *The Waste Land.* Edgar Allan Poe, however, denies that a long poem could exist:

> That degree of excitement which would entitle a poem to be so called at all cannot be sustained throughout a composition of any great length. After the lapse of half an hour, at the very utmost, it flags—fails—a revulsion ensues—and then the poem is, in effect, and in fact, no longer such. ("The Poetic Principle")

Some poets draw a rather arbitrary limit at a hundred lines; anything over that length, they argue, would go on too long to sustain its poetic intensity.

   A long poem today could be construed as anything over three pages in length. More reasonably, a long poem must sustain something beyond the lyric impulse. Sequences of short poems or numbered sections may characterize the shortest of long poems. Narratives usually require room to tell their stories and often qualify as long poems. However, Robert McDowell has identified narrative poems of four to twelve pages as "middle length." How short is long enough for a "long poem"? The question is still unresolved.

The most traditional kind of long poem is the *epic, which might constitute twenty-four books (in the sense of "chapters" or "long sections") and hundreds of pages. Many twentieth-century epics, such as Ezra Pound's *The Cantos*, reject traditional narrative (except in short bursts) and have experimented with other methods of organization: juxtaposition of scenes and images, alternation of themes. A lyric poem (or a short narrative poem) is to the short story as a long poem is to the novel or novella.

Recent book-length long poems include Carolyn Forché's *The Angel of History* and A.R. Ammons's *Garbage* (whose eighteen sections of couplets were composed on adding machine tape).

LUC-BAT (Vietnamese, "six-eight") A Vietnamese form consisting of alternating lines of six and eight syllables; the end-rhymes of each pair of eight-syllable and six-syllable lines are echoed by an *internal rhyme in the next line, positioned at the sixth syllable; a new rhyme then begins at the eighth syllable. (*See* WELSH POETIC FORMS *for some similar rhyming patterns.*)

Luc-bat occurs in folk poetry as well as literary works such as Nguyen Du's *The Tale of Kieu*, a verse novel of 3,250 lines. The following translation imitates the syllabic meter and rhyme scheme of the original: "sum" echoed by "come," "blows" by "flows" and "go-," and so on.

PROLOGUE AND OPENING OF CHAPTER ONE OF
KIM-VAN-KIEU (*THE TALE OF KIEU*) /
Nguyen Du (1765–1820; tr. John Drury)

> In life, a century's sum,
> Talent and fate may come to blows.
> You pass through ebbs and flows,
> Sickened by what is going on.
> Something gained, something gone,
> Fair cheeks are set upon by spite.

Manuscripts by lamplight
And bamboo texts relate the Ming
Period of Kia-Tsing
When peace was prevailing among
The people. In the Vuong
Family there was a young man, last
Son of a clerk whose modest
But literary past he knew,
And daughters named Thuy-Kieu
And Thuy-Van, both slim, beautiful,
In their two ways equal.

LYRIC POETRY One of the three main genres of poetry (the others being *dramatic poetry and *narrative poetry). It is poetry in which music predominates over story or drama.

Much lyric poetry expresses personal emotion—or at least suggests a real person thinking out loud, however impersonalized that speaker may be. Friedrich Nietzsche declares that the lyric poet "always says 'I' and sings us through the full chromatic scale of his passions and desires."

Originally, lyric poetry was sung, chanted, or recited to a musical accompaniment. The word *lyric* refers to the poet's lyre, the harplike instrument the poet or a musician would play. Today that music is more likely to be a suggestion at best, like a vestigial memory. Lyric poetry now tends to be quiet, inward, and mental, while we use the word *song* to denote "words and music." If a poem contemplates something at length, it is called *meditative poetry*.

L

MADRIGAL (mad'-rih-gul; the origin of the word is in dispute; according to the *Oxford English Dictionary*, it derives from the Italian for "herd" or "fold," in the sense that it is a *pastoral song; according to *The American Heritage Dictionary*, it derives from the Italian for "simple," from the Late Latin "invented," and is related to the Latin words for "womb" and "mother") A brief *song performed in several vocal parts, often with intricate rhyme schemes and varying line lengths within the text. Madrigals first appeared in Italy in the late thirteenth century. The following madrigal by Sir Philip Sidney was probably the first written in English, around 1580, and appears in *The Old Arcadia*.

AN EVENING MADRIGAL / Sir Philip Sidney (1554–1586)

Why dost thou haste away,
O Titan fair, the giver of the day?
Is it to carry news
To Western wights, what stars in East appear?
Or dost thou think that here
Is left a sun, whose beams thy place may use?
Yet stay, and well peruse
What be her gifts, that make her equal thee;
Bend all thy light to see
In earthly clothes enclosed a heavenly spark.

Thy running course cannot such beauties mark;
No, no, thy motions be
Hastened from us with bar of shadow dark,
Because that thou, the author of our sight,
Disdain'st we see thee stained with other's light.

MAD-SONG STANZA A five-line stanza, rhymed *Xabba* with the feet, *beats, or *accents arranged 3-3-2-2-3.

Typically used since the Renaissance for songs in the voice of a madman, the form resembles the *limerick, except the mad-song tends to be in loose *iambic meter (ˇ ´) while the limerick favors triple meter such as *anapestic (ˇ ˇ ´) and *amphibrachic (ˇ ´ ˇ). And while both forms indulge in nonsense, the limerick is comic, lightweight, and often lewd; the mad-song is visionary. The anonymous "Tom o' Bedlam's Song" (called "Loving Mad Tom" in Robert Graves's edition) is probably the best-known example. Here is one of its stanzas:

I know more than Apollo,
For oft, when he lies sleeping,
I see the stars
At bloody wars
In the wounded welkin weeping.

MASCULINE ENDING (also called *rising ending*) A line that ends with a *stressed syllable, such as "Something there is that doesn't love a wall" (Robert Frost). A line that adds an unstressed syllable after the final stress is called *feminine. *(See* ACCENTUAL-SYLLABIC METER *and* FOOT.*)*

MELOPOEIA (mel'-oh-pee'-uh) Ezra Pound's term for the use of sound effects in poetry, "inducing emotional correlations by the sound and rhythm of the speech," one of the three means by which a poet can "charge language with meaning." *(See* LOGOPOEIA *and* PHANOPOEIA.*)*

M

MEMORY A source of poetry, limiting if entrusted too literally, debilitating if spent too recklessly. The muses, the Greek inspirers of the creative arts, were the daughters of Memory, or Mnemosyne. Memory supplies the necessary raw materials of imagination.

Memorization, learning a poem by heart, is one of the best ways to absorb the craft and techniques of poetry. It is a kind of mental ingestion, akin to saving a file on a computer.

*Rhymed, metrical *verse is an especially useful tool in constructing memory aids or mnemonic devices, as in the weather proverb "Mackerel skies and mares' tails / Make lofty ships carry low sails."

METAPHOR (met'-uh-for; Greek, "to carry across") A comparison that likens two different things by identifying one as the other.

In mathematical symbols, a metaphor would require an equal sign, asserting that $A = B$, as in "that strange flower, the sun," a line from Wallace Stevens's "Gubbinal" that equates the sun with a "strange flower." Unlike a *simile, metaphor does not use linking words ("like," "as," "such as") to indicate similarity between two otherwise different things.

Metaphor, however, is also the general term for any comparison, including simile, metaphor, conceit, and analogy. In his column in *Natural History*, Stephen Jay Gould writes:

> One day, as I sat at an alfresco lunch spot enjoying a view of the Acropolis, a small truck pulled up to the curb and blocked the Parthenon. I was annoyed at first, but later wonderfully amused as I watched the moving men deliver some furniture to the neighboring house. Their van said Metaphora. Of course, I realized. *Phor* is the verb for "carrying," and *meta* is a prefix meaning "change of place, order, condition, or nature." A moving truck helps you change the order of something by carrying it from one spot to another—and is surely a metaphor. ... A metaphor carries you from one object (which may be difficult to understand) to another (which may be more accessible and therefore helpful, by analogy, in grasping the original concern).

M

Metaphors, as Gould asserts, are "carriers" which help readers make "imaginative leaps." But it is the poet who must be the moving man, covering that distance and transporting the goods.

I.A. Richards invented the terms *tenor* and *vehicle* to denote the two parts of a metaphor. The tenor is the literal subject; the vehicle is the figurative connection, the likeness, the thing that is compared to the subject, or the carrier—like the moving van Stephen Jay Gould saw in Greece. For example, the first stanza of Robert Lowell's "For the Union Dead" contains the metaphor "a Sahara of snow"; the tenor is snow, while the vehicle is the Sahara desert. The terms can apply to similes as well. In Robert Burns's line, "O my luve's like a red red rose," the tenor is "my luve" and the vehicle is "a red red rose."

When a metaphor is extended and elaborated (like the image of "twin compasses" John Donne develops through twelve lines of "A Valediction: Forbidding Mourning"), it is called a *conceit*.

METAPHYSICAL POETS A group of English poets, including John Donne, Abraham Cowley, George Herbert, and Henry Vaughan, who lived during the early seventeenth century and whose poems are characterized by elaborate *forms and *rhyme schemes, extensive use of *metaphor and conceit, wit and cleverness, intellectual daring, wide-ranging vocabulary (including scientific terms), and interests in religion and (in Donne's case especially) erotic love.

The term was coined by Dr. Samuel Johnson in his piece on Abraham Cowley in *Lives of the Poets*:

> The metaphysical poets were men of learning, and to show their learning was their whole endeavour; but unluckily resolving to show it in rhyme, instead of writing poetry they only wrote verses, and very often such verses as stood the trial of the finger better than of the ear, for the modulation was so imperfect that they were only found to be verses by counting the syllables.

M

Johnson adds, "The most heterogeneous ideas are yoked by violence together; nature and art are ransacked for illustrations, comparisons, and allusions. ... "

Samuel Taylor Coleridge comments similarly on the nature of metaphysical poetry in his *epigram "On Donne's Poetry," which imitates some of Donne's metaphorical ingenuity:

> With Donne, whose muse on dromedary trots,
> Wreathe iron pokers into truelove knots;
> Rhyme's sturdy cripple, fancy's maze and clue,
> Wit's forge and fire-blast, meaning's press and screw.

In this poetry Coleridge sees a camel instead of a winged horse, knots made of twisted metal, a cripple, a maze, a torture chamber of meaning where everything's wrenched out of natural shape.

In the early twentieth century, T.S. Eliot led a reappraisal and revival of metaphysical poetry. In his essay "The Metaphysical Poets," Eliot concludes that Donne and some of the others "are in the direct current of English poetry." He also notes that those who "tell us to 'look in our hearts and write'" do not look deep enough: "One must look into the cerebral cortex, the nervous system, and the digestive tracts."

In the following poem, rhymed *abbacdcdee* and using a stress-pattern of 4-2-5-5-4-4-5-5-5-5 in each stanza, John Donne plucks the sun right out of the sky and places it in his own bedroom. The images and rich complication of the poem show the love of the physical in metaphysical poetry.

THE SUN RISING / John Donne (1572–1631)

> Busy old fool, unruly sun,
> Why dost thou thus,
> Through windows and through curtains call on us?
> Must to thy motions lovers' seasons run?
> Saucy pedantic wretch, go chide
> Late school boys and sour prentices,
> Go tell court huntsmen that the king will ride,
> Call country ants to harvest offices;
> Love, all alike, no season knows nor clime,
> Nor hours, days, months, which are the rags of time.

> Thy beams, so reverend and strong
>> Why shouldst thou think?
> I could eclipse and cloud them with a wink,
> But that I would not lose her sight so long;
>> If her eyes have not blinded thine,
>> Look, and tomorrow late tell me,
>> Whether both th' Indias of spice and mine
>> Be where thou leftst them, or lie here with me.
> Ask for those kings whom thou saw'st yesterday,
> And thou shalt hear, All here in one bed lay.

>> She's all states, and all princes, I,
>> Nothing else is.
> Princes do but play us; compared to this,
> All honor's mimic, all wealth alchemy.
>> Thou, sun, art half as happy as we,
>> In that the world's contracted thus;
>> Thine age asks ease, and since thy duties be
>> To warm the world, that's done in warming us.
> Shine here to us, and thou art everywhere;
> This bed thy center is, these walls, thy sphere.

METER 1. The rhythmic measure of a line of verse. 2. The regular measure that a group of lines have in common, despite variations. 3. The way(s) of measuring certain poems that are written in *verse or lines (rather than in *prose).

In English verse, there are essentially three elements that can be measured: accents (also called beats or stresses), number of syllables, and length of syllables. The most common English meter, *accentual-syllabic verse, counts both accents and syllables. *Accentual verse counts only the accents. *Syllabic verse counts only the number of syllables. *Quantitative verse counts the length of syllables (long or short) as well as their number; although used by poets such as the Elizabethan poet-composer Thomas Campion and suggested in *The Cantos* of American expatriate Ezra Pound, it is more of a feat or

M

stunt in English than a viable meter; it is, however, the meter of ancient Greek poets such as Homer, Pindar, Sophocles, and Sappho.

In their essay "The Neural Lyre: Poetic Meter, the Brain, and Time," Frederick Turner and Ernst Pöppel argue that there's a neurological basis—and need—for meter in poetry. They discuss "the three-second LINE ... tuned to the three-second present moment of the auditory information-processing system." They assert that, in many different languages, a line of verse, however it may be measured, takes about three seconds to utter.

Other explanations of meter describe it as a "breath unit," a memory aid (especially in the oral tradition of bards like Homer), and a musical tempo (such as 4/4 time). Meter imposes order, and hence can seem artificial. But that regularity can induce a kind of hypnotic state in the reader or listener, casting a rhythmic spell. It affects the body in the same way music does. On the other hand, too much regularity can quickly become monotonous and tiresome, so poets try to use variation in their rhythms—much as a composer shapes a melody over the drumbeat. Some notes will be shortened, some lengthened, and there may be pauses as well. The actual words of a poem form the melody, which flows musically above the implied, mechanical tick-tock of the meter.

METONYMY (meh-tahn'-uh-mee) A figure of speech in which a thing is represented by something closely associated with it, like "the White House" used to represent "the President of the United States."

MINOR IONIC (eye-ahn'-ik; also called a "double iamb") A *double foot consisting of two unstressed syllables followed by two stressed syllables (a *pyrrhic and a *spondee, marked ˘ ˘ ´ ´). It is very common in English verse, probably because of phrases constructed as *preposition-article-adjective-noun*, like the opening words (here italicized) in a line by Theodore Roethke: "*In a dark time* I came into my own."

MONOSTICH (mon'-oh-stik; Greek, "one line") A one-line stanza or poem. Many twentieth-century poets make use of one-line stanzas, either interspersed through a poem or at the end, where a single isolated line is especially emphatic. David St. John's "Iris," for example, begins with a monostich—

> There is a train inside this iris:

—and then alternates couplets and monostichs throughout the poem.

A poem that consists of a single isolated line can be a definition, aphorism, image, fragment, joke (responding to the title like a punch line), or the kind of inscription one might find on a tomb. But it must stand out, without the interplay and assistance that other lines could provide.

BYGONES / Charles Wright (b. 1935)

> The rain has stopped falling asleep on its crystal stems.

MONOSYLLABIC FOOT (mon'-oh-sih-lab'-ik; Greek, "one syllable") A stressed syllable that stands by itself, usually because an unstressed syllable has been omitte\

d, either at the beginning of an *iambic or *anapestic line, the end of a *trochaic or *dactylic line, or within a line to create a pause, surprise, or syncopation ("springing" the line).

An unstressed syllable by itself is not really a foot, although it is very common because of the frequency of the *feminine ending. In an *iambic trimeter line with a feminine ending, such as "Shĕ's tiéd | iť iñ | hĕr áp-| rŏn" (from the anonymous ballad "Mary Hamilton"), the extra unstressed syllable is simply left hanging, like a tassel. One could conceivably scan the last foot as an *amphibrach ("hĕr áprŏn"), but this is not usually done. *(See* CATALEXIS.)

MOVEMENT, THE A group of British poets of the 1950s, including Philip Larkin, Donald Davie, Kingsley Amis, and the historian Robert Conquest, known for formal poetry, conservative views, skepticism, and wit. Conquest edited and introduced their work in the anthology *New Lines* (1956). These poets rejected the frag-

M

intelligent, compressed, often narrative style. The thrust of the Movement is antiromantic.

COMING / Philip Larkin (1922–1985)

On longer evenings,
Light, chill and yellow,
Bathes the serene
Foreheads of houses.
A thrush sings,
Laurel-surrounded
In the deep bare garden,
Its fresh-peeled voice
Astonishing the brickwork.
It will be spring soon,
It will be spring soon—
And I, whose childhood
Is a forgotten boredom,
Feel like a child
Who comes on a scene
Of adult reconciling,
And can understand nothing
But the unusual laughter,
And starts to be happy.

MOVEMENTS AND SCHOOLS OF POETRY Groups of poets banded together either to promote their ideas of what poetry should be—as well as their own poems—or to classify poetry that shares stylistic traits or the same historical period. Generally, the poets themselves organize the first kind of movement, while critics and scholars (who may in fact be poets) recognize the second. Movements led by poets who issued manifestoes and founded magazines or issued anthologies include the *Pre-Raphaelites, *Surrealists, *Imagists, *Fugitives, *Black Mountain School, *Language poets, and *New Formalists. Movements that may not have codified their programs but recognized their poetic comrades include *Sons of Ben,

*Symbolists, *Harlem Renaissance, *Beats, *Confessional poets, *Deep Image poets, *The Movement, and the *New York School. Some of these movements, including the Pre-Raphaelite Brotherhood, Surrealism, and the New York School, were vitally connected with new developments in the visual arts.

Critics have named some historical movements long after the poets wrote, as Samuel Johnson (in *Lives of the Poets 1779–1781*) dubbed Abraham Cowley, John Donne, and similar seventeenth-century poets *Metaphysical. Other historical schools include Neoclassical or Augustan poets (John Dryden and Alexander Pope), Romantic poets (William Wordsworth, John Keats, Percy Bysshe Shelley, Lord Byron), Lake poets (Wordsworth, Samuel Taylor Coleridge, Robert Southey), and Modernists (T.S. Eliot, Ezra Pound, Wallace Stevens, Gertrude Stein). A more recent example would be the *Elliptical poets.

English poetry is often classified by the name of the reigning monarch, although there is necessarily much overlapping. Thus we have Tudor poetry, in particular that written during the reign of Henry VIII (Thomas Wyatt and Henry Howard, Earl of Surrey), Elizabethan (Edmund Spenser, Sir Philip Sidney, William Shakespeare, Christopher Marlowe), Jacobean, referring to King James I (Shakespeare, John Donne, Ben Jonson), Victorian (Alfred, Lord Tennyson and Robert Browning), and Georgian (John Masefield, A.E. Housman, Edward Thomas).

Movements are like political parties, publicity vehicles that go faster and hit harder than a lone stroller. But William Butler Yeats (himself a member of the Rhymers' Club of the 1890s and a Symbolist) declared, "Out of the quarrel with others we make rhetoric; out of the quarrel with ourselves we make poetry." Movements necessarily involve quarreling with others—the unenlightened, the hidebound, the enemy—and demand rhetoric.

The notion of "strength in numbers" does not necessarily work when it comes to poetic movements. Yeats remarked at a meeting of the Rhymers' Club that "we are too many." At best, a movement or school serves to draw attention to deserving work, persuade poets to write more inventively, show readers how to read more attentively,

M

and change (or restore) the way we look at poetry and the world itself. At worst, a movement bullies in the name of self-aggrandizement, like a literary street gang.

Yeats also says, "All movements are held together more by what they hate than by what they love, for love separates and individualises and quiets, but the nobler movements, the only movements on which literature can found itself, hate great and lasting things." One could argue, for example, that Ezra Pound's promotion of Imagism was based largely upon a hatred of the rhetoric, Latinization, Puritanism, loftiness, manhandled syntax, thunderous blank verse, and sheer length of John Milton's *Paradise Lost*.

MUSE 1. The spirit, force, or person that inspires or impels a poet to create.

2. The deity which epic poets such as Homer invoke at the beginning of their poems, specifically one of the Greek goddesses, daughter of Mnemosyne (or Memory), who spoke through the artists she inspired.

Like other epic poems, *The Odyssey* begins with an invocation to the muse (translated here by Robert Fitzgerald):

> Sing in me, Muse, and through me tell the story
> of that man skilled in all ways of contending,
> the wanderer, harried for years on end,
> after he plundered the stronghold
> on the proud height of Troy.

The Greeks recognized nine muses, associated with different arts or sciences: Calliope (epic poetry), Clio (history), Erato (love poetry), Euterpe (lyric poetry), Melpomene (tragedy), Polyhymnia (songs to the gods), Terpsichore (dance), Thalia (comedy), and Urania (astronomy).

In a lecture on "professional standards in English poetry," Robert Graves defines the responsibility of poets:

> the desire to deserve well of the Muse, their divine patroness, from whom they receive their unwritten commissions, to whom

they eat their solitary dinners, who confers her silent benedic-
tion on them, to whom they swear their secret Hippocratic oath,
to whose moods they are as attentive as the stockbroker is to
his market.

More specifically, the poet finds this divine inspirer in the bodily
form of the beloved, the "personal Muse for whom he has written
the poem."

MUSIC POEM A poem that deals with music in some way, imitating a musical form or a work of music, narrating the lives of real or
imaginary musicians, or perhaps describing a musical instrument.
Of course, many poems consist of words meant to be sung, either
written for a particular melody or set to music by a composer.

In one of the following poems, Paul Celan imitates the repetitive
form of the fugue. In this intricate musical form, one voice or
instrument states a melodic phrase; when a second voice enters and
takes up the original melody, the first voice moves on to a new melody
that harmonizes with the old one. More voices come in, and the
accumulating melodies interweave, repeat, turn themselves upside
down, change from major to minor and back again, and perform all
sorts of sonic gymnastics. Similar to the fugue is the round, like "Row,
row, row your boat." Johann Sebastian Bach wrote the greatest fugues,
including a musical treatise, *The Art of Fugue.* The effect is more or
less impossible in poetry, since a fugue is polyphonic (several melodies
occurring simultaneously), but it can be suggested through patterns
of repetition. Dana Gioia's "Lives of the Great Composers" and Weldon
Kees' "Round" are other poems that imitate the contrapuntal techniques of music.

In his translation of Celan's "Deathfugue," John Felstiner adds a musical device to the fugue-like recurrences and recombinations of the
original. His version gradually switches certain English words back into
German, an effect like modulating to a different key in music. These
changes are clear and simple: "master" to "Meister," for example.
Paradoxically, they reinforce the sense of repetition, simply because we

M

notice the metamorphosis of the words. In a poem about the Holocaust, switching back to German suggests the brutal power of the Nazis. But it also leads the reader back to the original words of Paul Celan, who was both German and Jewish. Felstiner devotes a chapter of his book *Paul Celan: Poet, Survivor, Jew* to "Todesfuge."

Michael S. Harper's poem below captures the syncopation of John Coltrane's jazz masterpiece, *A Love Supreme*. Another jazz poem, Michael Stillman's "In Memoriam John Coltrane," uses a *haiku stanza as the basis for its riffs. More poems about jazz musicians, meditations on jazz, and improvisations based on jazz appear in *The Jazz Poetry Anthology*, edited by Sascha Feinstein and Yusef Komunyakaa.

Donald Justice, who studied musical composition with Carl Ruggles, has written many music poems, including two "Sonatinas" and *The Sunset Maker*, a book of verse and prose centered around music and memories of the study of music:

> One small, tight fist clutching the dread Czerny.
> Back then time was still harmony, not money.

As Ezra Pound remarks, the poet should "behave as a musician, a good musician, when dealing with that phase of [his] art which has exact parallels in music." (*See* BLUES, RAP, SONG, *and* SPIRITUAL.)

DEATHFUGUE / Paul Celan (1920–1970; tr. John Felstiner)

> Black milk of daybreak we drink it at evening
> we drink it at midday and morning we drink it at night
> we drink and we drink
> we shovel a grave in the air where you won't lie too cramped
> A man lives in the house he plays with his vipers he writes
> he writes when it grows dark to Deutschland your golden
>   hair Margareta
> he writes it and steps out of doors and the stars are all
>   sparkling he whistles his hounds to stay close
> he whistles his Jews into rows has them shovel a grave in
>   the ground
> he commands us play up for the dance

Black milk of daybreak we drink you at night
we drink you at morning and midday we drink you at evening
we drink and we drink
A man lives in the house he plays with his vipers he writes
he writes when it grows dark to Deutschland your golden
    hair Margareta
Your ashen hair Shulamith we shovel a grave in the air
    where you won't lie too cramped

He shouts dig this earth deeper you lot there you others
    sing up and play
he grabs for the rod in his belt he swings it his eyes
    are so blue
dig your spades deeper you lot there you others play on
    for the dancing

Black milk of daybreak we drink you at night
we drink you at midday and morning we drink you at evening
we drink and we drink
a man lives in the house your goldenes Haar Margareta
your aschenes Haar Shulamith he plays with his vipers

He shouts play death more sweetly this Death is a master
    from Deutschland
he shouts scrape your strings darker you'll rise up as smoke
    to the sky
you'll then have a grave in the clouds where you won't lie
    too cramped

Black milk of daybreak we drink you at night
we drink you at midday Death is a master aus Deutschland
we drink you at evening and morning we drink and we drink
this Death is ein Meister aus Deutschland his eye it is blue
he shoots you with shot made of lead shoots you level
    and true
a man lives in the house your goldenes Haar Margarete

M

179

he looses his hounds on us grants us a grave in the air
he plays with his vipers and daydreams der Tod ist ein
   Meister aus Deutschland

dein goldenes Haar Margarete
dein aschenes Haar Shulamith

DEAR JOHN, DEAR COLTRANE / Michael S. Harper (b. 1938)

a love supreme, a love supreme
a love supreme, a love supreme

Sex fingers toes
in the marketplace
near your father's church
in Hamlet, North Carolina—
witness to this love
in this calm fallow
of these minds,
there is no substitute for pain:
genitals gone or going,
seed burned out,
you tuck the roots in the earth,
turn back, and move
by river through the swamps,
singing: *a love supreme, a love supreme*;
what does it all mean?
Loss, so great each black
woman expects your failure
in mute change, the seed gone.
You plod up into the electric city—
your song now crystal and
the blues. You pick up the horn
with some will and blow
into the freezing night:
a love supreme, a love supreme—

Dawn comes and you cook
up the thick sin 'tween
impotence and death, fuel
the tenor sax cannibal
heart, genitals and sweat
that makes you clean—
a love supreme, a love supreme—

Why you so black?
cause I am
why you so funky?
cause I am
why you so black?
cause I am
why you so sweet?
cause I am
why you so black?
cause I am
a love supreme, a love supreme:

So sick
you couldn't play *Naima*,
so flat we ached
for song you'd concealed
with your own blood,
your diseased liver gave
out its purity,
the inflated heart
pumps out, the tenor kiss,
tenor love:
a love supreme, a love supreme—
a love supreme, a love supreme—

MYTH (Greek, "fable") Fantastic stories that explain some puzzle of nature—human or cosmic. Myths are the tales we live by, the talismans we wear around our necks and touch for luck, passed along

M

from generation to generation or made up individually as we go along. They can be cultural artifacts (like the myth of Orpheus descending to Hades to rescue his love, Eurydice, but then losing her as he glances back). Or they can be what we conjure up or fantasize to help us live our lives, to find our way out of a psychological labyrinth (as the Greek hero Theseus did).

Poets can retell known myths, interpreting and changing them, or they can invent new ones. Often, though, the poet simply alludes to myth in the course of a poem, invoking the ancient stories, hauling a big catch out of the depths.

EURYDICE / Linda Gregg (b. 1942)

I linger, knowing you are eager (having seen
the strange world where I live)
to return to your friends
wearing the bells and singing the songs
which are my mourning.
With the water in them, with their strange rhythms.
I know you will not take me back.
Will take me almost to the world,
but not out to house, color, leaves.
Not to the sacred world that is so easy
for you, my love.

Inside my mind and in my body is a darkness
which I am equal to, but my heart is not.
Yesterday you read the Troubadour poets
in the bathroom doorway
while I painted my eyes for the journey.
While I took tiredness away from my face,
you read of that singer in a garden
with the woman he swore to love forever.

You were always curious what love is like.
Wanted to meet me, not bring me home.
Now you whistle, putting together

M

the new words, learning the songs
to tell the others how far you traveled for me.
Singing of my desire to live.

Oh, if you knew what you do not know
I could be in the world remembering this.
I did not cry as much in the darkness
as I will when we part in the dimness
near the opening which is the way in for you
and was the way out for me, my love.

M

NARRATIVE POETRY Poetry that tells a story. It is one of the three main genres of poetry (the others being *dramatic poetry and *lyric poetry).

Narrative poetry presents characters and leads them through a plot. Its oldest form is the *epic, such as Homer's *The Iliad*. Traditional *ballads are also narrative. "The Demon Lover," for example, tells the story of a woman who is seduced and taken away by a man who changes into a demon as soon as their ship reaches the high seas; he sinks the ship to the bottom. The rise of the prose novel diverted more and more of the narrative impulse away from poetry, but some late-twentieth-century poets, such as Louis Simpson, Andrew Hudgins, and Jimmy Santiago Baca, have brought storytelling back into verse.

NASHERS A *light-verse form, invented by Ogden Nash, in which lines ranging from very short to extremely long *rhyme comically in *couplets.

Some of those comic rhymes will inevitably be *wrenched rhymes*, which the poet forces to fit together. To wrench a rhyme, the poet matches words that sound off-key (not quite close enough to take seriously), alters the spelling of one rhyme word so it stumbles into alignment with the other, or adds unexpected suffixes—all so the second rhyme more closely resembles its mate, as in this couplet from Nash's "Kindly Unhitch That Star, Buddy":

> Some people think they will eventually wear diamonds
>   instead of rhinestones
> Only by everlastingly keeping their noses to their
>   ghrinestones.

In the same poem, he also rhymes "failure"/"azalea," "seraphim"/ "sheriffim," and "correspondence"/"brunettance and blondance." The effect is like poetic slapstick, as if a line of rambling prose slipped on a banana peel (the word to be rhymed) and fell splat on the floor (the mismatched mate to the first rhyme word).

NEGATIVE CAPABILITY John Keats coined this term for a quality that he believed helped to form a poet, the capability of "being in uncertainties, mysteries, doubts, without any irritable reaching after fact and reason." He cites Shakespeare as possessing this highly receptive quality. Robert Frost speaks of something similar when he says that poets "stick to nothing deliberately, but let what will stick to them like burrs where they walk in the fields."

NEW FORMALISM A movement that arose in the 1980s to revive formal verse, with the intention of reaching out to a wider public and rejecting the limits of *academic poetry.

Some poets, such as Richard Wilbur and James Merrill, had continued to write rhymed, metrical poems through the period dominated by *free verse (beginning in the late 1950s). But the New Formalists, according to Dana Gioia, "put free verse poets in the ironic and uncomfortable position of being the *status quo*. Free verse, the creation of an older literary revolution, is now the long-established, ruling orthodoxy; formal poetry the unexpected challenge." In addition to Gioia himself, New Formalist poets include Charles Martin, Timothy Steele, Molly Peacock, R.S. Gwynn, Julia Alvarez, and Gjertrud Schnackenberg.

A related movement, the New Narrative, calls for a return to storytelling in verse. Mark Jarman and Robert McDowell have offered a checklist of what a successful New Narrative poem requires: a beginning, middle, and end; observation; compression of time;

containment; illumination of private gestures; understatement; humor; location; memorable characters; a compelling subject. New Narrative poets include David Mason, Frederick Turner, Andrew Hudgins, and Dick Allen. *New Expansive Poetry*, edited by R.S. Gwynn, contains essays by the poets of both movements (which are grouped together as *expansive poetry*).

Here are two examples of New Formalist poetry:

THE NEXT POEM / Dana Gioia (b. 1950)

How much better it seems now
than when it is finally done—
the unforgettable first line,
the cunning way the stanzas run.

The rhymes soft-spoken and suggestive
are barely audible at first,
an appetite not yet acknowledged
like the inkling of a thirst.

While gradually the form appears
as each line is coaxed aloud—
the architecture of a room
seen from the middle of a crowd.

The music that of common speech
but slanted so that each detail
sounds unexpected as a sharp
inserted in a simple scale.

No jumble box of imagery
dumped glumly in the reader's lap
or elegantly packaged junk
the unsuspecting must unwrap.

But words that could direct a friend
precisely to an unknown place,
those few unshakeable details
that no confusion can erase.

And the real subject left unspoken
but unmistakable to those
who don't expect a jungle parrot
in the black and white of prose.

How much better it seems now
than when it is finally written.
How hungrily one waits to feel
the bright lure seized, the old hook bitten.

WHERE IS HOME? / Molly Peacock (b. 1947)

Our homes are on our backs and don't forget it.
But we don't stay in them; we think them.
Homes are from our minds. Once I tried to fit,
repairing through remembering, the stem
of a favorite glass back on its head. No loss.
A man in dirty overalls swung down
from his truck grabbing the bag of shards to toss
into the maw of his truck. To me he was a clown
reaching a powdered hand into the garbage bag
and plucking out the glass intact. Thus in my mind
I'd everything I had. And please tag
along home with me now. The paths are blind
with wet new grass behind the rusty gate
where my low blurry child home lies in state.

NEW YORK SCHOOL A group of poets first active in New York
City in the 1950s.

Trumpeted by Donald Allen's anthology, *The New American
Poetry 1945–1960*, the New York School paralleled the Abstract-
Expressionist painters of the Manhattan art scene in the fifties,
especially the "action painters" like Jackson Pollock, who flung and
dribbled paint at canvases laid out flat on the floor. The best-known
"New York" poets include Frank O'Hara, John Ashbery, Kenneth
Koch, and James Schuyler. Their work differs greatly, but they are
all daring, funny, passionate, and casual. *Free verse predominates

in their work, although they take pleasure in complex forms such as the *sestina.

The following poem shows the breezy style and the interest in popular culture typical of the New York School. But the voice is unmistakably Frank O'Hara's—hip and urban, funny, emotional, and knowing. He would call it an "I do this, I do that" poem. As he says in his mock manifesto, "Personism," a poet "goes on his nerves." *(See another O'Hara poem in* CITY POEM.*)*

POEM / Frank O'Hara (1926–1966)

> Lana Turner has collapsed!
> I was trotting along and suddenly
> it started raining and snowing
> and you said it was hailing
> but hailing hits you on the head
> hard so it was really snowing and
> raining and I was in such a hurry
> to meet you but the traffic
> was acting exactly like the sky
> and suddenly I see a headline
> LANA TURNER HAS COLLAPSED!
> there is no snow in Hollywood
> there is no rain in California
> I have been to lots of parties
> and acted perfectly disgraceful
> but I never actually collapsed
> oh Lana Turner we love you get up

NONCE FORM A poetic form invented for a particular poem. Fixed forms necessarily begin as nonce forms, although their origins may be murky and undiscernible. However, the *villanelle as we know it began with a pattern invented by Jean Passerat; earlier villanelles, including his own, had simply been imitations of Italian country songs using *refrains but with no fixed pattern. The popularity of Passerat's arrangement hardened a nonce form into a fixed form. *(See* INVENTED FORMS AND STANZAS.*)*

NONSENSE VERSE Playful verse whose words seem to resist ordinary understanding.

Here is a celebrated example of nonsense verse, the first stanza of Lewis Carroll's "Jabberwocky" (1855):

> 'Twas brillig, and the slithy toves
>> Did gyre and gimble in the wabe;
> All mimsy were the borogroves,
>> And the mome raths outgrabe.

Although both Carroll himself and Humpty Dumpty (in *Through the Looking-Glass*, 1871) supply glosses for these words, the pleasure in reading and remembering the poem comes not from a translation into the commonplace but from a reveling in the funny, peculiar language.

Carroll's contemporary, Edward Lear, is the other great nineteenth-century master of nonsense verse. But the uses of nonsense stretch back to the *mad-song stanza and the mad scenes in Shakespeare's *Hamlet* and forward to Modernist experimenters such as Gertrude Stein, James Joyce, Wallace Stevens, and Theodore Roethke. Karl Shapiro even remarks that the "meaning of poetry, as far as language is concerned, is the meaning of *hey-nonny-nonny*"—a popular Elizabethan nonsense phrase.

NUMBERED SECTIONS Poems are sometimes divided into numbered sections that can function as separate chapters, different perspectives, or alternate views or "takes," as in Wallace Stevens's "Thirteen Ways of Looking at a Blackbird." *Sequences, such as William Shakespeare's *sonnets, are often numbered. In some poems, such as John Keats's *odes, each *stanza is numbered. The poet may use either Roman or Arabic numerals.

Numbers can serve as indications of pauses or changes in direction. They can also substitute for titles (although sometimes the numbers come with titles, subtitles, dates, or epigraphs). Asterisks are sometimes used instead of numbers to indicate the breaks between sections.

Pat Mora's "La Migra" uses numbered sections to separate the parts in a role-playing game, first "I" and then "you" pretending to

N

be the border patrol—with very different results. *(See* ACCENTUAL
METER, DEEP IMAGE POETRY, EPITHALAMION, FREE VERSE, HAIKU,
RESPONSE, SEQUENCE, TERZA RIMA, *and* TRIOLET *for other examples
of poems in numbered sections.)*

LA MIGRA / Pat Mora (b. 1942)

1

Let's play La Migra.
I'll be the Border Patrol.
You be the Mexican maid.
I get the badge and sunglasses.
You can hide and run,
but you can't get away
because I have a jeep.
I can take you wherever
I want, but don't ask
questions because
I don't speak Spanish.
I can touch you wherever
I want but don't complain
too much because I've got
boots and kick—if I have to,
and I have handcuffs.
Oh, and a gun.
Get ready, get set, run.

2

Let's play La Migra.
You be the Border Patrol.
I'll be the Mexican woman.
Your jeep has a flat,
and you have been spotted
by the sun.
All you have is heavy: hat,
glasses, badge, shoes, gun.

I know this desert,
where to rest,
where to drink.
Oh, I am not alone.
You hear us singing
and laughing with the wind,
Agua dulce brota aquí, aquí, aquí,
but since you can't speak Spanish,
you do not understand.
Get ready.

NOTE: Pat Mora writes that La Migra is a term "used along the United States/Mexican border for United States Immigration agents." "Agua dulce brota aquí, aquí, aquí" means "Sweet water flow here, here, here."

NUMBERS An older term for metrical *rhythms, based on the counting of syllables in poetic measures such as *iambic pentameter. Sir Philip Sidney refers to "that numbrous kind of writing which is called verse." Alexander Pope observes, "But most by Numbers judge a Poet's song; / And smooth or rough, with them is right or wrong." *(See* ACCENTUAL-SYLLABIC METER, FOOT, METER, *and* VERSE.)

NURSERY RHYME A poem or *song, typically attributed to Mother Goose, full of *rhymes, strong *rhythms, and nonsense, telling stories of kingdoms, farms, and families.

Nursery rhymes include "Jack and Jill," "Old Mother Hubbard," and "Little Boy Blue." In "Some Remarks on Rhythm," Theodore Roethke writes, "What do I like? Listen:

Hinx, minx, the old witch winks!
The fat begins to fry!
There's nobody home but Jumping Joan,
And father, and mother, and I."

In a letter of 1878, Gerard Manley Hopkins discusses *sprung rhythm (which is meter scanned "by accents or stresses alone, without any account of the number of syllables, so that a foot may be one strong syllable or it may be many light and one strong"); he quotes from nursery rhymes to demonstrate this principle: "Here are instances— 'Díng, dóng, béll; Pússy's ín the wéll; Whó pút her ín? Líttle Jóhnny Thín. Whó púlled her oút? Líttle Jóhnny Stóut.' For if each line has three stresses or three feet it follows that some of the feet are of one syllable only. So too 'Óne, twó, Búckle my shóe'. …"

The poem below by Donald Justice imitates the nursery rhyme "This Little Piggy Went to Market."

COUNTING THE MAD / Donald Justice (1925–2004)

This one was put in a jacket,
This one was sent home,
This one was given bread and meat
But would eat none,
And this one cried No No No No
All day long.

This one looked at the window
As though it were a wall,
This one saw things that were not there,
This one things that were,
And this one cried No No No No
All day long.

This one thought himself a bird,
This one a dog,
And this one thought himself a man,
An ordinary man,
And cried and cried No No No No
All day long.

O

OBJECT POEM A poem about an inanimate object. It may give us a fresh look at something ordinary, or it may transform a strange object into something familiar.

The term is a translation of the German *Dinggedicht*, or "thing poem," and some of the best object poems are by Rainer Maria Rilke, including his "Archaic Torso of Apollo." Don Bogen has written object poems such as "Card Catalog," "Salver," "Necklace," "Among Appliances," and "Bullhorn" (which he calls "A gun / for the mouth"). Charles Simic's "Fork," which appears on the next page, has two companion poems, "Knife" and "The Spoon."

A NAVAJO BLANKET / May Swenson (1919–1989)

Eye-dazzlers the Indians weave. Three colors
are paths that pull you in, and pin you
to the maze. Brightness makes your eyes jump,
surveying the geometric field. Alight, and enter
any of the gates—of Blue, of Red, of Black.
Be calmed and hooded, a hawk brought down,
glad to fasten to the forearm of a Chief.

You can sleep at the center,
attended by Sun that never fades, by Moon
that cools. Then, slipping free of zigzag and

hypnotic diamond, find your way out
by the spirit trail, a faint Green thread that
secretly crosses the border, where your mind
is rinsed and returned to you like a white cup.

FORK / Charles Simic (b. 1938)

This strange thing must have crept
Right out of hell.
It resembles a bird's foot
Worn around the cannibal's neck.

As you hold it in your hand,
As you stab with it into a piece of meat,
It is possible to imagine the rest of the bird:
Its head which like your fist
Is large, bald, beakless and blind.

OBJECTIVE CORRELATIVE T.S. Eliot's term for a set of specific objects (images and actions) that will evoke a specific, correlated emotion in the reader. In an essay on Shakespeare's *Hamlet* (1919), Eliot defines it as "a set of objects, a situation, a chain of events which shall be the formula of that *particular* emotion; such that when the external facts, which must terminate in sensory experience, are given, the emotion is immediately evoked." In "The Love Song of J. Alfred Prufrock," Eliot presents images that serve as objective correlatives for the speaker's loneliness, timidity, and withdrawal from emotional relationships, as in the lines "I should have been a pair of ragged claws, / Scuttling across the floors of silent seas."

OCCASIONAL VERSE Poem written to commemorate an occasion; a poem commissioned by someone to celebrate some happening, like the Olympian odes of Pindar or the coronation ode by a poet laureate.

The term is often used dismissively to label a poem as a kind of "work for hire," inspired not by imagination but by something external. However, real poems do arise out of (and for) particular occasions. It matters, perhaps, who does the choosing. Ellen Bryant Voigt's "The Last Class" begins:

> Put this in your notebooks:
> All verse is occasional verse.

Some kinds of occasional verse have time-honored names from the Greek. An *epithalamion* celebrates a wedding. A *genethliacon* or *genethliacum (jen-eth-lie´-uh-con or -cum)* is a birthday ode, like Dylan Thomas's "Poem on His Birthday," or a poem that celebrates a birth, like Helen Frost's "First Deep Breath," which was written as a blessing for poet Annie Finch's newborn daughter.

Occasional verse might also be written on the spur of the moment, about a time of day, for a birthday or holiday, or for a day of the week—anything that represents a quick sketch of the ephemeral, of time fleeing.

OCTAVE (Latin, "eight") An eight-line *stanza. An octave serves as the first eight lines of a Petrarchan (or Italian) *sonnet, rhymed *abbaabba*. When used as a stanza in its own right, it is called a *brace octave*, and can also rhyme *abbacddc*. A *common octave* rhymes *ababcdcd* or leaves the odd-numbered lines unrhymed: *XaXaXbXb*. *Ottava rima*, which Lord Byron uses in Don Juan, rhymes *abababcc*. *(See* TRIOLET.*)*

ODE (Greek, "song") 1. A *song or lyric, often passionate, expansive, exuberant, rhapsodic.

2. A poem in any of several song-like forms:

• Pindaric or choral ode (used by the Greek poet Pindar and Greek playwrights such as Sophocles): written in triads (groups of three *stanzas), beginning with a **strophe (stro´-fee)* and *antistrophe (an-tih´-struh-fee)* that are metrically identical, followed by an *epode (eh´-pode)* that diverges from that pattern. An ode may consist of one or more triads. The three parts are also called *turn, counter-turn,* and *stand*. The terms refer to dance movements, since these odes were originally musical numbers commissioned to celebrate the victors of athletic events in Ancient Greece. Wayne Koestenbaum's "Ode to Anna Moffo" is a contemporary Pindaric ode.

• Horatian ode (used by or modeled after the Roman poet Horace): regular matching stanzas or metrical units; often in *quatrains such as the *Sapphic stanza, the *Alcaic stanza, or Andrew Marvell's quatrain in "An Horatian Ode upon Cromwell's Return from Ireland" (two iambic tetrameter lines followed by two trimeter lines, rhymed *aabb*):

> 'Tis time to leave the Books in dust,
> And oyl th' unused Armours rust:
> > Removing from the Wall
> > The Corslet of the Hall.

NOTE: *corslet*: armor, breastplate

John Keats's odes are Horatian in that the stanzas in any given ode have the same number of lines. "Ode on a Grecian Urn" and "Ode to a Nightingale," for example, consist of ten-line stanzas rhymed *ababcdecde*.

• Cowleyan or Irregular ode (also "False Pindaric"; named after Abraham Cowley [pronounced cool´-ee; 1618–1667]): lines of irregular length and irregular rhyme scheme, stanzas (if any) not matching each other in meter, line length, or rhyme; free to be anything but regular. Here is the second stanza of Cowley's "Ode upon Doctor Harvey." The "she" of this stanza stands for "Coy Nature," pursued by the heroic Dr. Harvey, who discovered the movement of the bloodstream:

> Here sure shall I be safe (said she,)
> None will be able sure to see
> > This my retreat, but only He
> > Who made both it and me.
> The heart of Man, what Art can e'er reveal?
> > A Wall impervious between

Divides the very parts within,
And doth the very Heart of Man ev'n from itself conceal.
   She spoke, but e're she was aware,
   Harvey was with her there,
And held this slippery *Proteus* in a chain,
Till all her mighty Mysteries she descry'd,
Which from his Wit th' attempt before to hide
Was the first Thing that Nature did in vain.

The rhyme scheme is *aaaabccbddeffe*; the pattern of iambic feet in the lines is 4-4-4-3-5-4-4-7-4-3-5-5-5-5 (not like any of the ode's other four stanzas). If each stanza followed this pattern, the ode would be Horatian; if the first two stanzas followed it but every third one diverged, the ode would be Pindaric. (Proteus, incidentally, was a Greek god who changed his shape; captured and held long enough, he would stop metamorphosing and reveal the truth, as Nature reveals the circulatory system to Dr. Harvey.)

William Wordsworth's "Ode: Intimations of Immortality from Recollections of Early Childhood" is perhaps the best-known Cowleyan ode. Here are the first two of its eleven stanzas (each with its own rhyme scheme, number of feet for different lines, and indented shape):

There was a time when meadow, grove and stream,	a	5
The earth, and every common sight,	b	4
To me did seem	a	2
Appareled in celestial light,	b	4
The glory and the freshness of a dream.	a	5
It is not now as it hath been of yore—	c	5
Turn whereso'er I may,	d	3
By night or day,	d	2
The things which I have seen I now can see no more.	c	6
The Rainbow comes and goes,	e	3
And lovely is the Rose,	e	3
The Moon doth with delight	b	3

Look round her when the heavens are bare,	f	4
Waters on a starry night	b	4
Are beautiful and fair;	f	3
The sunshine is a glorious birth;	g	4
But yet I know, where'er I go,	h/h	4
That there hath passed away a glory from the earth.	g	6

These stanzas happen to contain the same number of lines (nine), but the ode's other stanzas contain seventeen, twenty-two, twenty, eight, twenty-three, twenty-one, thirty-nine, nineteen, and seventeen lines.

• Elemental ode (invented by Pablo Neruda, sometimes translated as "elementary ode"): short-lined free-verse poems about everyday things; passionate and rhapsodic about the ordinary, lavishing attention and affection on subjects such as watermelons.

The term *ode* is now used very loosely. A sense of rapture, elevation, mystical oneness with nature, and "the voice of the bard" typify poems like Walt Whitman's "Out of the Cradle Endlessly Rocking" and Dylan Thomas's "Fern Hill." In odes, the poet usually comments on—and praises—things apart from himself, even though the ostensible subject may be his own childhood.

OLYMPIA 4 / Pindar (518 or 522–438 or 442 B.C.E.; tr. Richmond Lattimore)

Mightiest driver of the weariless speed in the
    lightning's feet,
Zeus: the circling Hours, your own,
have brought me to testify
to highest achievements   *strophe*
by virtue of song and the lyre's intricacy.
At friends' good luck the noble will rise to welcome
the sweet message.
O son of Kronos, lord of Aitna,
blast-furnace to hundred-headed Typhon's bulk,
in the name of the Graces
accept this song of Olympic victory,

light at long last from the wide strength of valor.
For it rides the wheels of Psaumis,
who, his brow shaded in olive
of Pisa, comes home, bringing glory   *antistrophe*
on Kamarina. May God be kindly
to his prayers hereafter; I have praise for him.
A keen handler of horses,
he rejoices in hospitality to his friends;
and his face, with clean purpose, is turned toward
      Concord, who loves cities.
I will not steep my speech
in lies; the test of any man lies in action.

So the son of Klymenos
was set free from being scorned
by Lemnian women.
As he won the race in bronze armor   *epode*
and came to Hypsipyle for his garland, he spoke:
"Here am I in my speed.
My hands are as good as my heart.
Many a time even on young men gray hairs
appear, against the likelihood of their youth."

NOTE: *son of Kronos*: Zeus, king of the gods, wielder of lightning; *Aitna*: Mt. Etna in Sicily; *Typhon*: a flame-breathing giant under Mt. Etna; *Psaumis of Kamarina, Sicily*: the winner of the chariot race in the Olympian games of 452 B.C.E.; *son of Klymenos*: Erginos, one of Jason's Argonauts; *Lemnos*: island in northern Aegean Sea; *Hypsipyle*: Queen of the Lemnian women.

ODES, Book I, ix / Horace (65–8 B.C.E.; tr. John Frederick Nims)

You see how, white with snows to the north of us,
Soracte looms; how snow's over everything;
      the burdened pines no longer buoyant,
            streams at a stand in the winter weather.
So, rout the cold! Load logs on the andirons
as good hosts should do. Logs! And no rationing
      your wine, young fellow there! Your Sabine,
            hustle it out from the crusty wine-jars.

Then let the heavens see to the rest of it.
When once they've lulled the winds at their weltering
 on whitened surf, no cypress quivers,
  never a breath in the ancient alder.
What comes tomorrow, never you mind about.
Each day on waking reckon, "Another!" and
 chalk up your one more gain. Don't spurn the
  pleasure of love in your time for dancing,
while youth's in bloom, while moody decrepitude's
remote. Now haunt the malls and the stadium.
 When little whispers stir in starlight,
  make very sure you arrange to be there,
where—who's in hiding?—giveaway laughter from
the dark, a girl's laugh, muffled ... lovely ...
 her bracelet tussled for in fun, or
  ring from a teasingly tightened finger.

NOTE: This ode uses the Alcaic stanza.

ODE TO SALT / Pablo Neruda (1904–1973; tr. Robert Bly)

I saw the salt
in this shaker
in the salt flats.
I know
you
will never believe me,
but
it sings,
the salt sings, the hide
of the salt plains,
it sings
through a mouth smothered
by earth.
I shuddered in those deep
solitudes
when I heard

the voice
of
the salt
in the desert.
Near Antofagasta
the entire
salt plain
speaks:
it is a
broken
voice,
a song full
of grief.
Then in its own mines
rock salt, a mountain
of buried light,
a cathedral through which light passes,
crystal of the sea, abandoned
by the waves.

And then on every table
on this earth,
salt,
your nimble
body
pouring out
the vigorous light
over
our foods.
Preserver
of the stores
of the ancient ships,
you were
an explorer
in the ocean,

O

substance
going first
over the unknown, barely open
routes of the sea-foam.
Dust of the sea, the tongue
receives a kiss
of the night sea from you:
taste recognizes
the ocean in each salted morsel,
and therefore the smallest,
the tiniest
wave of the shaker
brings home to us
not only your domestic whiteness
but the inward flavor of the infinite.

ONOMATOPOEIA (ahn'-uh-mah-tuh-pee'-uh; Greek, "making a name") The use of a word that imitates the sound of what the word means, like *splat*, *sizzle*, *buzz*, and *puff*.

Expressive sound effects, such as onomatopoeia, have an important place in poetry. In a passage from "An Essay on Criticism," Alexander Pope says:

The sound must seem an echo to the sense.
Soft is the strain when Zephyr gently blows,
And the smooth stream in smoother numbers flows;
But when loud surges lash the sounding shore,
The hoarse, rough verse should like the torrent roar.
When Ajax strives some rock's vast weight to throw,
The line too labors, and the words move slow ...

The "smooth stream" of words is called *euphony (yoo´-fuh-nee; Greek, "sounding well")*: mellifluous sound, pretty noise, a smooth, pleasant, and harmonious flow of words. The "hoarse, rough" words are called *cacophony (kuh-kah´-fuh-nee; Greek, "sounding ill")*: unpleasant sound, a jangle of clashing words, what the Elizabethan songwriter John Dowland calls "hellish, jarring sounds."

OTTAVA RIMA (aw-tah'-vuh ree'-muh; Italian, "eighth rhyme")
Eight-line *stanza form, in which the *iambic pentameter lines
rhyme *ababacc.*

Adapted, perhaps, from the Sicilian *strambotto* (discussed in
SONNET), ottava rima is credited to Boccaccio in fourteenth-cen-
tury Italy. It became the heroic form of Italian poetry, used in
Ariosto's *Orlando Furioso* and Tasso's *Jerusalem Delivered.* Thomas
Wyatt was the first English poet to use ottava rima frequently.
Anthony Burgess's *Byrne,* a verse novel published in 1995, is writ-
ten in ottava rima.

The stanza is flexible and potent, the first two rhyme sounds
alternating three times and followed by the "bang" of a *couplet
using a third rhyme sound. It gives a wonderful sense of buildup
and completion, equally suitable for the comic and the serious.
Lord Byron's ottava rima stanzas in *Don Juan* are generally humorous, partly because he often uses preposterous, polysyllabic
rhymes, usually in the final couplets, as in the following lines from
Canto IV:

> Here I might enter on a chaste description,
>   Having withstood temptation in my youth,
> But hear that several people take exception
>   At the first two books having too much truth;
> Therefore I'll make Don Juan leave the ship soon,
>   Because the publisher declares, in sooth,
> Through needles' eyes it easier for the camel is
> To pass, than those two cantos into families.

The following example, which Byron calls "a mere speculation," is
not so jocular (though humor is still present in his brief rethink-
ing of Hamlet's soliloquy.) William Butler Yeats's stanzas in ottava rima, on the other hand, always sound serious and stately. He
uses the form for many of his meditations, including "Among
School Children," "The Circus Animals' Desertion," and "Sailing
to Byzantium."

from *DON JUAN* (Canto XIV, 4–6) / George Gordon, Lord Byron
(1788–1824)

A sleep without dreams, after a rough day
    Of toil, is what we covet most; and yet
How clay shrinks back from more quiescent clay!
    The very Suicide that pays his debt
At once without installments (an old way
    Of paying debts, which creditors regret)
Lets out impatiently his rushing breath,
Less from disgust of life than dread of death.

'Tis round him, near him, here, there, everywhere;
    And there's a courage which grows out of fear,
Perhaps of all most desperate, which will dare
    The worst to *know* it:—when the mountains rear
Their peaks beneath your human foot, and there
    You look down o'er the precipice, and drear
The gulf of rock yawns,—you can't gaze a minute
Without an awful wish to plunge within it.

'Tis true, you don't—but, pale and struck with terror,
    Retire: but look into your past impression!
And you will find, though shuddering at the mirror
    Of your own thoughts, in all their self confession,
The lurking bias, be it truth or error,
    To the *unknown*; a secret prepossession,
To plunge with all your fears—but where? You know not,
And that's the reason why you do—or do not.

OULIPO (oo-lee-poe'; acronym for "Ouvroir de littérature poten-
tielle," *ouvroir* meaning a "workroom in a convent," *littérature poten-
tielle* meaning "potential literature") A poetic movement founded in
1960 by a group of poets and mathematicians, led by Raymond Queneau.

This group explored a number of existing, game-like poetic forms,
such as the *sestina (which uses six "end-words," in place of rhymes,

in a set order through six stanzas), *cento (poem composed from passages taken from other poems), and *rhopalic verse, which they also call "snowball" (lines in which each word has one syllable more than the previous word, such as "I disdain rhopalic composition un-repentently"). A "melting snowball" would go in the opposite direction, from words of many syllables (or letters) to monosyllabic or one-letter words ("O!").

Here are some of the other forms used by Oulipo poets:

• Holorhyming verse: line in which every syllable must rhyme (for example, "Why sigh, I cry, my sly, shy guy?")

• Lipogram: text that does not use certain letters (for example, es-chewing or eliminating any words containing the letter *s*)

• Permutational poem: verse in which the lines can be read in any order

• Tautogram: text in which each word begins with the same letter (like the "A" chapters of Walter Abish's novel *Alphabetical Africa*, which begins "Ages ago, Alex, Allen and Alva arrived at Antibes …")

The Oulipo poets also experimented with computer generation of texts and created a number of new poetic forms:

• Antonymic translation: a method in which antonyms are substitut-ed for the words of a text, transforming an utterance into its opposite

• Boolean poem: text that uses the words common to two selected poems to generate a new poem (Considering those two poems a "set," the poet draws words from their "intersection")

• Haikuization: a method by which the poet keeps the rhyming parts of a poem but gets rid of the rest, so that the last stanza of Yeats's "Sailing to Byzantium" might become "Never take / any natural thing. / Make / enameling /awake. / Sing / of Byzantium / to come."

• Perverb: a mixing of the first half of one proverb with the second half of another, such as "The Lord helps those who / gather no moss" or "Still waters / starve a fever." (The word *perverb* does the same thing: per[verted pro]verb.)

0

• S + 7: a transformation method by which the poet replaces each noun (substantive) in a text with the seventh noun after it in a dictionary (Andrew Marvell's "Had we but world enough, and time, / This coyness, lady, were no crime" might become, through the S + 7 method, "Had we but worry enough, and timeserver, / This crab, laetrile, were no crinoline." The results depend upon the dictionary and the accuracy of the noun-counter.)

The Oulipo poets are interested in exploiting most *rhetorical devices and in word oddities such as:

• Palindrome: a word, phrase, or sentence that reads the same frontwards and backwards, such as "Madam, I'm Adam"

• Portmanteau word: a nonce word that combines part of one word with part of another, as Lewis Carroll, who coined the term, combined "chuckle" and "snort" to invent "chortle"

• Spoonerism: the switching of initial sounds between nearby words, named after the Reverend W.A. Spooner, 1844–1930, who once said in a sermon, "Our Lord is indeed a shoving leopard."

More of their methods appear in *Oulipo: A Primer of Potential Literature*, edited by Warren F. Motte, Jr.

OXYMORON (oc-see-more'-ahn; Greek, "sharp" + "dull, foolish") An expression that combines opposite, contradictory qualities, seemingly nonsensical but capturing some psychological or emotional extreme of ambivalence. Romeo's complaint to Benvolio in Act I, Scene I of *Romeo and Juliet* is a good example: "Feather of lead, bright smoke, cold fire, sick health!"

PALINODE (pal'-ih-node; Greek, "singing again") 1. A poem that retracts or takes back something previously said. In the first palinode, Stesichorus of Himera (sixth century B.C.E.) recants an earlier attack against Helen of Troy. Here is Richmond Lattimore's translation of the fragment:

> That story is not true.
> You never sailed in the benched ships.
> You never went to the city of Troy.

Charles Simic's "*errata*" (which imitates a scholarly book's list of its own errors) is a contemporary palinode. Here are its opening lines:

> Where it says snow
> read teeth-marks of a virgin

2. A variant of the Greek *ode; a form in which four *stanzas are arranged as follows:

Stanza	1	Ode	Strophe A
	2	Ode	Strophe B
	3	Palinode	Antistrophe B (same form as Strophe B)
	4	Palinode	Antistrophe A (same form as Strophe A)

PANTOUM (pan-toom'; also *pantun*) A Malay repeating form, written in *quatrains, in which the second and fourth lines of each *stanza become the first and third lines of the next one.

In the last stanza, ideally, the second and fourth lines repeat the opening stanza's first and third lines, bringing the pantoum full circle. David Mason's "Gusev," included below, exemplifies this circular structure—and follows the traditional *abab* *rhyme scheme. One variation appears in Donald Justice's "In the Attic," which repeats end-words (as in a *sestina) rather than whole lines. Each repeated line is called a *repeton*.

The pantoum was introduced to the West in the notes to Victor Hugo's *Les Orientales*. The poem that Hugo chose demonstrates another characteristic of a Malay pantoum. In each quatrain, lines one and two are independent of lines three and four; they deal with different subjects entirely. In the original, rhyme links the disparate halves of each quatrain in a scheme of *abab*.

In the nineteenth century, the pantoum was a popular form in France and England, used by poets such as Charles Baudelaire, Théodore de Banville, and Austin Dobson. In America, John Ashbery's "Pantoum," which begins, "Eyes shining without mystery," popularized the form in the late fifties, especially among the poets of the *New York School.

MALAY PANTOUM (*Les papillons jouent à l'entour sur leurs ailes*; tr. John Drury, from the French version of Ernest Fouinet included in the notes to Victor Hugo's *Les Orientales*, 1829)

Butterflies dip and flutter on their wings;
They fly to the sea, near a chain of rocks.
My heart has felt ill in my chest
From my earliest days to the present hour.

They fly to the sea, near a chain of rocks ...
The vulture soars on the way to Bandam.
From my earliest days to the present hour
I have admired the young.

The vulture soars on the way to Bandam ...
And glides down to Patani.
I have admired the young,
But none compares to the one I choose.

He glides down to Patani ...
Look! Two young pigeons!
No young man compares to the one I choose,
Skilled as he is at touching the heart.

GUSEV / David Mason (b. 1954)

from the story by Anton Chekhov

The wind has broken free of its chain.
The sea has neither sense nor pity,
and what befalls us falls like rain.
The water's hot as new-made jelly.

The sea has neither sense nor pity.
One dies while playing a game of cards.
The water's hot as new-made jelly.
Above it there are curious clouds.

One dies while playing a game of cards.
Pavel insists he is getting well.
Above the ship are curious clouds
like lions leaping over the swell.

Pavel insists he is getting well
and dies still hating the peasant class.
Lions leaping over the swell
turn to scissors as they pass.

He dies still hating the peasant class
while Gusev lies in a fevered state.
Clouds turn to scissors as they pass
and dead men find it hard to hate.

Gusev lies in a fevered state,
wishing he didn't have to die,
and though he finds it hard to hate
he's saddened when he sees the sky.

Wishing he didn't have to die,
he goes below to suffocate,
saddened now he's seen the sky.
He thinks of snow, the village gate,

and goes below to suffocate,
his dreams increasingly absurd.
He sleighs through snow, the village gate,
sleeps two days, dies on the third.

His dreams increasingly absurd,
he tosses the fever from his bed,
sleeps two days, dies on the third.
They sew the sail-cloth over his head.

He tosses the fever from his bed.
The fever smiles and crawls back in.
They sew the sail-cloth over his head.
Below deck someone's dying again.

The fever smiles and crawls back in.
The wind has broken free of its chain.
Below deck someone's dying again,
and what befalls us falls like rain.

PARODY (pare'-uh-dee; Greek, "song sung beside") A poem that satirizes or ridicules another poem (by imitating its mannerisms) or a poet (by lampooning his stylistic tics).

In his "daydream college for bards," W.H. Auden would require that the only critical exercise be the writing of parodies. *Imitation, whether for fun or intellectual profit, remains one of the great ways of learning the craft of poetry.

A *pastiche (pass-teesh´; Italian, "pie")* is a kind of parody, denoting either a hodgepodge of borrowed passages, as in a *cento, or an imitation of another work, not usually meant to ridicule. Other words used for designating parodies include *burlesque, caricature, lampoon,* and *travesty.*

Lord Byron's parody of Wordsworth's "Peter Bell" appears in QUINTAIN. Beth Gylys parodies Dylan Thomas's "Do Not Go Gentle into That Good Night" (which appears in VILLANELLE) as "Do not dive head-first in that puddle of mud." Her other refrain is "Wade, wade slowly into the brackish crud." In the following parody, Lewis Carroll pokes fun at the rather indestructible "Twinkle, Twinkle, Little Star" by Jane Taylor.

from *ALICE'S ADVENTURES IN WONDERLAND* /
Lewis Carroll (1832–1898)

> Twinkle, twinkle, little bat!
> How I wonder what you're at!
> Up above the world you fly,
> Like a tea-tray in the sky.

PASTORAL (pass´-tur-ul) A poem that describes country life in an idealized way.

The pastoral began with Theocritus, a Sicilian poet of the third century B.C.E., who wrote about the lives of shepherds. (A "pastor" is one who leads a flock.) There are three major kinds of pastoral:

• Complaint: a shepherd's love song praising his beloved and moaning about her cruelty

• Eclogue: a *dialogue, usually representing a singing contest between two shepherds

• Pastoral elegy: a shepherd's lament for another shepherd who has died *(See* ELEGY.*)*

Several terms are used interchangeably with pastoral: *bucolic, *eclogue, *georgic,* and *idyll* (or *idyl*).

A bucolic *(byoo-kol´-ik; Latin, "pastoral," Greek, "ox-herd")* refers to herders or shepherds in an idealized landscape. In the mystery *Saratoga Haunting*, poet Stephen Dobyns writes, "Traditionally a bucolic setting includes shepherds, farmlands, lush foliage. But even the bucolic can suffer the pangs of modernization and in the present instance the ox has been replaced by a bright yellow backhoe, the herdsman by the backhoe operator."

A *georgic deals with the work of farming and often takes the form of a *how-to poem.

Theocritus's pastorals are in fact called *idylls*. The opening lines of his twenty-seventh idyll present a dialogue between Daphnis, a shepherd, and Chloris, the girl he pursues. Here is John Dryden's translation (written in *heroic couplets, although the original is unrhymed):

> DAPHNIS. The shepherd Paris bore the Spartan bride
>   By force away, and then by force enjoy'd;
>   But I by free consent can boast a bliss,
>   A fairer Helen, and a sweeter kiss.
>
> CHLORIS. Kisses are empty joys, and soon are o'er.
>
> DAPHNIS. A kiss betwixt the lips is something more.
>
> CHLORIS. I wipe my mouth, and where's your kissing then?
>
> DAPHNIS. I swear you wipe it to be kiss'd again.
>
> CHLORIS. Go, tend your herd, and kiss your cows at home;
>   I am a maid, and in my beauty's bloom.

But by the end of this idyll, the shepherd has seduced the girl:

> DAPHNIS. The noble deed is done! My herds I'll cull;
>   Cupid, be thine a calf; and, Venus, thine a bull.
>
> CHLORIS. A maid I came, in an unlucky hour,
>   But hence return without my virgin flow'r.

In conclusion, the poet comments:

First rose the maid, and with a glowing face,
Her downcast eyes beheld her print upon the grass;
Thence to her herd she sped herself in haste:
The bridegroom started from his trance at last,
And piping homeward jocundly he pass'd.

This idyll combines several features of pastoral poetry: a peaceful, beautiful, and isolated rural setting; a shepherd and a girl; a dialogue; some narration by the poet; a lover's complaint; and a seduction that is likened to animal husbandry.

PATTERN POEM (also called *calligramme, carmen figuratum, concrete poem, emblematic verse, figured poem, shaped poem, visual poem*) A poem in which the words or letters form a typographical picture, either imitating how something looks or suggesting what the subject does (like a wavy left-hand margin suggesting a snake, or the movement of a river, or the meandering of thoughts).

Pattern poems appeared in Ancient Greek (depicting a monument) and in several poems by the seventeenth-century poet George Herbert (depicting an altar and a pair of wings). In *Alice's Adventures in Wonderland,* Lewis Carroll presents a mouse's tale in the typographical shape of a mouse's tail that curls back and forth down the page in a thin column, the type getting smaller and smaller.

Guillaume Apollinaire coined the term *calligramme (cah-lee-grahm´),* a word similar to "calligraphy," in his 1918 volume, *Calligrammes.* Among other things, these poems depict the Eiffel Tower and rainfall.

John Hollander's *Types of Shape* consists entirely of pattern poems. The shapes include a key, lightbulb, harpsichord, bell, sundial, lazy Susan, kitty, kitty with bug, the state of New York, a double helix, and a swan with its reflection. These poems, however, can still be read aloud.

In the twentieth century, some poets began experimenting with *concrete poetry*, which often departs entirely from a readable text and presents something closer to graphic art. One sign of this shift is that such a poem can be reduced to an explanation of how it looks (such as a poem in the shape of an apple, using the word *apple* over and over, but replaced in one spot by the word *worm*). An explanation, in place of the picture-poem itself, would be an example of *conceptual poetry*.

Richard Kostelanetz, a leading experimenter with concrete poetry, suggests a new term for the pattern poem: "word-imagery, which encompasses the two major genres of the form—imaged words and worded images." May Swenson has written some of the finest pattern poems. Her shapes are sometimes abstract, sometimes specific, but tend to look expressively askew, often more suggestive than literal.

EASTER WINGS / George Herbert (1593–1633)

Lord, who createdst man in wealth and store,
Though foolishly he lost the same,
Decaying more and more
Till he became
Most poore;
With thee
O let me rise
As larks, harmoniously,
And sing this day thy victories;
Then shall the fall further the flight in me.

My tender age in sorrow did beginne;
And still with sicknesses and shame
Thou didst so punish sinne,
That I became
Most thinne.
With thee
Let me combine,
And feel this day thy victorie;
For if I imp my wing on thine,
Affliction shall advance the flight in me.

OUT OF THE SEA, EARLY / May Swenson (1919–1989)

A bloody
egg yolk. A burnt hole
spreading in a sheet. An en-
raged rose threatening to bloom.
A furnace hatchway opening, roaring.
A globular bladder filling with immense
juice. I start to scream. A red hydrocepha-
lic head is born, teetering on the stump of
its neck. When it separates, it leaks rasp-
berry from the horizon down the wide esca-
lator. The cold blue boiling waves cannot
scour out that band, that broadens, slid-
ing toward me up the wet sand slope. The
fox-hair grows, grows thicker on the
upfloating head. By six o'clock,
diffused to ordinary gold,
it exposes each silk thread and rumple in the carpet.

PHANOPOEIA (fan'-oh-pee'-uh) Ezra Pound's term for the use of imagery in poetry, "throwing the object (fixed or moving) on to the visual imagination," one of the three means by which a poet can "charge language with meaning." (*See* LOGOPOEIA *and* MELOPOEIA.)

POEM (Greek, a "made thing") A text or verbal composition, often written in lines, whose language is compressed and resonant and which conveys an experience, an emotion, or simply an aesthetically pleasing arrangement of words. Samuel Taylor Coleridge defines a poem as "that species of composition, which is opposed to works of science, by proposing for its *immediate* object pleasure, not truth; and from all other species (having *this* object in common with it) it is discriminated by proposing to itself such delight from the *whole*, as is compatible with a distinct gratification from each component *part*." John Crowe Ransom says that a poem is "a loose logical struc-ture with a good deal of local texture." William Carlos Williams defines a poem as "a small (or large) machine made of words." According to Wallace Stevens, "Every poem is a poem within a poem: the poem of the idea within the poem of the words." As Robert Frost says, "It begins in delight and ends in wisdom."

P

POET (Greek, a "maker") One who creates poems, or one who has created them, or one who thinks and feels like a poet (winged horse at the hitching post), or one who prepares to write poems or attempts writing them or otherwise stays alert for words, images, and experiences that might coalesce into the nucleus of a poem. Ralph Waldo Emerson says that the poet is "the sayer, the namer, and represents beauty."

There are many synonyms for poet. A *bard* (Irish for "poet") was originally a minstrel poet; now, any poet. A *scop* is an Anglo-Saxon court poet. A *makar* is a Scottish poet. The German word, *Dichter*, is interesting because the verb *dichten* (from which it derives) means "to condense" as well as "to write poems." *Minstrel* and *troubadour* both denote Medieval poets who sang of courtly love, but the terms are now used jocularly (and more often for singer-songwriters, like the "Troubadours of Folk"). *Poetaster, rhymer, rhymester, sonneteer,* and *versifier* are terms of ridicule and deprecation.

POETRY (Greek, "making") The art made up of *poems, texts with charged, compressed language. The word *poetry* is used more generally than the word *poem* (which refers to a particular "made thing" in words). It can refer to a body of poems, as in "the poetry of Emily Dickinson." It can also be used as a term of praise for anything extraordinary, transcendent, or superlative, as in the phrase "poetry in motion." It applies to texts containing acute perceptions, vivid impressions, compressed language, the musically rhythmic use of language, a heightened sense of attentiveness, and an overall intensification coupled with intensity of detail. Poetry is singing thought.

Robert Graves, however, asserts that poetry is "not an art, but a way of thinking." He also calls it "the fusion of contradictory ideas." William Wordsworth defines poetry as "the spontaneous overflow of powerful feelings: it takes its origin from emotion recollected in tranquility." Percy Bysshe Shelley calls poetry "a mirror which makes beautiful that which is distorted." Sir Philip Sidney defines *poesy* (a synonym for poetry, though now used mostly in a jocular or derisive way) as a "speaking picture." Horace asserts that its purpose is "to delight and instruct at once." Gertrude Stein defines poetry as the "calling upon names." Howard Nemerov says poetry is "a way of getting something right in language, poetry is language doing itself right."

Some poets, aptly enough, use *metaphors to define poetry. Ezra Pound says, "Poetry is a centaur. The thinking word-arranging, clarifying faculty must move and leap with the energizing, sentient, musical faculties." Wallace Stevens says, "Poetry is a pheasant disappearing in the brush."

Prose, *free verse*, and *metrical verse* are the three principal modes of poetry. (One could possibly add the *pattern poem*, which is shaped typographically, as a fourth category.) Prose is what we ordinarily read in newspaper articles, fiction, essays, and letters; it is written in sentences and paragraphs and printed with a justified right-hand margin, without regard for which words are located on that margin, hyphenating words as needed. Verse is written in lines, although it also uses sentences; any line must end where the poet says it ends, not where a typesetter might like to terminate it. If the lines are not measured in some way, they are *free verse; if they are measured by a regular count of syllables, or accents, or both, they are metrical. (*See* ACCENTUAL VERSE, ACCENTUAL-SYLLABIC VERSE, FOOT, METER, *and* SYLLABIC VERSE.)

The following three poems all appear in James Wright's *This Journey*. The first is a *prose poem; the second is a free-verse poem; the third is a metrical poem, a *sonnet rhymed *ababcdcd eefggf*.

THE FOX AT EYPE / James Wright (1927–1980)

He knows that all dogs bounding here and there, from the little vales all the way to the cliff-meadows and Thorncombe Beacon and beyond, are domestically forbidden to kill him. So every evening just before the end of twilight he emerges softly from the hedge across the lane and sits elegantly till darkness, gazing, with a certain weary amusement, into the middle distance of the sea.

OHIOAN PASTORAL / James Wright (1927–1980)

On the other side
Of Salt Creek, along the road, the barns topple
And snag among the orange rinds,
Oil cans, cold balloons of lovers.
One barn there
Sags, sags and oozes
Down one side of the copperous gulley.
The limp whip of a sumac dangles
Gently against the body of a lost
Bathtub, while high in the flint-cracks
And the wild grimed trees, on the hill,
A buried gas main
Long ago tore a black gutter into the mines.
And now it hisses among the green rings
On fingers in coffins.

READING A 1979 INSCRIPTION ON BELLI'S MONUMENT / James Wright (1927–1980)

It is not only the Romans who are gone.
Belli, unhappy a century ago,
Won from the world his fashionable stone.
Where it stands now, he doesn't even know.
Across the Tiber, near Trastevere,
His top hat teetered on his head with care,
Brushed like a gentleman, he cannot see
The latest Romans who succeed him there.

One of them bravely climbed his pedestal
And sprayed a scarlet MERDA on his shawl.
This afternoon, I pray his hidden grave
Lies nameless somewhere in the hills, while rain
Fusses and frets to rinse away the stain.
Rain might erase when marble cannot save.

NOTE: Giuseppe Belli (1791-1863) was a native of Rome who wrote many sonnets.

POETRY IN FICTION 1. Works of fiction that are considered poetic, such as James Joyce's *Ulysses* and Herman Melville's *Moby-Dick*.

2. Works of fiction that contain poems or are partly written in verse, such as Richard Powers's *The Gold Bug Variations*, Vladimir Nabokov's *Pale Fire*, D.M. Thomas's *The White Hotel*, E.L. Doctorow's *Loon Lake*, and John Barth's *The Sot-Weed Factor* (and several of his other novels).

POETRY READING Public recitation of poetry, often by the author, but also by other poets, actors, and fans of the author. *(See* POETRY SLAM.*)*

Readings may take place in coffeehouses, auditoriums, private homes, libraries, theaters, museums, classrooms, public memorials, parks, bars, and even stadiums. Most poets read from book or typescript, but some recite from memory. Styles range from plain speaking to chanting to declaiming to singing. Most readers, however, "say" their poems (as Robert Frost put it) in a natural voice, indicating line breaks subtly—if at all.

Basil Bunting, who liked to read his autobiographical poem *Briggflatts* to an accompaniment of harpsichord sonatas by Domenico Scarlatti, argues for the primacy of reading aloud:

> Poetry, like music, is to be heard. It deals in sound—long sounds and short sounds, heavy beats and light beats, the tone relation of vowels, the relations of consonants to one another which are like instrumental colour in music. Poetry lies dead on the page, until some voice brings it to life, just as music on the stave is no more than instructions to the player. A skilled musician can imagine the sound, more or less, and a skilled reader can try to hear, mentally, what his eyes see in print; but nothing will satisfy either of them till his ears hear it as real sound in the air. Poetry must be read aloud.

Robert Graves, however, asserts that a poem best reveals itself through close, silent reading:

Although every poem should be suited for reading aloud, with full value given to every sound, pause, and rhythmic idiosyncrasy, a poem read silently in private yields far more of its magic truth than a poem read in a concert hall.

P

POETRY SLAM Competition, usually held in a bar or café, in which poets recite or perform their work, are rated by judges, and may receive titles (such as "Grand Slam Champion") and prizes. *(See* POETRY READING *and* RENGA.*)*

In "The Sidewalk of High Art," an introduction to the anthology *Aloud: Voices from the Nuyorican Poets Cafe*, Miguel Algarín describes the judging:

Judges, who have been selected whimsically from the audience, are introduced with such "qualifications" as being born in Brooklyn or having never been to a Slam before. These judges will rate the poem from zero ("a poem that should never have been written") to ten ("mutual simultaneous orgasm") using the "Dewey decimal rating system" to avoid ties and "the dreaded Sudden-Death Haiku Improv overtime round." Here we are in the realm of literate humor, with no discerning of "high" and "low," all in the service of bringing a new audience to poetry via a form of entertainment meant to tune up fresh ears to a use of language as art that has been considered dead by many.

Algarín credits the creation of the poetry slam to Marc Smith, "who continues his weekly bare-knuckles events at the Green Mill in Chicago."

The history of poetic competition goes back at least to the ancient Greeks, who held competitions at the yearly Dionysian festival between the tragedies written in verse by poet-playwrights such as Aeschylus and Sophocles. Richard Wagner dramatized poetic competitions, based on historical events and real poets, in two of his operas, *Tannhäuser* and *Die Meistersinger von Nürnberg* (in which prospective master-singers are judged by a "marker," who scratches a mark on his slate for each mistake in versification).

Miguel Algarín mentions other examples of poetic competitions, "from the Greek mythological tale of Apollo and Marsyas to the African griots, from the *Sanjurokunin sen*, or imaginary poetry team competitions, of tenth-century Japanese court poet Fujiwara no Kinto to the African-American 'dozens.'" (*Dozens* is a traditional African-American game of taunting in rhymed couplets, trading insults back and forth. Langston Hughes makes use of the dozens in his poem "Ask Your Mama.") Algarín notes that this tradition continues in present-day Puerto Rico,

> where El Trovador improvises in the plaza, spontaneously pulling into the verse the life of the folks in the small town, the tragedies that have occurred in their families, the gossip that surrounds their private lives, and the celebratory passages that talk about births, deaths, weddings, and baptisms. All of this is compacted into ten-syllable lines with end-rhymes.

POULTER'S MEASURE A meter consisting of alternating lines of *iambic hexameter (six stresses, twelve syllables) and iambic heptameter (seven stresses, fourteen syllables). The name derives from the egg seller's practice of offering fourteen eggs, instead of twelve, for each second dozen bought. The lines tend to break into halves (stressed 3-3 and 4-3) so the lines sound like elongated ballads. The effects of singsong rhythm and monotony led to the meter's demise after the sixteenth century, when poets such as Thomas Wyatt and Sir Philip Sidney still used it on occasion. Here is an example of poulter's measure by George Gascoigne (ca. 1542–1577):

> I could not though I would: good Lady say not so,
> Since one good word of your good wil might soone
>   redresse my wo
> Where would is free before, there could can never fayle:
> For profe, you see how gallies passe where ships can beare
>   no sayle.
> The weary mariner when skies are overcast,
> By ready will doth guyde his skill and wins the haven at last.

PRE-RAPHAELITE BROTHERHOOD A group of painters and poets active in Victorian England.

In 1848 several young painters formed an organization called the Pre-Raphaelite Brotherhood, devoted to countering academic, formal art by harking back to the Italian painters before Raphael (in other words before the sixteenth century). One of the founding members, Dante Gabriel Rossetti, happened to be a gifted poet as well as a painter. The brotherhood lasted only a few years, but the movement it fostered thrived over four decades, adding poets such as William Morris, Christina Rossetti, George Meredith, and Algernon Charles Swinburne. Pre-Raphaelite poetry is characterized by dreaminess, romanticism, and an almost religious view of art. Late in his life, however, Rossetti dismissed the initial brotherhood: "As for the prattle about Pre-Raphaelitism, I confess to you I am weary of it, and long have been. Why should we go on talking about the visionary vanities of half-a-dozen boys?" The movement was also ridiculed as the "Fleshly School of Poetry."

LILITH / Dante Gabriel Rossetti (1828–1882)

FOR A PICTURE

Of Adam's first wife, Lilith, it is told
   (The witch he loved before the gift of Eve,)
That, ere the snake's, her sweet tongue could deceive
And her enchanted hair was the first gold.
And still she sits, young while the earth is old,
   And, subtly of herself contemplative,
   Draws men to watch the bright net she can weave,
Till heart and body and life are in its hold.

The rose and poppy are her flowers; for where
   Is he not found, O Lilith, whom shed scent
And soft shed kisses and soft sleep shall snare?
   Lo! as that youth's eyes burned at thine, so went
   Thy spell through him, and left his straight neck bent,
And round his heart one strangling golden hair.

PROEM (pro'-em; Greek, "opening, prelude") A prefatory poem, such as Hart Crane's "To Brooklyn Bridge," which introduces his long poem *The Bridge*; the opposite of a *coda* or an *epilogue*, which is a poetic afterword.

PROSE POEM A brief work in prose that is considered a poem because of its intense, condensed language or because of some other similarity to poems in verse.

Some poets, such as James Wright, have thought of them more as prose sketches. Often it is difficult to distinguish a short-short story from a narrative prose poem. But this blurring of genres is a blessing to some, an incitement to experiment. *Language poets, such as Leslie Scalapino, move easily from prose to verse. It need not be a problem, except to the harried taxonomist.

Some critics, however, distinguish more harshly. Lewis Turco asserts that a prose poem is anything "not written in verse—in a metrical prosody." By that definition, all *free verse would, in fact, be prose. But the distinction is a useful one to maintain. Anything written in lines, metrical or unmetrical, strict or free, is verse. Anything not written in discrete lines is prose. The lines in prose are nothing but a typographical necessity. Given wide enough margins, a Proustian paragraph could go on for miles. The prose writer does not dictate where one line ends and another begins.

The prose poem began as a conscious form in nineteenth-century France, pioneered by Aloysius Bertrand and Charles Baudelaire. The form represented a kind of reaction against the strict poetic dictates of the French Academy (which remains imperious, having prohibited foreign words, such as *le drugstore*, which might corrupt the language). Baudelaire happens to be a master of the classical forms: the *alexandrine and the *sonnet. He wrote companion versions, for example, of "Invitation to the Voyage": one in rhymed verse, one in prose.

In his introduction to *Little Poems in Prose* (also called *Paris Spleen*), Baudelaire asks:

> Which of us, in his ambitious moments, has not dreamed of the miracle of a poetic prose, musical, without rhyme and without rhythm, supple enough and rugged enough to adapt itself to the lyrical impulses of the soul, the undulations of the psyche, the prickings of consciousness?

In his anthology *The Prose Poem: An International Anthology*, Michael Benedikt defines the prose poem:

> a genre of poetry, self-consciously written in prose, and characterized by the intense use of virtually all the devices of poetry, which includes the intense use of devices of verse. The sole exception to access to the possibilities, rather than the set priorities of verse is, we would say, the line break.

In his essay "The Prose Poem as an Evolving Form," Robert Bly says of the prose poem, "Its mood is calm, more like a quiet lake than a sea." He mentions several kinds of prose poem: the *fable (both ancient, in the work of Aesop, and contemporary, in the work of Russell Edson and David Ignatow), the "fire-prose" or "illumination" invented by the nineteenth-century French poet Arthur Rimbaud, and the *object poem (as in the work of Francis Ponge and Juan Ramon Jimenez), which "centers itself not on story or image but on the object, and it holds on to its fur, so to speak." Bly adds:

> The fact that no critics have yet laid out formal standards for the prose poem is a blessing. Sometimes a fox and a human being play together best when no loud sounds are heard. When relaxed and aware of no rigid patterns, the mind sometimes gracefully allows itself to play with something equally graceful in nature, and the elegance of the prose poem appears in that play.

Both Benedikt and Bly have written prose poems, and they agree that it is a genre not for beginners but for more advanced writers. *(See* HAIBUN *and* POETRY.*)*

GET DRUNK! (*Enivrez-vous*) / Charles Baudelaire (1821–1867;
tr. Michael Benedikt)

Get drunk and stay drunk. That's it; that's the sole solution to our greatest problem. So as not to feel the terrible burden of time breaking your back and bowing you ever closer to the earth, you must remain incessantly, relentlessly, constantly intoxicated.

But intoxicated with what? With wine, with poetry, or with virtue: whatever you prefer. But get drunk!

And if now and then you happen to come to, on the steps outside a palace, amid the green grass of some ditch or in the dreary solitude of your room; and you discover that your drunkenness is leaving you, or has already vanished, ask wind and wave, ask star, bird and clock; ask every fleeting thing, every flowing thing, everything that can sing or speak or croak or cry out:—ask them: "What time is it now?" And wind and wave, star, bird and clock will all answer: "It's time to get drunk! Yes, if you are not merely to live out your lives as the martyred slaves of Time, make sure you stay drunk, too! With wine, poetry, or virtue, whatever you prefer."

THE COLONEL / Carolyn Forché (b. 1950)

What you have heard is true. I was in his house. His wife carried a tray of coffee and sugar. His daughter filed her nails, his son went out for the night. There were daily papers, pet dogs, a pistol on the cushion beside him. The moon swung bare on its black cord over the house. On the television was a cop show. It was in English. Broken bottles were embedded in the walls around the house to scoop the kneecaps from a man's legs or cut his hands to lace. On the windows there were gratings like those in liquor stores. We had dinner, rack of lamb, good wine, a gold bell was on the table for calling the maid. The maid brought green mangoes, salt, a type of bread. I was asked how I enjoyed the country. There was a brief commercial in Spanish.

His wife took everything away. There was some talk then of how difficult it had become to govern. The parrot said hello on the terrace. The colonel told it to shut up, and pushed himself from the table. My friend said to me with his eyes: say nothing. The colonel returned with a sack used to bring groceries home. He spilled many human ears on the table. They were like dried peach halves. There is no other way to say this. He took one of them in his hands, shook it in our faces, dropped it into a water glass. It came alive there. I am tired of fooling around he said. As for the rights of anyone, tell your people they can go fuck themselves. He swept the ears to the floor with his arm and held the last of his wine in the air. Something for your poetry, no? he said. Some of the ears on the floor caught this scrap of his voice. Some of the ears on the floor were pressed to the ground.

PROSODY (proz'-uh-dee; Greek, "accent, song sung to music") The study of sound and rhythm in *poetry, of *meter and *versification (how to compose lines of verse).

Prosodical marks include the symbols used to scan verse and note rhyme schemes. Syllables can be stressed (´) or unstressed (˘); or a weak syllable can receive a metrical stress (˘́); or, for the prosodist who wants to mark other levels of accenting, the medium stresses can be marked secondary (`) and the light stresses marked tertiary (!). In the *quantitative meter used in the classical poetry of Greece and Rome, the length of syllables is marked long (–) and short (˘). Breaks can be marked: between metrical feet (|), at a *caesura or pause in the middle of a line (||), for the end of a line (/, when several lines are quoted in a prose sentence), and for the end of a *stanza (//). Rhyme schemes use the letters of the alphabet to indicate rhyme groups, perhaps reserving capital letters for *refrains (repeated lines) and X for unrhymed lines. Some prosodists have used musical notation (quarter notes, for example). Karl Shapiro and Robert Beum use dots for unstressed syllables and x's for stressed syllables in *A Prosody Handbook. (See*

SCANSION *for further discussion and for the elements of Derek Attridge's beat-offbeat system of prosody.)*

PSALM (sawm; Greek, "twitching" or "twanging" [of harp strings]) A sacred song or hymn.

The Book of Psalms, originally written in Hebrew and considered the compositions of King David of Israel, contains 150 of these religious lyrics. The psalms are written in a kind of long-lined free verse whose *prosody is governed by repetition (exemplified in Psalm LXX by the repeated "Let," which begins several lines, an instance of *anaphora) and by variation (in the first line, "O God" changes to "O Lord" and interrupts "Make haste … to deliver me," while the latter phrase follows "Make haste to help me"). *(See* BIBLICAL VERSE *and* FREE VERSE.)

PSALM LXX (King James Version of the Bible)

Make haste, O God, to deliver me; make haste to help me, O Lord.

Let them be ashamed and confounded that seek after my soul: let them be turned backward, and put to confusion, that desire my hurt.

Let them be turned back for a reward of their shame that say, Aha, aha!

Let all those that seek thee rejoice and be glad in thee: and let such as love thy salvation say continually, Let God be magnified.

But I am poor and needy: make haste unto me, O God: thou art my help and my deliverer; O Lord, make no tarrying.

PYRRHIC (peer'-ik; Greek, a metrical foot used in a war dance) A metrical foot consisting of two unstressed syllables (˘ ˘).

No English words are pyrrhic, since one of the word's two syllables would have to be accented, however slightly. A pyrrhic phrase such as "in a" requires something stressed to follow it and complete the prepositional phrase. If that something is a spondee, the pyrrhic survives: "in a big town," for example.

Pyrrhic

Pyrrhic meter is impossible in English, since any noun or verb or even adjective that turned up would be hailed with a rousing stress. And even in a hypothetical poem composed of prepositions, articles, and conjunctions, our speech patterns and rhythmic sense would impose relative stresses every so often. *(See* MINOR IONIC *and* SPONDEE.*)*

P

QUANTITATIVE METER A *meter that measures the length of syllables, long (‾) and short (˘), and counts their number in lines of verse. The word *quantity* refers to the duration of a syllable; generally, two short syllables (such as *tin* and *man*) equal one long syllable (such as *moan*).

This metrical system was the basis of ancient Greek poetry, adopted by Latin poets and attempted with varying success by English poets such as Sir Philip Sidney and Thomas Campion. English poetry takes its terms for *accentual-syllabic feet (such as *iamb* and *trochee*) from quantitative meter. (*A list appears in* FOOT.)

One type of quantitative meter is called *hendecasyllabics (Greek, "eleven syllables")*. Here is the pattern of long and short syllables:

‾ ˘ ‾ ˘ ˘ ‾ ˘ ‾ ˘ ‾ ˘

In *Poems in Classical Prosody*, a set of experiments with quantitative meter in English, Robert Bridges (1844–1930) writes the following hendecasyllabics in "The Fourth Dimension":

> If this be not a holy consolation
> More than plumpudding and a turkey roasted,
> Whereto you but address a third dimension,
> Try it, pray, as a pill to aid digestion:
> I can't find anything better to send you.

The problem with using this metrical system in English is that *stress is more powerful than the duration of syllables. The first line above is actually a perfect example of *iambic pentameter with a *feminine ending. *(See* ALCAICS, ELEGIAC DISTICH, ODE, *and* SAPPHICS.*)*

QUATRAIN (kwot'-rane; French, "group of four") A four-line *stanza.

Although quatrains can be rhymed or unrhymed (or partly rhymed), written in *meter or *free verse, the names given to specific types of quatrains refer to distinct patterns of *rhyme and line length. An unrhymed quatrain, for instance, may be called a *tetrastich* (especially if it is written in iambic pentameter). Several types of rhymed quatrains are listed below.

• Alternating Quatrain: *abab.* The rhyming alternates: lines one and three together, lines two and four together. When the lines are 4-3-4-3 iambic feet in length, it is called the *hymn stanza.* When the lines are *iambic pentameter, it is called the *heroic quatrain* or *Sicilian quatrain* (which is used in Shakespearean *sonnets). When lines two and four of one stanza become lines one and three of the next, it is called a **pantoum* (although many contemporary pantoums omit rhyming altogether). The following quatrains are in iambic pentameter:

DIVERNE'S WALTZ / Marilyn Nelson (b. 1946)

Diverne stands in the kitchen as they dance,
laughing and flirting, on the bare parlor floor.
She's taken up the rug, glad for the chance,
at last, to beat it free of sins outdoors.

Her fancy cakes are popular, her punch
has earned light giggles from Miss Atwood's friends.
She'd struggled at Miss Atwood's back to cinch
that tiny waist. *Miss Atwood look right grand.*

Mister Tyler asks for a water-glass of rye:
he's just enlisted, a drop-out from law school.
She notices something dangerous in his eye:
Crazy damn white man, acting like a fool.

Taking her hands, Henry Tyler gives her a twirl
and off they waltz. He swirls Diverne so fast
her head kerchief unknots itself. He smiles
down at Diverne's embarrassment, and gasps:

They blush! Hearing the whispers from the walls,
he sees men grin. His father shakes his head.
But (*That dark rose ...*) he dances. *What the hell,
who knows? next week, next month, I could be dead.*

Q

• Envelope Quatrain: *abba*. The outer lines rhyme with each other;
the inner lines rhyme with each other. When the lines are iambic
tetrameter, it is called the *In Memoriam stanza, after a poem by
Alfred, Lord Tennyson. When the lines are iambic pentameter, it is
called the *brace stanza* or *Italian quatrain* (as in the first four lines of
the Petrarchan sonnet).

NEUTRAL TONES / Thomas Hardy (1840–1928)

We stood by a pond that winter day,
And the sun was white, as though chidden of God,
And a few leaves lay on the starving sod;
   —They had fallen from an ash, and were gray.

Your eyes on me were as eyes that rove
Over tedious riddles of years ago;
And some words played between us to and fro
   On which lost the more by our love.

The smile on your mouth was the deadest thing
Alive enough to have strength to die;
And a grin of bitterness swept thereby
   Like an ominous bird a-wing. ...

> Since then, keen lessons that love deceives,
> And wrings with wrong, have shaped to me
> Your face, and the God-curst sun, and a tree,
>   And a pond edged with grayish leaves.

• Couplet Quatrain: *aabb*. Two rhymed *couplets join in a single stanza. Trochaic quatrains, such as William Blake's "The Tyger," are usually rhymed in couplets. The following poem is written in what Robert Frost would call "loose" iambic tetrameter.

GOOD HOURS / Robert Frost (1874–1963)

> I had for my winter evening walk—
> No one at all with whom to talk,
> But I had the cottages in a row
> Up to their shining eyes in snow.
>
> And I thought I had the folk within:
> I had the sound of a violin;
> I had a glimpse through curtain laces
> Of youthful forms and youthful faces.
>
> I had such company outward bound.
> I went till there were no cottages found.
> I turned and repented, but coming back
> I saw no window but that was black.
>
> Over the snow my creaking feet
> Disturbed the slumbering village street
> Like profanation, by your leave,
> At ten o'clock of a winter eve.

• Even-Rhymed Quatrain: *XaXa*. Lines two and four rhyme; lines one and three do not. The opposite, an "odd-rhymed" quatrain (*aXaX*), is rare, but William Stafford's "Clash" is an example. When the even-rhymed quatrain contains lines that are 4-3-4-3 stresses in length, it is called the *ballad stanza*.

SOME KEEP THE SABBATH GOING TO CHURCH /
Emily Dickinson (1830–1886)

Some keep the Sabbath going to Church—
I keep it, staying at home—
With a Bobolink for a Chorister—
And an Orchard, for a Dome—

Some keep the Sabbath in Surplice—
I just wear my Wings—
And instead of tolling the Bell, for Church,
Our little Sexton—sings.

God preaches, a noted Clergyman—
And the sermon is never long,
So instead of getting to Heaven, at last—
I'm going, all along.

• Monorhymed Quatrain: *aaaa*. All four lines rhyme on the same sound. Few poets use this quatrain, because of the difficulty of finding so many rhymes, over and over again. The repetitions can become tedious, even ludicrous. But the relentless rhyming may be especially suitable for conveying obsession, as in Rossetti's poem below.

THE WOODSPURGE / Dante Gabriel Rossetti (1828–1882)

The wind flapped loose, the wind was still,
Shaken out dead from tree and hill:
I had walked on at the wind's will—
I sat now, for the wind was still.

Between my knees my forehead was—
My lips, drawn in, said not Alas!
My hair was over in the grass,
My naked ears heard the day pass.

My eyes, wide open, had the run
Of some ten weeds to fix upon;
Among those few, out of the sun,
The woodspurge flowered, three cups in one.

> From perfect grief there need not be
> Wisdom or even memory:
> One thing then learnt remains to me—
> The woodspurge has a cup of three.

A rhyme sound in one quatrain can recur in the following stanza. Robert Frost uses interlocking rhyme in "Stopping by Woods on a Snowy Evening": *aaba bbcb ccdc dddd*, a four-lined variation on *terza rima. Isolated out of context, without those carried-over rhymes, each stanza would be a *rubai except the last, which is monorhymed.

(*See* ALCAICS, ODE *[for some kinds of Horatian ode]*, RHYME SCHEME, SAPPHICS.)

QUINTAIN (quin'-tun; Latin, "fifth") A five-line stanza, sometimes called a *cinquain* (although the term is now usually applied to a stanza developed by Adelaide Crapsey), a *quintet* (although the term suggests a musical ensemble), or a *pentastich* (especially if the stanza is unrhymed).

Various rhyme schemes are possible. Thomas Wyatt's "My Lute, Awake" (whose stanzas rhyme *aabab*) begins:

> My lute, awake! Perform the last
> Labor that thou and I shall waste,
> And end that I have now begun;
> For when this song is sung and past,
> My lute, be still, for I have done.

George Herbert's "The Pulley" uses a rhyme scheme of *ababa* for each of its four stanzas:

> When God at first made man,
> Having a glass of blessings standing by,
>   "Let us," said he, "pour on him all we can.
> Let the world's riches, which dispersèd lie,
>   Contract into a span."

The five-line stanzas of Edmund Waller's "Song" rhyme *ababb*. The poem begins:

> Go, lovely rose!
> Tell her who wastes her time and me
> That now she knows,
> When I resemble her to thee,
> How sweet and fair she seems to be.

William Wordsworth's "Peter Bell," a long narrative in five-line stanzas, rhymes *Xabba*. Here is the poem's last stanza:

> And Peter Bell, who, till that night,
> Had been the wildest of his clan,
> Forsook his crimes, renounced his folly,
> And, after ten month's melancholy,
> Became a good and honest man.

Lord Byron, who was never one to renounce his own follies, parodies Wordsworth's poem in "Epilogue," using the same rhyme scheme:

> And now I've seen so great a fool
> As William Wordsworth is for once;
> I really wish that Peter Bell
> And he who wrote it were in hell
> For writing nonsense for the Nonce.

Other quintains include the *cinquain, *limerick, *mad-song stanza, *quintilla, and *tanka.

QUINTILLA (quin-tee'-yuh) Spanish five-line stanza containing eight syllables per line and rhyming *ababa, abbab, abaab, aabab,* or *aabba*. Each stanza must have two rhymes (*a* and *b*) and the last two lines may not be a couplet. Originally the quintilla was called a *redondilla.

R

RANN (rahn, with the *r* trilled; Irish, "division" or "stanza") Four-line stanza in Irish verse. It is often written in seven-syllable lines and rhymed *abab* or *XaXa* (although the unrhymed *X* may consonate with *a*). *Alliteration in Irish verse is somewhat different than in English. Vowels as well as consonants may alliterate, and any stressed word with a different sound will block the alliteration. *Consonance also differs from the English sense, so that in consonant words the vowel lengths must be the same and the consonants must belong to the same class. An English approximation might match short vowels (or long vowels) and consonant groups such as plosives (*b, p; t, d; g, k*), nasals (*n, m, ng*), or liquids (*l, r*). Examples of this kind of consonance might include reed/late and dim/pun.

Irish meters may specify (1) the number of syllables in different rhyme words (an *a* rhyme might consist of three syllables, while *b* might consist of two), (2) consonance between rhyme words and the last words of unrhymed lines, (3) the position and frequency of alliteration and *internal rhyme, and (4) alliteration from the end of one line to the beginning of the next. Sometimes the odd-line rhymes are stressed and the even are not. Eleanor Knott gives the English example of *bit/rabbit*. The stressed rhyme is called *rinn*, the unstressed one *airdrinn (ar´-drin)*. (Notice how the terms demonstrate the technique.) In all of these Irish meters, the poem begins and ends with the same syllable, word, or line, a technique called *dunadh (doo´-nuh)*.

Irish verse is a branch of Celtic prosody, with rules and practices similar to those used in *Welsh poetic forms. For further information, see Eleanor Knott's *An Introduction to Irish Syllabic Poetry of the Period 1200–1600.*

RAP A contemporary form of popular song, invented by African-Americans and dating from about 1976, in which an outpouring of rhymed lines (similar to *skeltonics) is declaimed, not sung, over a driving beat usually provided by a drum machine or by rhythmically scratching a phonograph record.

Nikki Giovanni calls rap "an honest voice of an anguished people." And yet the anger is typically matched by the humor of slangy phrasing, topical wisecracks, and clever rhyming. The form owes a great deal to the fast patter of rhythm-and-blues disc jockeys.

One of the most influential early rap songs was "The Message" (1982), by Grandmaster Flash & the Furious Five. Its lyrics are both flashy and furious, a blend of rage and comic rhyming, as in "Got a bum education, double-digit inflation / Can't train to the job, there's a strike at the station." *(See* POETRY SLAM, RHYME, *and* SONG.*)*

READER (also *audience) 1. The one to whom the poet presents or submits her work.

2. The person that the poet imagines reading her work; the ideal audience.

3. What a poet must be in order to write something worth reading.

REDONDILLA Spanish *quatrain consisting of four eight-syllable lines, usually rhymed *abba.* If rhymed *abab,* it can also be called a *serventesio.* If there are fewer than eight syllables per line (six is a common variant), the stanza is a *redondilla menor. (See* QUINTILLA.*)*

REFRAIN A line that is repeated, like the *chorus of a song, especially at the end of a *stanza; also called a *burden.*

Sometimes, as in Robert Frost's "The Pasture," included below, a refrain will not rhyme with any other lines in a poem. Part of the listening pleasure then comes from one kind of repetition (a string of words) being set off against another (the rhymes). Sometimes the refrain rhymes with one or more lines in each stanza. In "Crazy Jane Grown Old Looks at the Dancers," William Butler Yeats uses a rhyme scheme of *abacacB* (the capital letter representing a repeated line), so that the refrain, "Love is like the lion's tooth," appears at the end of each stanza and rhymes with the second line.

The wording of a refrain can change from stanza to stanza, but at least a recognizable phrase must remain constant. A number of forms require refrains: *ballade, *kyrielle, *rondeau, *rondel, *rondelet, *roundel, *triolet, and *villanelle. In a *sea shanty*, the leader sings a line and then a chorus of sailors joins in; each stanza uses two different refrains, and the second may be considerably longer than the first, as in the folk song "Shenandoah" (in which the refrains are italicized):

> Oh, Shenandoah, I love your daughter
> *Away, you rolling river*
> I'll take her cross the rolling water
> *Away, I'm bound away,*
> *Across the wide Missouri.*

In a poem not necessarily meant to be sung, the refrain must be interesting in itself. It helps if it can conclude each stanza with a different shade of meaning.

THE PASTURE / Robert Frost (1874–1963)

> I'm going out to clean the pasture spring;
> I'll only stop to rake the leaves away
> (And wait to watch the water clear, I may):
> I shan't be gone long.—You come too.
>
> I'm going out to fetch the little calf
> That's standing by the mother. It's so young
> It totters when she licks it with her tongue.
> I shan't be gone long.—You come too.

REGIONAL POETRY Poetry that is firmly, obviously, often proudly set in a particular locale and is saturated with the look and feel of that place. Richard Hugo's Northwest (Washington and Montana in particular), James Dickey's South (Georgia and South Carolina), Ted Kooser's Midwest (Nebraska), and N. Scott Momaday's Southwest (Arizona and New Mexico) represent kinds of regional poetry. So do Thomas Hardy's poems about Wessex, his composite of the southwest part of England, especially Dorset.

RELATIVE STRESS A syllable that is accented slightly because of the unstressed syllables around it. This kind of stress usually occurs when a weak syllable falls on a place that would normally be stressed, like the sixth syllable ("in") of Shakespeare's "Th'expense of spirit in a waste of shame." *(See* SCUD.*)*

RENGA A Japanese collaborative form, also called *linked verse.*

This form derives from *tanka*, which is arranged syllabically in a stanza pattern of 5-7-5-7-7 (although a tanka is usually complete in itself, even when included as part of a sequence). In renga, the first poet writes the first three lines (the *hokku* or *haiku*), the second poet writes the next two (each consisting of seven-syllables), and they continue trading verses back and forth, a conversation in form, a literary pastime. More than two poets can take part, continuing in a kind of circle. Haiku as a separate form grew out of the practice of renga teachers such as Matsuo Basho, recognized as the first master of haiku. If renga is necessarily a *dialogue, a communal exercise, haiku then is the proverbial "one hand clapping" of the Zen koan, the first half of a tanka isolated and answered by silence, an exercise of the solitary self in the midst of the universe. *(See* cadavre exquis *in chance poetry.)*

REPETEND (rep'-uh-tend) A word, phrase, or line that is repeated in some irregular, seemingly random way, unlike a *refrain or *repeton. In T.S. Eliot's "The Love Song of J. Alfred Prufrock," the phrase "Let us go" is a repetend, appearing in the first line, "Let us go then, you and I, / When the evening is spread out against the sky," and recurring as "Let us go, through certain half-deserted streets" and "Let us go and make our visit."

REPETITION The recurrence of words, phrases, *lines, groups of lines, *rhyme sounds, consonants, vowels, *images, *symbols, *themes, or ideas.

Repetition is a coming back, a going over, a completion of a circle, an obsessive returning to something emotionally magnetic or rhythmically compelling—and is essential to much, perhaps most, poetry. Its opposite is *variation, changing to something different instead of repeating the same thing. Most often, repetition and variation work together, as when different stanzas end with the same *refrain. In the following poem, Richard Howard uses a refrain twice in each stanza, but the sixth word of the refrain changes with each repetition.

LIKE MOST REVELATIONS / Richard Howard (b. 1929)

after Morris Louis

It is the movement that incites the form,
discovered as a downward rapture—yes,
it is the movement that delights the form,
sustained by its own velocity. And yet

it is the movement that delays the form
while darkness slows and encumbers; in fact
it is the movement that betrays the form,
baffled in such toils of ease, until

it is the movement that deceives the form,
beguiling our attention—we supposed
it is the movement that achieves the form.
Were we mistaken? What does it matter if

it is the movement that negates the form?
Even though we give (give up) ourselves
to this mortal process of continuing,
it is the movement that creates the form.

REPETON (rep-uh-tahn'; French *répéton*) Line that is repeated once in an interlocking form such as the *pantoum and the terzanelle. *(See* INVENTED FORMS AND STANZAS*).*

RESPONSE A poem written in reaction to another poem (or, more broadly, to anything); an answer or reply to something the poet has read; a poem written on the same subject as another poem but from a different point of view.

Some responses are written in the voice of a person addressed in the original poem. For example, in Anthony Hecht's "The Dover Bitch," the woman addressed in Matthew Arnold's "Dover Beach" responds to the speaker of that poem.

Many poets have written responses to "The Passionate Shepherd to his Love" by Christopher Marlowe (1564–1593). An example of *pastoral poetry, it begins with this *quatrain:

> Come live with me and be my love,
> And we will all the pleasures prove
> That valleys, groves, hills, and fields,
> Woods, or steepy mountain yields.

Sir Walter Raleigh (1552–1618) provides the lady's answer in "The Nymph's Reply to the Shepherd," which begins:

> If all the world and love were young,
> And truth in every shepherd's tongue,
> These pretty pleasures might me move
> To live with thee and be thy love.

In "The Bait," John Donne (1572–1631) offers a racier, wittier invitation from the speaker to the woman:

> Come live with me, and be my love,
> And we will some new pleasures prove,
> Of golden sands, and crystal brooks:
> With silken lines, and silver hooks.

R

Other responses to Marlowe's poem include C. Day Lewis's "Song" (beginning "Come, live with me and be my love") and Delmore Schwartz's "The Passionate Shepherd to His Love" (beginning "Come live with me and be my wife").

In the following poem, Wallace Stevens responds to William Carlos Williams's "El Hombre" (Spanish for "The Man"), which he quotes in its entirety as an *epigraph.

NUANCES OF A THEME BY WILLIAMS / Wallace Stevens (1879–1955)

It's a strange courage
you give me, ancient star:

Shine alone in the sunrise
toward which you lend no part!

I
Shine alone, shine nakedly, shine like bronze,
that reflects neither my face nor any inner part
of my being, shine like fire, that mirrors nothing.

II
Lend no part to any humanity that suffuses
you in its own light.
Be not chimera of morning,
Half-man, half-star.
Be not an intelligence,
Like a widow's bird
Or an old horse.

RHETORIC The art of discourse, the means by which a writer or speaker can persuade and move an audience.

Classical rhetoric constitutes a system through which to compose one's thoughts, "not so much to persuade," as Aristotle points out in *Rhetoric*, "as to find out in each case the existing means of persuasion." These means include argumentation and style.

Although argumentation—the gathering of evidence, the use of logic and chains of reasoning, the avoidance and detection of fallacies, the establishing of proofs—might seem more at home in a court of law, it has a traditional place in poetry (enough so that *Symbolist poets rejected the rigors of logic in favor of the suggestiveness of music and imagery). Many *sonnets are constructed on a logical framework, filling in a kind of *if ... then ... therefore* structure, as in Sonnet 138 by William Shakespeare (whose logical connective words are *when, thus, but*, and *therefore*):

> When my love swears that she is made of truth,
> I do believe her, though I know she lies,
> That she might think me some untutor'd youth,
> Unlearned in this world's false subtleties.
> Thus vainly thinking that she thinks me young,
> Although she knows my days are past the best,
> Simply I credit her false-speaking tongue,
> On both sides thus is simple truth suppress'd:
> But wherefore says she not she is unjust?
> And wherefore say not I that I am old?
> O, love's best habit is in seeming trust,
> And age in love loves not to have years told.
>> Therefore I lie with her, and she with me,
>> And in our faults by lies we flatter'd be.

In poetry, *argument usually means the "plot" of a poem, or a synopsis ("plot summary") that may precede it.

Style comprises diction (word choice), syntax (word order), paragraphing, euphony (melodious sounds), and figures of speech (also called rhetorical devices). These figures, which include such essential poetic tools as *metaphor, *irony, and *alliteration, represent ways of transforming either the order or the sense of words, to make the writing more vivid, emphatic, and memorable. (See RHETORICAL DEVICES.)

There is also a negative sense of the word *rhetoric*, associating it with bombast, falsity, trickery, or empty talk, like the "rhetoric" of politicians. But rhetoric itself is simply the art of expressive speech, and its devices provide a wide range of tools for the writer. They are aids in invention, means of transforming the raw materials of language into imaginative work.

RHETORICAL DEVICES (also called *figures of speech*) Ways of transforming the natural order or literal meaning of words, in order to make a text more inventive, emphatic, rhythmic, impressive, or memorable. There are two main kinds: *schemes* (changes in word order) and *tropes* (changes in word sense).

Schemes involve a transformation in the order or arrangement of a word, phrase, clause, sentence, or line. Here are some of the most common schemes:

• *Alliteration: repetition of consonants (such as the repeated *w* in e e cummings's "what if a much of a which of a wind")

• Anadiplosis *(an-uh-dih-plo´-sis)*: repetition of the last word or phrase at the beginning of the next line, phrase, clause, or sentence, as in these lines from an anonymous nursery rhyme, "This Is the Key":

> Flowers in a basket;
> Basket on the bed;
> Bed in the chamber;
> Chamber in the house;
> House in the weedy yard;
> Yard in the winding lane;
> Lane in the broad street;
> Street in the high town;
> Town in the city;
> City in the Kingdom ...

• *Anaphora: repetition of the first word or phrase at the beginning of successive lines, as in the opening lines of John Donne's "On His Mistris":

By our first strange and fatall interview,
By all desires which thereof did ensue,
By our long starving hopes, by that remorse ...

In these lines, the repeated word "By" begins successive lines, but it also begins successive phrases (the fourth instance, not capitalized, appears in the middle of line three).

• Anastrophe *(uh-nas´-truf-fee)*: inversion of natural word order, as in George Peele's "His Golden lockes, Time hath to Silver turn'd," which begins with the direct object; the natural word order would be "Time hath turn'd his Golden lockes to Silver," which would change the meter and lose the rhyme—serious defects in a poem written to be set to music (as it was by the Elizabethan lutanist John Dowland)

• Antimetabole *(an-tih-muh-tab´-uh-lee)*: repetition of the words in a phrase in reverse order, as in Molière's "One should eat to live, not live to eat"

• Antithesis *(an-tih´-thuh-sis)*: the juxtaposition of conflicting ideas or images, usually arranged in parallel structure, as in Alexander Pope's "What oft was thought, but ne'er so well express'd," contrasting *often* and *never*, or in John Dryden's "But what we gain'd in Skill we lost in Strength"

• Aposiopesis *(uh-pos-ee-oh-pee´-sis)*: a breaking-off or trailing-off of a sentence, leaving something unsaid, usually indicated by an ellipsis (...)

• Apposition *(ap-oh-zih´-shun)*: word or phrase that follows another and identifies it, as in Ralph Waldo Emerson's "Daughters of Time, the hypocritic Days" or Walt Whitman's "Walt Whitman, a kosmos, of Manhattan the son"

• *Assonance: repetition of vowels, like the long *o* sounds in Lord Byron's "So, we'll go no more a roving"

• Asyndeton *(uh-sin´-deh-tahn)*: omission of conjunctions between series of clauses, as when Walt Whitman says,

> All this I swallow, it tastes good, I like it well, it
>   becomes mine,
> I am the man, I suffered, I was there.

The last line could be a pacifist's version of Julius Caesar's "I came, I saw, I conquered" (another example of asyndeton). A related term is *parataxis (pare-uh-tak´-sis)*, the *juxtaposition of phrases or clauses without any connecting words between them, as in "Rains came; rivers overflowed"

• Chiasmus *(key-az´-mus)*: reversal of grammatical structures in successive phrases or clauses, as in Alexander Pope's "Each strengthens Reason, and Self-Love restrains"; also called criss-cross

• Ellipsis *(uh-lip´-sis)*: omission of a word or phrase that is implicit, as in the opening lines of a lute-song by John Dowland (words attributed to Sir Edward Dyer):

> The lowest trees have tops, the Ant her gall,
> The flie her spleene, the little sparke his heate …

The verb *has* is implicit after "Ant," "flie," and "sparke."

• Epanalepsis *(uh-pan-uh-lep´-sis)*: repetition at the end of a line, phrase, clause, or sentence of the word that began it, as when Shakespeare's King Lear says "Nothing will come of nothing"

• Epanorthosis *(uh-pan-or-tho´-sis)*: the recalling of a word or phrase to substitute something more exact; a revision or second thought displayed in the writing, as when Elizabeth Bishop qualifies her initial placement of the flowers in "Brazil, January 1, 1502":

> and flowers, too, like giant water lilies
> up in the air—up, rather, in the leaves—

• *Epistrophe: repetition of a word or phrase at the end of successive lines or clauses, as in the repetition of "nothing" in T.S. Eliot's "'Do / 'You know nothing? Do you see nothing? Do you remember / 'Nothing?'" (from *The Waste Land*)

• Epizeuxis *(ep-ih-zook´-sis)*: the repetition of a word for emphasis, as in John Keats's "more happy happy love!" (from "Ode on a Grecian Urn")

• Isocolon *(eye-so-co´-lun)*: parallel structure between clauses (and this parallel, or parison, must be exact), as in these lines from Shakespeare's *A Midsummer Night's Dream*:

> DEMETRIUS. Well roar'd, Lion.
>
> THESEUS. Well run, Thisbe.
>
> HIPPOLYTA. Well shone, Moon.

• Parenthesis *(puh-ren´-thuh-sis)*: insertion of words that interrupt the sentence flow, as when "who knows?" interrupts Elizabeth Bishop's line "impractically shaped and—who knows?—self-pitying mountains"

• Parison *(pare´-ih-zon)* or parallelism: use of matching structures in related words, phrases, clauses, or lines, as in John Dowland's "to see, to heare, to touch, to kisse, to die" (from "Come Again"), in which the parallel unit is the infinitive; in Alexander Pope's "It stopt, I stopt; it mov'd, I mov'd again," (from *The Dunciad*), a structure of *pronoun-verb, different pronoun-same verb* is repeated

• Polyptoton *(pah-lip-toe´-tun)*: repetition of words derived from the same root, a kind of play on words or pun, as when Shakespeare's Hamlet says to Polonius, "Conception is a blessing, but not as your daughter may conceive"

• Polysyndeton *(pah-lee-sin´-deh-tahn)*: repetition of conjunctions, such as "and," as in these verses from Genesis:

> And the earth was without form, and void; and darkness was upon the face of the deep: and the Spirit of God moved upon the face of the waters.
> And God said, Let there be light: and there was light.
> And God saw the light, that it was good: and God divided the light from the darkness.

Polysyndeton is what Elizabeth Bishop refers to as "Everything only connected by 'and' and 'and.'"

One stanza in Walt Whitman's "Out of the Cradle Endlessly Rocking" uses several of these schemes within six lines:

> *Shake out carols!*
> *Solitary here, the night's carols!*
> *Carols of lonesome love! death's carols!*
> *Carols under that lagging, yellow, waning moon!*
> *O under that moon where she droops almost down into the sea!*
> *O reckless despairing carols!*

The repeated word "*carols*" appears at the end of the first three lines (epistrophe), at both the beginning and end of line three (epanalepsis), and at the beginning of lines three and four (anaphora). The omission of "*carols*" in line five is also rhetorical, a kind of ellipsis, as if to suggest "*O [carols] under the moon …*" The word returns at the end of line six, continuing the epistrophe of the opening lines, as if rhyming on the same word, "*carols*."

Tropes (literally "turns," as in "turns of phrase") involve transformations of meaning. Here are some of the most common tropes:

• *Allegory: story in which characters stand for concepts, as in Edmund Spenser's *The Faerie Queen*

• Anthimeria *(an-thih-meer´-ee-uh)*: substitution of one part of speech for another, as when the noun *impact* is used as a verb ("News leaks impact upon the trial") or an adjective is used as an adverb ("Be sure to act proper" instead of "properly")

• *Apostrophe: direct address to someone absent or to something abstract, as in "O Spring!" (The Whitman stanza quoted above is an apostrophe addressed to "*carols*")

• Auxesis *(awk-zee´-sis)*: use of a more impressive word to exaggerate the importance of something, perhaps ironically, such as calling a shouting match a "brawl" or "riot"; the opposite of *meiosis*

• Hyperbole *(hie-pur´-buh-lee)*: overstatement or exaggeration, such as "Paying the fine killed me"

• *Irony: a discrepancy between what is said and what is meant or understood, or between appearance and reality; the use of a word to convey the opposite of its usual meaning, such as "That was fun cleaning the oven"

• Litotes *(lie´-tuh-tees or lie-toe´-tees)*: understatement, a deliberate way of seeming to make less of something in order to make more, such as "the plan was not uninteresting"

• Meiosis *(my-oh´-sis)*: a "lessening," the use of a less impressive word to minimize the importance of something, such as calling a fist fight a "misunderstanding"; the opposite of *auxesis*

• *Metaphor: comparison between two things, such as the "yellow fog" that is a cat (which "rubs its muzzle," "Licked its tongue," and "Curled once about the house") in T.S. Eliot's "The Love Song of J. Alfred Prufrock"

• *Metonymy: use of an associated word for what is really meant, such as "hired gun" for "gunslinger"

• *Onomatopoeia: word or phrase whose sound imitates the sense, such as "plop" or "screech"

• *Oxymoron: word combination that seems like a contradiction, such as "happy sorrow"

• Paralipsis *(pare-uh-lip´-sis)*: the trick of pretending to avoid discussing something while nevertheless revealing it, of seeming to keep something in while actually letting it out; a kind of irony, as in Marc Antony's "Friends, Romans, countrymen" speech in Shakespeare's *Julius Caesar*

• Periphrasis *(puh-rif´-ruh-sis)* or antonomasia *(an-tuh-nuh-may´-zhuh)*: substitution of a nickname or descriptive phrase, or of a proper name in place of a thing or concept, as in "Jim Crow" for "racial segregation"

R

• Prosopopoeia *(pruh-so-puh-pee´-yuh)* or personification: attachment of human qualities to something abstract or non-human, like the pig speaking in Philip Levine's "Animals Are Passing from Our Lives" (which appears in SYLLABICS)

• Pun: play on words, of which there are three kinds:

> Antanaclasis *(an-tuh-nak´-luh-sis)*: repetition of a word in different senses, as in Ben Franklin's "If we don't hang together, we'll hang separately"

> Paronomasia *(pare-uh-no-may´-zhuh)*: words alike in sound but different in meaning, as in the riddle "What's black and white and red all over?" (a newspaper, whose pages of newsprint are read)

> Syllepsis *(sih-lep´-sis)*: word with different meanings in relation to two other words, for example a verb with two objects (as in "I'll strike the first blow and a match"); called *zeugma (zoog´-muh)* when one of those two "yoked" elements is grammatically incompatible with the word that governs them, as in "I struck the first blow, and may you too" (meaning "may strike you too")

• Rhetorical question or erotema *(air-uh-tee´-muh)*: a question asked without the expectation of a reply, as in Percy Bysshe Shelley's "If Winter comes, can Spring be far behind?"

• *Simile: comparison using a connecting word such as "like," as in W.B. Yeats's "ancient faces like rain-beaten stones"

• *Synecdoche: a part standing for the whole, as in "hired hand" for "farm worker"

George Puttenham, an Elizabethan rhetorician, tried to replace the Greek rhetorical terms with English equivalents, such as "the echo found" (epanalepsis), "the loud liar" (hyperbole), and the "cuckoo's call" (epizeuxis). They didn't take hold, possibly because the teachers who pounded Greek terms into the heads of their students saw no need to relearn a terminology that served perfectly well.

RHOPALIC VERSE (Greek, "like a club," thicker toward the end, like the club used by Hercules; also called *wedge verse*) A gamelike form in which each word in a line is one syllable longer than the word before it. Here is an example: "The circus performer hypnotizes pediatricians." *(See* OULIPO.*)*

RHYME (also *rime*) A word that echoes the vowel-consonant combination (or sometimes just the vowel) of another word, as in *rhyme/chime*.

In mathematical terms, most rhymes comprise a constant and a variable. (The exception is *rime riche*, in which the words rhymed are exactly the same—all constant, no variable, except in the meaning and often the spelling of those homonyms.) In the most common type of *true* or *full rhyme*, a variable consonant precedes either a fixed vowel and fixed consonant (*brake/shake*) or a fixed vowel by itself (*so/go*).

In *slant rhyme*, one of those fixed elements becomes variable (*brake/spoke, brake/brave; so/gay, so/say*). Sometimes both the preceding and following consonants become fixed, sandwiching a changeable vowel (*brake/broke*). Slant rhyme does its work at an angle, tilted away from what a carpenter would call true.

Rhymes can be grouped not only by how closely the words look or sound alike, but also by where they occur and recur. *End-rhymes* appear at the end of lines. The farther apart they appear, the fainter their repetition will sound. *Couplets, therefore, tend to clang; rhymes separated by one or more intervening lines are progressively harder to distinguish. Rhymes that are end-stopped protrude more prominently than rhymes that are *enjambed, in which the sense runs on swiftly to the next line. Sometimes a poet needs the obvious echo, and sometimes she will choose to hide or disguise that echo. Rhymes in which at least one of the rhyme words occurs within a line are called *internal rhymes*. In *leonine rhyme*, the internal rhyme occurs at the halfway point of a line (often just before a pause, or *caesura) and is echoed by the end-word, as in Alfred, Lord Tennyson's "The splendor falls on castle walls."

Rhymes differ according to the number of syllables that are echoed. The most common kind in English is called *single, masculine*, or *per-*

R

fect rhyme (also *rime suffisante*), in which the rhyme falls on a single stressed syllable, as in the conclusion of Sylvia Plath's "Lady Lazarus":

> I rise with my red hair
> And I eat men like air.

But the stressed syllable can be part of a polysyllabic word and its stress can be fairly weak, although it must be stronger than the syllable preceding it, as in Thomas Hardy's "The Convergence of the Twain":

> In a solitude of the sea
> Deep from human vanity,

Poets tend to place the monosyllabic word first, before the polysyllabic word whose last syllable rhymes with it.

In *double full, feminine,* or *light rhyme,* two-syllable words that are *trochaic (a stressed syllable followed by an unstressed syllable, such as *thicken/quicken*) are used for the rhyme sounds, as in Richard Wilbur's "Seed Leaves":

> And making crusty rubble.
> It comes up bending double,
> And looks like a green staple.
> It could be seedling maple,

This kind of rhyming is less common than single rhyme. In Wilbur's thirty-four-line poem, for example, these four lines are the only ones with double-full rhymes.

Rhyming more than two syllables almost always sounds comic. *Triple rhyme* contributes to the humor of Lord Byron's *Don Juan*:

> He learned the arts of riding, fencing, gunnery,
> And how to scale a fortress—or a nunnery.

The list below classifies various kinds of rhyme. But the poet's ear (and the critic's judgment) are better arbiters of when an exact rhyme is required and when a slant rhyme is permissible.

Types of Rhyme

• True, full, or perfect rhyme; chime (sounding alike, though possibly looking different):

> Aunt Jennifer's tigers prance across a screen,
> Bright topaz denizens of a world of green.
>
> —Adrienne Rich, "Aunt Jennifer's Tigers"

> The wrinkled sea beneath him crawls;
> He watches from his mountain walls,
>
> —Alfred, Lord Tennyson, "The Eagle"

• Eye or sight rhyme (looking the same, sounding different):

> For, unless ways are changing here at home,
> You might not have it if I had not come.
>
> —Edwin Arlington Robinson, "The Prodigal Son"

• Historical rhyme (once perfect, now sounding different):

> Good-nature and good-sense must ever join;
> To err is human, to forgive, divine.
>
> —Alexander Pope, "An Essay on Criticism" (II)

Types of Slant Rhyme

(Also called *approximate*, *embryonic*, *half*, *imperfect*, *near*, *oblique*, *off*, *partial*, and *part rhyme*; *paraphone* or *pararhyme*)

• Consonant rhyme (final consonant the same, vowel different):

> There, in his night, the black-tongued bells
> The sleepy man of winter pulls
>
> —Dylan Thomas, "I See the Boys of Summer"

Consonant rhyme can be monosyllabic, as in *floods/tides* and *threads/voids* in Thomas's poem, or disyllabic, as in *mothers/weathers* in the same poem.

• Double-consonant rhyme (vowel different, surrounding consonants the same):

> Was it for this the clay grew tall?
> —O what made fatuous sunbeams toil
>
> —Wilfred Owen, "Futility"

• Assonant rhyme (vowel the same, final consonant different):

> When he came to the king's gate,
> He sought a drink for Hind Horn's sake.
>
> —"Hind Horn," anonymous popular ballad

Assonant rhyme is especially common in folk songs and in contemporary popular songs, because the vowels echo so audibly, especially long vowels.

• Rhyming on the weak syllable of a two-syllable word, such as *flower/tatter* or *slimy/gravy*.

Other Types of Rhyme

• Apocopated rhyme (rhyming the penultimate or antepenultimate syllable in one line with the final syllable in the next):

> Till on glass rigid with his own seizure
> At length the sucking jewels freeze.
>
> —James Merrill, "The Octopus"

• Broken rhyme (in which one of the rhyme sounds is the first part of a hyphenated word; perhaps another kind of "wrenched rhyme"):

> I did: through last July's parenthesis,
> I worked, walked, ate, grew brown, wiry and lis-
> some climbing paths ...
>
> —Marilyn Hacker, "Lacoste I"

• Diminishing rhyme (in which a word loses its preceding consonants as they are repeated):

> What open force, or hidden charm
> Can blast my fruit, or bring me harm,
> While the inclosure is thine arm?
>
> —George Herbert, "Paradise" (lines 4–6)

The rhymes, of course, could progress in the opposite direction, building up instead of diminishing.

• Initial rhyme (used rarely), in which the first syllables in adjacent lines rhyme, as the following couplet rhymes *Yea/May* (and also *blest/palimpsest* in the more usual end position):

> Yea, Love, sole music-master blest,
> May read thy weltering palimpsest.
>
> —Sidney Lanier, "The Symphony"

• Mosaic rhyme (intentionally comic feminine or triple rhymes in which at least one of the rhymes consists of more than one word):

> She snatched it, and refused another morsel,
> Saying, he had gorged enough to make a horse ill.
>
> —George Gordon, Lord Byron, *Don Juan*

• Wrenched rhyme (in which a word is misspelled or mispronounced or garbled in some way to "rhyme" with another word; the effect is usually comic):

> Farewell, farewell, you old rhinoceros,
> I'll stare at something less prepocerous!
>
> —Ogden Nash, "The Rhinoceros"

Although double-consonant rhyme (*stick/stock*) is acceptable and often used, *alliteration alone is not very satisfying when used for rhyming. The vowel or the final consonant needs to echo as well.

Finally, some poets who once used rhyme, such as John Milton and Thomas Campion, came to detest it, partly because it was not countenanced by Classical tradition (specifically Ancient Greek poetry, which does not rhyme), partly because it seemed merely decorative and ornamental. (Milton's Puritanism was aesthetic, too.) And most *free verse (with the prominent exception of Robert Creeley's) eschews rhyming as strongly as it rejects *meter, since both techniques are means of establishing regularity and order, of satisfying expectations instead of constantly subverting them.

RHYME ROYALE (also *Chaucer stanza, Troilus stanza,* and *rime royal*) A seven-line *stanza rhyming *ababbcc*, usually in *iambic pentameter.

This stanza form was introduced into English poetry by Geoffrey Chaucer, who used the stanza for *Troilus and Criseyde, The Parliament of Fowls,* and several of *The Canterbury Tales* (The Man of Law, The Clerk, and the Second Nun). Other poets, such as Thomas Wyatt, William Shakespeare, William Wordsworth, and W.H. Auden have also used it. The name may derive from the poems in this stanzaic form written by King James I of Scotland.

THEY FLEE FROM ME / Thomas Wyatt (1503–1542)

> They flee from me, that sometime did me seek,
> With naked foot stalking in my chamber.
> I have seen them, gentle, tame, and meek,
> That now are wild, and do not remember
> That sometime they put themselves in danger
> To take bread at my hand; and now they range,
> Busily seeking with a continual change.
>
> Thanked be Fortune it hath been otherwise,
> Twenty times better; but once in special,
> In thin array, after a pleasant guise,
> When her loose gown from her shoulders did fall,
> And she me caught in her arms long and small,
> And therewith all sweetly did me kiss
> And softly said, "Dear heart, how like you this?"
>
> It was no dream, I lay broad waking.
> But all is turned, thorough my gentleness,

Into a strange fashion of forsaking;
And I have leave to go, of her goodness,
And she also to use newfangleness.
But since that I so kindely am served,
I fain would know what she hath deserved.

NOTE: *newfangleness*: fickleness; *kindely*: naturally.

RHYME SCHEME The pattern of rhymes in a poem, represented by letters of the alphabet.

Although a poet is free to make up new rhyme schemes, there are names for many of them. *(See* STANZA *for a list and* QUATRAINS *for examples of schemes in four-line stanzas.)* In the following poem in *iambic trimeter by N. Scott Momaday, all of the lines rhyme, but not in a pattern the reader might expect in a *quatrain. Instead, it plays off the 6-2 structure of the rhyme scheme *(abcabc dd)* against the 4-4 structure of the quatrains.

TO A CHILD RUNNING WITH OUTSTRETCHED ARMS IN CANYON DE CHELLY / N. Scott Momaday (b. 1934)

You are small and intense	a
In your excitement, whole,	b
Embodied in delight.	c
The backdrop is immense;	a
The sand banks break and roll	b
Through cleavages of light	c
And shadow. You embrace	d
The spirit of this place.	d

RHYTHM (Latin, "time, harmony") The way sounds move against the flow of time. In language, rhythm is the melody of words together: how they rise and fall, how they repeat, how they adhere (or do not adhere) to patterns.

Rhythm must be distinguished from *meter, which may or may not appear in poetry. All writing has rhythm, both prose and verse, although that rhythm may not seem as prominent in expository writing as in a poem. Writing is a temporal art (or act); it necessarily involves words moving against or along with time. Meter, however, is a pattern of measurement, a way of counting words, syllables, accents, or the length of syllables. It is like the time signature in music. Rhythm in metrical poetry resembles the way melody plays around a steady beat: rising, falling, slowing down, speeding up, pausing.

RIDDLE A poem that playfully or mysteriously hides its subject, describing it but not naming it, presenting a puzzle to be solved by the reader, as in the following poem (which is about a hummingbird).

R

A ROUTE OF EVANESCENCE / Emily Dickinson (1830–1886)

A Route of Evanescence
With a revolving Wheel—
A Resonance of Emerald—
A Rush of Cochineal—
And every Blossom on the Bush
Adjusts its tumbled Head—
The mail from Tunis, probably,
An easy Morning's Ride—

RIME COUÉE (reem coo-ay'; French, "tail rhyme") Six-line stanza, rhymed *aabaab*, in which the *a* lines (one, two, four, and five) are longer than the short *b* lines (three and six). *(See* BURNS STANZA *and* TAILED SONNET.*)*

RIME RICHE (reem' reesh'; French, "rich rhyme") *Rhyme made up of words that are pronounced or spelled the same. Rime riche is common in French poetry but not used much in English. In "Nostalgia of the Lakefronts," however, Donald Justice rhymes "prizes" and "surprises," "cockatoo" and "1942," "disappears" and "piers," "no" and "know." He also repeats some words (such as "distance") at the ends of lines. *(See* ECHO VERSE.*)*

RISPETTO (Italian, "respect"; plural, *rispetti*) A poetic form consisting of two *quatrains, usually rhymed *abab ccdd*, often in *iambic tetrameter. Originally this Tuscan form, used by Lorenzo de' Medici, contained between six and twelve lines per stanza. Traditionally, it paid "respect" to a woman.

RONDEAU (ron-doe'; plural, *rondeaux*; French, meaning something round or circular, referring specifically to a dance, the "round," for which such lyrics were composed) A form consisting of fifteen lines (sometimes fewer) arranged in three parts and rhyming *aabba aabR aabbaR*. The R indicates a *refrain or rentrement that repeats the first word or phrase of the opening line.

R

The terms *rondeau*, *rondel*, *roundel*, and *roundelay* were once used interchangeably for certain French forms that use intricate rhyming on two different rhyme sounds (*a* and *b*) and repeat part of a line, a whole line, or two whole lines as refrains. Although all of these terms denote what are called fixed forms, the original distinctions between them were extremely loose. To further complicate this nomenclature, what we now call a *triolet was once the simplest, shortest kind of rondeau. The chart in which the currently recognized forms of "Five Similar Repeating French Forms" appear will clarify matters for the reader or writer who prefers strict rules to casual practice. In any case, the terms have now been fairly stable for hundreds of years. *(See* BALLADE, RONDEAU REDOUBLÉ, RONDEL DOUBLE, RONDELET, *and* VILLANELLE.*)*

The first of the following rondeaux uses fewer than the usual fifteen lines. François Villon omits three lines (two, seven, and eleven) and rhymes *abbaabR abbaR*. All of these omitted lines would have rhymed on the same sound: *a*. Since there are eight *a* rhymes and only five *b* rhymes (plus the two unrhymed refrains) in the full, fifteen-line form of the rondeau, it makes sense to drop some of the *a* rhymes. Dropping the *b* rhymes, however, would magnify the disproportion rather than alleviate it.

Paul Laurence Dunbar's rondeau adheres to the standard pattern. The "We" in "We Wear the Mask" refers to African-Americans.

Rondeau

Using a fixed form, in this case, may be analogous to putting on a mask.

TO DEATH, OF HIS LADY / François Villon (1431–1463?; tr. Dante Gabriel Rossetti)

Death, of thee do I make my moan,
　　Who hadst my lady away from me,
　　Nor wilt assuage thine enmity
Till with her life thou hast mine own:
For since that hour my strength has flown.
　　Lo! what wrong was her life to thee,

Death?

Two we were, and the heart was one;
　　Which now being dead, dead I must be,
　　Or seem alive as lifelessly
As in the choir the painted stone,

Death!

WE WEAR THE MASK / Paul Laurence Dunbar (1872–1906)

We wear the mask that grins and lies,
It hides our cheeks and shades our eyes—
This debt we pay to human guile;
With torn and bleeding hearts we smile,
And mouth with myriad subtleties.

Why should the world be over-wise,
In counting all our tears and sighs?
Nay, let them only see us, while
　　We wear the mask.

We smile, but, O great Christ, our cries
To thee from tortured souls arise.
We sing, but oh the clay is vile
Beneath our feet, and long the mile;
But let the world dream otherwise,
　　We wear the mask!

Five Similar Repeating French Forms

Rondel	Rondeau	Roundel	Rondelet	Triolet
A	a	a	A	A
B	a	b	b	B
b	b	a	A	a
a	b	B	a	A
	a		b	a
a		b	b	b
b	a	a	A	A
A	a	b		B
B	b			
	refrain	a		
a		b		
b	a	a		
b	a	B		
a	b			
A	b			
(B)	a			
	refrain			

NOTE: Capital *A* or *B* indicates a refrain on that rhyme sound. "Refrain" indicates one or more unrhymed words from the first line. Parentheses indicate a line that is optional. Spaces indicate the usual positions for stanza breaks.

RONDEAU REDOUBLÉ (reh-doo-blay'; "double rondeau") A form related to the *rondeau but longer, in which twenty-five lines are arranged in a pattern of *ABA´B´ babA abaB babA´ abaB´ babaR*. Here's what the algebra means: Capital letters indicate *refrain lines;

each line of the opening *quatrain serves once as a refrain at the end of the next four quatrains; refrains *A* and *A´* rhyme, as do refrains *B* and *B´*; letters rhyme whether they are upper or lower case; finally, the *R* signifies a *rentrement* made up of the first two words or first phrase of the opening line.

The man responsible for this complication is the sixteenth-century French poet Clément Marot. Jean de La Fontaine and Dorothy Parker also wrote in the form, which is especially suited to *light verse.

RONDEL (ron-del'; French, "round") A form consisting of thirteen lines arranged in three parts and rhyming *ABba abAB abbaA* (the capital letters being *refrain lines). A *rondel prime* (or *supreme*) adds a fourteenth line, repeating the *B* refrain.

The rondel differs from the *rondeau in that it repeats whole lines as refrains, rhymes them, and is usually (though not always) two lines shorter; the rondeau, on the other hand, repeats only the first part of the opening line as a refrain and does not rhyme it with anything else. The rhyme schemes differ as well, although both forms use just two rhyme sounds (*a* and *b*). Each form consists of three stanzas.

*Roundel was used synonymously with the other terms, but in the nineteenth century the English poet A.C. Swinburne settled upon a specific pattern and wrote many poems in the form. This confusion in terms can be seen in the following rondel, which is called "Rondeau"—an instance of how freely the terms were used and how similar the forms really are.

RONDEAU / Charles d'Orléans (1391–1465; tr. Richard Wilbur)

The year has cast its cloak away
That was of driving rains and snows,
And now in flowered arras goes,
And wears the clear sun's glossy ray.

No bird or beast but seems to say
In cries or chipper tremolos:
The year has cast its cloak away
That was of driving rains and snows.

Stream, brook and silver fountain play,
And each upon itself bestows
A spangled livery as it flows.
All creatures are in fresh array.
The year has cast its cloak away.

RONDEL DOUBLE (doo'-bluh) An expanded form of the *rondel in which four quatrains rhyme *ABBA abBA abba ABBA*. The capital letters indicate *refrains.

RONDELET (ron-deh-lay'; French, "little rondel") A form consisting of seven lines, with a *refrain and only two rhymes. The rhyme and refrain scheme is *AbAabbA* (capital *A* = refrain). The refrain lines (*A*) each contain four syllables; the other lines (*a* and *b*) each contain eight syllables.

ROUNDEL (rown-del') An eleven-line variant of the *rondeau, introduced into English by Algernon Charles Swinburne in his *A Century of Roundels*. The term *roundel* is not new; it was used in Geoffrey Chaucer's time to mean a "rondel," as in his "Merciles Beaute: A Triple Roundel." Swinburne's roundel consists of three stanzas rhymed *abaB bab abaB*. The *B* is a short phrase from the first part of the opening line; it is used as a *refrain and rhymes with *b* (lines two, five, seven, and nine). Metrically, the refrains are short and contain one or two stresses, while the rest of the lines contain four or five (the measure staying consistent throughout a given poem). Swinburne's roundels may be *trochaic (like the example below), *iambic, or *anapestic.

A NIGHT-PIECE BY MILLET / Algernon Charles Swinburne (1834–1909)

Wind and sea and cloud and cloud-forsaking
Mirth of moonlight where the storm leaves free
Heaven awhile, for all the wrath of waking
    Wind and sea.

Bright with glad mad rapture, fierce with glee,
Laughs the moon, borne on past cloud's o'ertaking
Fast, it seems, as wind or sail can flee.

One blown sail beneath her, hardly making
Forth, wild-winged for harbourage yet to be,
Strives and leaps and pants beneath the breaking
    Wind and sea.

NOTE: *Millet:* nineteenth-century French painter.

ROUNDELAY (rown-deh-lay') Sometimes used interchangeably with *rondeau, *rondel, and *roundel; in a more general sense, it is simply a *lyric with *refrain.

RUBAI (roo-bye'; Persian, "quatrain") A four-line *stanza rhymed *aaXa* or *aaaa*; usually an *occasional poem, spontaneous and witty, but grounded in the mystical Sufi tradition of Islam. A poem made up of these stanzas is called a *rubaiyat (roo'-bye-at or -yat).*

The rubai is also called the *Omar Khayyam stanza* or *Omar stanza,* after Edward FitzGerald's paraphrase of over one hundred quatrains from *The Rubaiyat of Omar Khayyam,* a twelfth-century work in Persian. Each rubai is independent from its neighboring *quatrains, although FitzGerald, who took many liberties with the original texts, arranged his stanzas in a coherent order. The first three quatrains below use the *aaXa* rhyme scheme (with *X* indicating an unrhymed line); the fourth is monorhymed (*aaaa*).

THE RUBÁIYÁT OF OMAR KHAYYÁM OF NAISHÁPÚR,
Stanzas I, VII, XII, and LXIII / Edward FitzGerald (1809–1883)

Wake! For the Sun, who scatter'd into flight
The Stars before him from the Field of Night,
    Drives Night along with them from Heav'n, and strikes
The Sultán's Turret with a Shaft of Light.

Come, fill the Cup, and in the fire of Spring
Your Winter-garment of Repentance fling;
    The Bird of Time has but a little way
To flutter—and the Bird is on the Wing.

A Book of Verses underneath the Bough,
A Jug of Wine, a Loaf of Bread—and Thou
    Beside me singing in the Wilderness—
Oh, Wilderness were Paradise enow!

Oh threats of Hell and Hopes of Paradise!
One thing at least is certain,—*This* Life flies;
    One thing is certain and the rest is Lies;
The Flower that once has blown forever dies.

RUNE, RUNIC VERSE (roon; Old English, "mystery") A chant or
incantation, associated with magic. Runes used the letters of the
Teutonic alphabet and were carved on swords, drinking vessels, and
stones. Rudyard Kipling's "The Runes on Weland's Sword" begins:

A Smith makes me
To betray my Man
In my first fight.

To gather Gold
At the world's end
I am sent.

The Gold I gather
Comes into England
Out of deep Water.

Like a shining Fish
Then it descends
Into deep Water.

SAPPHICS, SAPPHIC STANZA (saf'-ix, saf'-ik) *Quatrain in which the first three lines contain eleven syllables and the fourth line contains five syllables; named after the Greek poet Sappho, who lived in the seventh and sixth centuries B.C.E. and was the best-known practitioner of the form.

In Ancient Greek, the lines are arranged in *quantitative meter, based on the length of syllables (long or short) according to the following pattern:

	*Feet that can be spondaic (– –)
– ◡ | – ◡ | – ◡ ◡ | – ◡ | – ◡	2nd &/or 5th
– ◡ | – ◡ | – ◡ ◡ | – ◡ | – ◡	2nd &/or 5th
– ◡ | – ◡ | – ◡ ◡ | – ◡ | – ◡	2nd &/or 5th
– ◡ ◡ | – ◡	2nd

In the *accentual-syllabic meter of English verse, the long syllables (–) are usually replaced by *accents (´). The first three lines are *trochaic pentameter with an extra unstressed syllable in the third *foot (´ ◡ \| ´ ◡ \| ´ ◡ ◡ \| ´ ◡ \| ´ ◡). The fourth line consists of a *dactyl followed by either a *trochee or a *spondee (´ ◡ ◡ \| ´ ◡ or

′ ᵕ ᵕ | ′ ′). Some poets might choose to follow a syllabic pattern
of 11-11-11-5 or to suggest the form in *free verse by grouping three
longer lines with a short one, perhaps indented. Some poets rhyme
their sapphics, although Sappho did not.

The short fourth line is called an *adonic*. It effectively punctuates
the stanza, giving it variety and a quick punch appropriate either for
springing to the next stanza or ending a poem. It is also a natural
phrase rhythm in English, appearing frequently in expressions ("Put
up or shut up") and names (Abraham Lincoln, Eleanor Rigby,
Theodore Roethke).

POEM 1 / Sappho (circa 620–550 B.C.E.; tr. John Frederick Nims)

On your throne, a marvel of art, immortal
Aphrodite, daughter of Zeus, amused to
lead us on through folly and pain—you'd doom me
    body and soul now?
Come with help, if ever in days gone-by you
heard me praying desperately in the distance—
heard and hurried, leaving your father's home to
    harness your golden
car up. Had it yoked in a moment. Gamy
sparrows flew you quick as a wink around the
dusky earth, their wings in a blur, and sky-high
    diving through cover
spiraled down here. You (your immortal features
hid a half smile stirring the dimple) asked me:
"What's it now, love? Trouble again? And this time
    why the commotion?
What's your wild heart heaving to have, I wonder,
this time? Only tell me her name, the one you'd
have me wheedle round to your love. She's being
    cruel to you, Sappho?
Running off now? Soon she'll be running after.
Won't take gifts? Tomorrow she will—and give them.

Just can't love? Tomorrow she'll love—but you'll see—
    like it or not, dear."
Even so, though! Now's when I need you. End this
tossing, turning! All that I'm mad to have, you
know so well! Then work for it, standing with me
    shoulder to shoulder.

SAPPHICS AGAINST ANGER / Timothy Steele (b. 1948)

Angered, may I be near a glass of water;
May my first impulse be to think of Silence,
Its deities (who are they? do in fact they
    Exist? etc.).

May I recall what Aristotle says of
The subject: to give vent to rage is not to
Release it but to be increasingly prone
    To its incursions.

May I imagine being in the *Inferno*,
Hearing it asked: "Vergilio mio, who's
That sulking with Achilles there?" and hearing
    Vergil say: "Dante,

That fellow, at the slightest provocation,
Slammed phone receivers down, and waved his arms like
A madman. What Attila did to Europe,
    What Genghis Khan did

To Asia, that poor dope did to his marriage."
May I, that is, put learning to good purpose,
Mindful that melancholy is a sin, though
    Stylish at present.

Better than rage is the post-dinner quiet,
The sink's warm turbulence, the streaming platters,
The suds rehearsing down the drain in spirals
    In the last rinsing.

For what is, after all, the good life save that
Conducted thoughtfully, and what is passion
If not the holiest of powers, sustaining
    Only if mastered.

SATIRE (Latin, "platter of mixed fruits") A literary work that ridicules, scorns, mocks, or otherwise attacks the folly or evil of a person, an institution, an idea, or a culture.

Ezra Pound remarks that satire is "surgery, insertions and amputations" and that it "reminds one that certain things are not worth while. It draws one to consider time wasted." The Greek soldier-poet Archilochos, who lived in the seventh century B.C.E. and whose work survives in fragments, is considered the first satirist:

I know how to love those
Who love me, how to hate.
My enemies I overwhelm
With abuse. The ant bites!

        (from Fragment 43, tr. Guy Davenport)

Some of the best and earliest satire appears in the plays of Aristophanes, such as *Clouds*, which pokes fun at Socrates and other philosophers. But the terms used to classify the two main kinds of satire come from two Roman poets, Juvenal (c. 60–140 C.E.) and Horace (65–8 B.C.E.). *Juvenalian satire* is sharp-tongued, a morally outraged indictment of the evils of society. Its ridicule is fierce. Here is the opening of Samuel Johnson's "The Vanity of Human Wishes," which is subtitled "The Tenth Satire of Juvenal Imitated":

Let observation with extensive view,
Survey mankind, from China to Peru;
Remark each anxious toil, each eager strife,
And watch the busy scenes of crowded life;
Then say how hope and fear, desire and hate,

O'erspread with snares the clouded maze of fate,
Where wav'ring man, betray'd by vent'rous pride,
To tread the dreary paths without a guide,
As treach'rous phantoms in the mist delude,
Shuns fancied ills, or chases airy good;
How rarely reason guides the stubborn choice,
Rules the bold hand, or prompts the suppliant voice;
How nations sink, by darling schemes oppress'd,
When vengeance listens to the fool's request.
Fate wings with ev'ry wish th' afflictive dart,
Each gift of nature, and each grace of art,
With fatal heat impetuous courage glows,
With fatal sweetness elocution flows,
Impeachment stops the speaker's pow'rful breath,
And restless fire precipitates on death.

Horatian satire is gentler, using laughter more as a medicine than as a weapon. Here is the opening of the first poem in Horace's first book of *Satires*:

Maecenas, why is no one living
Happy where he is, whether he chose for himself or fate
For him? Everyone wants to be someone else.
"O blessed merchants!" cries the stiff old soldier,
His body broken by years of hard campaigning.
But the merchant, as the West wind tosses his ship,
Cries, "War is better. And why? There's a battle,
In a moment you're either dead or a hero."
The lawyer swears he'll return to the land, when
A client drags him out of bed at dawn.
The farmer who's signed a bond and is forced to travel
    to town
Swears the city's the only place.

(tr. Burton Raffel)

One of the *ironies of satire, of course, is that it confers a kind of fame—or notoriety, at least—on the victims of its barbs. But as W.H. Auden points out, regarding Alexander Pope's satirical epic, *The Dunciad*:

> [it] should never be read with notes, for to think that it matters who the characters were or why Pope was angry with them is to miss the whole point of the poem, which is best appreciated by supplying one's own contemporary list of the servants of the Goddess of Dullness.

Guy Davenport notes that the following satire by Archilochos was "provoked by the superstitious reaction to the solar eclipse of 14 March 711 B.C." The "late famous general" satirized by Jonathan Swift in another poem below is the Duke of Marlborough.

FRAGMENT 113 / Archilochos (7th century B.C.E.;
tr. Guy Davenport)

There's nothing now
We can't expect to happen!
Anything at all, you can bet,
Is ready to jump out at us.
No need to wonder over it.
Father Zeus has turned
Noon to night, blotting out
The sunshine utterly,
Putting cold terror
At the back of the throat.
Let's believe all we hear.
Even that dolphins and cows
Change place, porpoises and goats,
Rams booming along in the offing,
Mackerel nibbling in the hill pastures.
I wouldn't be surprised,
I wouldn't be surprised.

A SATIRICAL ELEGY ON THE DEATH OF A LATE FAMOUS GENERAL / Jonathan Swift (1667–1745)

His Grace! Impossible! what dead!
Of old age too, and in his bed!
And could that Mighty Warrior fall?
And so inglorious, after all!
Well, since he's gone, no matter how,
The last loud trump must wake him now:
And trust me, as the noise grows stronger,
He'd wish to sleep a little longer.
And could he be indeed so old
As by the news-papers we're told?
Threescore, I think, is pretty high;
'Twas time in conscience he should die.
This world he cumber'd long enough;
He burnt his candle to the snuff;
And that's the reason, some folks think,
He left behind *so great a s ... k.*
Behold his funeral appears,
Nor widow's sighs, nor orphan's tears,
Wont at such times each heart to pierce,
Attend the progress of his hearse.
But what of that, his friends may say,
He had those honours in his day.
True to his profit and his pride,
He made them weep before he dy'd.

Come hither, all ye empty things,
Ye bubbles rais'd by breath of Kings;
Who float upon the tide of state,
Come hither, and behold your fate.
Let pride be taught by this rebuke,
How very mean a thing's a Duke;
From all his ill-got honours flung,
Turn'd to that dirt from whence he sprung.

SCANSION (scan'-shun; Latin, "act of climbing") The marking of a poem to indicate its metrical structure and how it sounds. Traditionally, a reader scans a poem by noting the stressed and unstressed syllables, *feet, and *caesurae (pauses). A poem that adheres to some metrical pattern is said to "scan." The traditional metrical terms and marks for *prosody appear in the entries for FOOT and ACCENTUAL-SYLLABIC METER.

The first two lines of Shakespeare's Sonnet XXX can be scanned as follows, using the traditional prosodical marks:

> Whén to | the sés | sĭons ŏf | sweét sí | lĕnt thoúght
>
> Ĭ súm | mŏn úp | rĕmém | brănce ŏf | thĭngs pást,

The lines are in *iambic pentameter, whose basic pattern is: ˘ ´ |˘ ´ | ˘ ´ |˘ ´ |˘ ´. If each line followed that pattern strictly, however, the results could be monotonous. Shakespeare's lines play against the underlying drumbeat of the meter. According to this scansion, Shakespeare's first line consists of a *trochee, an *iamb, a *pyrrhic, a *spondee, and an iamb. (For a radically different reading of Shakespeare's opening line, as well as a dissenting view of how to scan English verse, refer to "The Audible Reading of Poetry" by Yvor Winters.)

In *The Rhythms of English Poetry*, Derek Attridge introduced his system of "beat-offbeat scansion." More recently, he and poet Thomas Carper have collaborated on *Meter and Meaning: An Introduction to Rhythm in Poetry*, which offers revised versions of Attridge's "symbol system." The rhythm markers used in Attridge's system appear below each line of the poem being scanned:

B beat [emphasized syllable]   **o** offbeat [unemphasized syllable]
b beat [unemphasized syllable]   **O** offbeat [emphasized syllable]

There are other markers, but the following two are especially useful: **-o-** (double offbeat, indicating two unemphasized syllables) and **ô** (implied offbeat, indicating not a syllable but a necessary rhythmical pause). Here are those two lines from Shakespeare's sonnet:

When to the sessions of sweet silent thought
B   -o-   B   -o-   B ô B o   B

I summon up remembrance of things past,
o B   o b   o B   -o-   B ô B

No metrical feet are marked—or necessary. The *minor ionic
(˘ ˘ ´ ´) becomes a "rhythmic figure" represented by **-o- B ô B**.

Although scansion may be held in the same repute as sentence diagramming, it is extremely useful in reading a poem closely and hearing it clearly—and subsequently in writing one's own.

SCUD Vladimir Nabokov's term for an *iambic *foot in which the stress is unaccented. In *Notes on Prosody*, he cites the opening foot in line twenty-seven of Lord Byron's "Mazeppa" as an example:

And in the depths of forests darkling,

"And in" sounds like a pyrrhic foot (˘ ˘), but the unstressed syllable ("in") receives a metrical stress because of the prevailing meter (iambic tetrameter). Nabokov rejects the notion of inverted feet, so that, in an iambic line, what we call a trochaic substitution (´ ˘) would be a "tilted scud." Nabokov remarks, "Any tilt is a tilted scud, since the stress in such feet is not accented. English theorists term tilted scuds 'inversion of stress'; a better description would be 'inversion of accent,' since it is the word stress that (more or less gracefully) feigns a surrender to the meter. The meter is basic and cannot succumb to the word." Nabokov calls the *minor ionic (˘ ˘ ´ ´) a "split reverse tilt."

SENTENCE A group of words that expresses a complete thought or utterance, including at least one subject and at least one main verb (in other words, at least one independent clause); a string of words that begins with a capital letter and continues unwinding until it reaches a period (or full-stop, as the British say).

Most poems feature an interplay between sentence and line, which may coincide but often do not. Sentences can be as short as a single word ("Stop!") or as long as an entire poem. They can be declarative ("I did it."), exclamatory ("I did it!"), interrogative ("Did I do it?"), or imperative ("Do it."). They can be simple ("I did it."), compound ("I did it, and that's that."), complex ("I did it, because I wanted to.") or compound-complex ("I did it, because I wanted to, and that's that.").

The following poem consists of a single sentence progressing through eight lines. Another one-sentence poem appears in BLACK MOUNTAIN SCHOOL, Robert Creeley's "I Know a Man."

PHOTOSYNTHESIS / A.R. Ammons (1926–2001)

> The sun's wind
> blows the fire
> green, sails the
> chloroplasts,
> lifts banks, bogs,
> boughs into flame:
> the green ash of
> yellow loss.

SENTENCE FRAGMENT A group of words that ends with a period but lacks either a subject or a main verb; a subordinate clause or a phrase or a single word standing by itself. Here are some examples of fragments (in one line of Geoffrey Hill's "Mercian Hymns"):

> A pet-name, a common name. Best-selling brand, curt graffito. A laugh; a cough. A syndicate. A specious gift. Scoffed-at horned phonograph.

A sentence fragment is a mistake, if used carelessly, but a valuable device if used expressively or rhythmically. *(See* FRAGMENT *and* FRAGMENTATION.*)*

SENTENCE SOUNDS Robert Frost based much of his own poetic method on what he called, in letters to his friend John T. Bartlett in 1913 and 1914, "the sound of sense" or "sentence sounds," the way real voices sound when people talk. "The best place to get the abstract sound of sense," Frost writes, "is from voices behind a door that cuts off the words." He offers a series of examples:

> You mean to tell me you can't read?
> I said no such thing.
> Well read then.
> You're not my teacher.

Frost believes that a writer must catch these sentence sounds "fresh from talk." He insists that the "ear is the only true writer and the only true reader." *(See* SPEAKER, SPEECH STRESS, *and* VOICE.*)*

SEQUENCE A group of poems, often numbered; a progression of poems or sections.

Poems in a sequence must be connected in some way, perhaps by title, theme, subject matter, stanza form, range of references, speaker(s), or an ongoing narrative. A sequence offers a good way to make a *long poem out of a number of short lyrics. Jim Harrison refers to such sequences as "suites," like an orchestral work composed of many brief movements. The best known, and most enduring, kind of sequence is the *sonnet sequence. Book-length sequences include Rita Dove's *Thomas and Beulah* and Marvin Bell's *The Book of the Dead Man. (See* NUMBERED SECTIONS.*)*

VEGETABLE POEMS / Katha Pollitt (b. 1949)

1. Potatoes
Blind knobby eyes feeling out
the chinks in the damp black earth
all summer long these tunnel under the fence
to throttle the open field of milkweed and Queen Anne's lace
or live for years in cellars
their softened, mealy flesh
rotting into the earth, indistinguishable from earth
but still flinging up roots and occasional leaves
white as fish in caves.

Feel them, the swollen sac
the baggy elephant skin:
if they are edible, it is only by accident.

2. Tomato

It is the female fruit: the plush
red flesh the fat
sac of seeds and oh
those silky membranes
plump and calm
it fits your palm just so
it is that perfect softball of your childhood
the one you always lost
you can stroke the sleek skin
you can thumb
the comfortable curve beneath:
here's
all soft gum
no sheer
secret murderous teeth.

3. Onion

The smoothness of onions infuriates him
so like the skin of women or their expensive clothes
and the striptease of onions, which is also a disappearing act.
He says he is searching for the ultimate nakedness
but when he finds that thin green seed
that negligible sprout of a heart
we could have told him he'd only be disappointed.
Meanwhile the onion has been hacked to bits
and he's weeping in the kitchen most unromantic tears.

4. Eggplant

Like a dark foghorn in a yellow kitchen
we imagine the eggplant's
melancholy bass

booming its pompous operatic sorrows
a prince down on his luck
preserving among peasants
an air of dignified, impenetrable gloom
or Boris, dying,
booming, *I still am Tsar.*

5. Nettles
Like neighbors not invited to the wedding
these show up anyway: fat stalks
dull hairy leaves
they stand at the edge of the garden and cry *I burn!*
Ugly, but tenacious,
they make themselves useful: in teas,
poultices, cures for baldness and rheumatic complaints.
From us, such homely uses are all they can hope for,
but they too have their dream:
to be the chosen food of their beautiful loves
the peacock
small tortoiseshell
and red admiral caterpillars.

SESTINA (ses-tee'-nuh; Italian, "sixth") A fixed form, developed in Provençal by the Troubadours, in which six end-words are repeated in an interwoven order through six *stanzas and in a final three-line *envoi* (also called *tornada*), which contains all six of those words.

After the first stanza establishes a sestina's six end-words, each of the following stanzas rearranges the previous stanza's end-words according to a prescribed numerological order: 6, 1, 5, 2, 4, 3. This arrangement can be remembered easily as a weaving pattern that moves from bottom to top and from outside to inside.

In the envoi, three of the end-words appear at the ends of lines, while the other three are embedded, one per line. The poet is free to arrange the end-words as needed. Since the envoi often sounds like a postscript anyway, some poets choose to omit it altogether.

In *The Spirit of Romance*, Ezra Pound calls the sestina "a thin sheet of flame folding and infolding upon itself." Marilyn Hacker describes it: "A camera on a rotating boom, / six words spin slowly round and pan the room."

Arnaut Daniel (who appears as a character in Dante's *Purgatorio*) wrote the earliest extant sestina in the twelfth century. (The original musical setting still exists.) It was promptly answered by Bertran de Born, whose sestina, "Certainly great vileness enters," uses the same end-words. His response is a *sirventes (sear-ven-tess´)*, a Troubadour poem that imitates the form and borrows the tune of another, usually for comic, bawdy, satirical, or political purposes. In the early twentieth century, Ezra Pound repopularized the form with his "Sestina: Altaforte," a dramatic monologue based on Bertran's life but not on any particular poem. Pound's sestina uses the end-words *peace, music, clash, opposing, crimson,* and *rejoicing.*

Although many poets write their sestinas in *iambic pentameter, Arnaut's original uses a syllabic pattern of 8-11-11-11-11-11 in each of its six-line stanzas. *Free-verse sestinas include Donald Justice's "Here in Katmandu," Edward Hirsch's "At Kresge's Diner in Stonefalls, Arkansas,"and John Ashbery's "Farm Implements and Rutabagas in a Landscape" (which features characters from the Popeye cartoons).

A *double sestina* consists of two sestinas with a single envoi, using the same six end-words throughout. Once the first set of six six-line stanzas concludes, another begins. After twelve six-line stanzas, the envoi finally shows up. An example is "Ye goat-herd gods, that love the grassy mountains," by the Elizabethan poet Sir Philip Sidney.

The repeated end-words (also called *teleutons*) do not ordinarily rhyme. But Sidney wrote another sestina, "Farewell, O sun, Arcadia's clearest light," whose end-words are *light, treasure, might, pleasure, direction,* and *affection*. Because of the set pattern of end-words, Sidney's *rhyme scheme changes from stanza to stanza.

Contemporary poets often feel free to alter the end-words of a sestina as they recur, adding or deleting suffixes, making use of puns or homophones or different meanings, or even using a slant rhyme (*boot* changing to *boat*, for example)—all to make the form more flexible and more surprising while keeping a sense of the repetitive structure. In one of the following sestinas, Donald Justice alters the end-words each time they recur—his poem is appropriately called "The Metamorphosis." He also omits the envoi.

James Cummins, whose "Echo" is included in the following examples, is the author of two book-length collections of sestinas: *The Whole Truth*, based on characters from the Perry Mason mysteries, and (in collaboration with David Lehman) *Jim and Dave Defeat the Masked Man*.

SESTINA

(*Lo ferm voler q'el cor m'intra*) / Arnaut Daniel
(twelfth century; tr. John Drury)

	Stanza	Line	End Word
The firm resolve that has entered	1	1	A
my heart cannot be ripped out by beak or nail		2	B
of flatterers who gab away their souls.		3	C
I don't dare batter them with stick or rod,		4	D
alone, without the aid of any uncle,		5	E
and so I'll love my love in grove or chamber.		6	F
When I recollect the chamber	2	1	F
where—my loss too—I know that no man enters		2	A
(and everyone's more strict than brother or uncle),		3	E
none of my parts is still, not even a nail,		4	B
just like a boy about to feel the rod—		5	D
I fear that she might overwhelm my soul.		6	C
May I be hers, body not soul,	3	1	C
so she'd agree to hide me in her chamber!		2	F
It strikes a blow to my heart, more than a rod's,		3	D
that where she is this servant may not enter.		4	A
I'll stay with her, close as flesh and nails,		5	B
ignoring the reproach of friend or uncle.		6	E
The sister of my uncle	4	1	E
I don't love nearly as much—upon my soul!		2	C

If she allowed me, close as fingernail	3	B
to finger, I'd advance into her chamber.	4	F
I'd bow to love that in my heart has entered	5	A
sooner than heed a hard man's flimsy rod.	6	D

Since the flowering of the dry rod	5	1	D
and Adam propagating nephews and uncles,		2	E
I can't believe the fine love that has entered		3	A
my heart has come before in body or soul.		4	C
Wherever she is, in plaza or in chamber,		5	F
my body doesn't stray the length of a nail.		6	B

And my body fastens with nails,	6	1	B
attached to her like bark on branching rod,		2	D
for she is joy's tower and palace and chamber,		3	F
lessening my love for brother, parent, or uncle;		4	E
in paradise, twice the joy for my soul		5	C
if any man who loves that well can enter.		6	A

Arnaut sends off his song of uncle and nail	Envoi	1	EB
to please the soul who arms him with a rod,		2	CD
his Desire, with honor entering the chamber.		3	AF

NOTE: "Desire" is Provençal *Desirat,* which is a *senhal (sen-yahl´)*, a secret sign or in-joke among Troubadour poets, though indecipherable now. It may refer to a lady or perhaps to the poet Bertran de Born ("Sir Desire, famed for chambers he has entered"). In the original, the envoi's end-words are arranged E B / D C / F A.

SESTINA / Elizabeth Bishop (1911–1979)

September rain falls on the house.
In the failing light, the old grandmother
sits in the kitchen with the child
beside the Little Marvel Stove,
reading the jokes from the almanac,
laughing and talking to hide her tears.

She thinks that her equinoctial tears
and the rain that beats on the roof of the house

were both foretold by the almanac,
but only known to a grandmother.
The iron kettle sings on the stove.
She cuts some bread and says to the child,

It's time for tea now; but the child
is watching the teakettle's small hard tears
dance like mad on the hot black stove,
the way the rain must dance on the house.
Tidying up, the old grandmother
hangs up the clever almanac

on its string. Birdlike, the almanac
hovers half open above the child,
hovers above the old grandmother
and her teacup full of dark brown tears.
She shivers and says she thinks the house
feels chilly, and puts more wood in the stove.

It was to be, says the Marvel Stove.
I know what I know, says the almanac.
With crayons the child draws a rigid house
and a winding pathway. Then the child
puts in a man with buttons like tears
and shows it proudly to the grandmother.

But secretly, while the grandmother
busies herself about the stove,
the little moons fall down like tears
from between the pages of the almanac
into the flower bed the child
has carefully placed in front of the house.

Time to plant tears, says the almanac.
The grandmother sings to the marvellous stove
and the child draws another inscrutable house.

THE METAMORPHOSIS / Donald Justice (1925–2004)

Past Mr. Raven's tavern
Up Cemetery Hill
Around by the Giant Oak
And Drowning Creek gone dry
Into the Hunting Woods
And that was how he went

At his back the wind
Blowing out of heaven
And at his feet foul weeds
That it was like to hell
And scarcely could he draw
Breath and the ribs did ache

No rest got under the oak
Nor water for the wound
Yet kept the way and drew
Home at length to haven
And the familiar hall
His key into the wards

Then owls cried out from the woods
And terrors of that ilk
So that the bitch at heel
A little moaned and whined
As she some fit were having
That back her long legs drew

Whereat his mouth stood dry
And without any words
Despite his heart heaving
And tongue working to speak
Some name to cast the wonder
Straight from his heart whole

Then bent he to the keyhole
Nor might his eyes withdraw
The while the hall unwound
That thing which afterwards
No man should know or its like
Whether dead or living

ECHO / James Cummins (b. 1948)

Lovers check each other—"How are you?"—
when love is going, but before it's gone.
"Oh, I'm better. The nausea's settled down.
The mad howling stopped the other night."
Some rueful laughter on the other end.
"Me, too," she whispers, in her quiet voice,

"me, too." He thinks: I love her quiet voice.
"Yesterday, at the market, I saw you"—
she catches, laughs. It's hard for love to end.
It's hard to wake up, certain that it's gone.
He says, "I thought about you all last night,
but I'm better. The nausea's settled down."

They never say that love has settled down,
that it no longer uses its sweet voice
to carry them in boats across the night.
If you deny love, love will deny you;
the nighttime of its daytime voice is gone,
as you will be. It's hard for love to end.

But any love is difficult to end;
all endings seem to whisper, then lie down—
an old man dying by the fire, soon gone,
as if he'd never lived. Her quiet voice,
that only yesterday spoke just to you,
will soon become a whisper in the night,

then disappear forever from the night.
And there's no preparation for that end.
She laughs again. "I want to be with you."
He understands. He puts the phone back down.
How will he live without her quiet voice?
What will he do, when she's finally gone?

Within a week the moving van is gone.
He works all day, and dreads the quiet night.
The day will come when he'll forget her voice;
he has no need for longing for that end.
He'd settle now for keeping dinner down.
He hears again: *I want to be with you.*

He stares into the pool of night, her voice
behind him, gone. He monitors the end:
he lies down, hears the faint refrain: "*... with you ...*"

SETTING The location (if any) where a poem takes place. John Donne's "The Sun Rising" (in METAPHYSICAL POETS) takes place in a lover's bedroom. Frank O'Hara's "A Step Away from Them" (in CITY POEM) takes place in Manhattan. But many poems, such as "The Descent" by William Carlos Williams (in TRIADIC LINE), do not have definable settings.

SIMILE (sim'-uh-lee; Latin, "like") A comparison that uses some linking word (*like, as, such as, how*) to make the likeness clear. A kind of *metaphor (though a true metaphor does not use linking words).

In mathematical symbols, a simile would require an approximate sign ($\approx$), meaning "similar to." In Dylan Thomas's "Fern Hill," there is "fire green as grass," and the poem ends:

> Time held me green and dying
> Though I sang in my chains like the sea.

A simile generally sounds more casual, and less emphatic, than a metaphor. Instead of a leap, it provides a visible bridge linking two things, indicating one likeness among many differences. It gives both pleasure and information.

SIXAIN (six'-ane) A six-line stanza.

Sixains appears most frequently in the *stave of six* (rhymed *ababcc*). In a *sonnet, a six-line stanza is called a *sestet*. Other six-line stanzas include the *Burns stanza* (rhymed *aaabab*) and the *sestina* (except for its three-line *envoi*).

The following poem by Robert Browning uses an envelope pattern (*abccba*), working inward and then out. The rhyme sounds in the middle are quite pronounced, while those on the outer edges of each stanza are more faintly heard.

MEETING AT NIGHT / Robert Browning (1812–1889)

> The gray sea and the long black land;
> And the yellow half-moon large and low;
> And the startled little waves that leap
> In fiery ringlets from their sleep,
> As I gain the cove with pushing prow,
> And quench its speed i' the slushy sand.
>
> Then a mile of warm sea-scented beach;
> Three fields to cross till a farm appears;
> A tap at the pane, the quick sharp scratch
> And blue spurt of a lighted match,
> And a voice less loud, thro' its joys and fears,
> Than the two hearts beating each to each!

SKELTONICS (skel-tahn'-ix) Rough, bounding verse, usually two accents per line, rhymed several lines in a row, as in the poems of John Skelton. Robert Graves's "In the Wilderness" is a twentieth-century poem in skeltonics. *(See* DIPODICS.*)*

TO MISTRESS MARGARET HUSSEY / John Skelton (1460–1529)

Merry Margaret,
As midsummer flower,
Gentle as falcon
Or hawk of the tower:
With solace and gladness,
Much mirth and no madness,
All good and no badness;
So joyously,
So maidenly,
So womanly
Her demeaning
In every thing,
Far, far passing
That I can indite,
Or suffice to write
Of Merry Margaret
As midsummer flower,
Gentle as falcon
Or hawk of the tower.
As patient and still
And as full of good will
As fair Isaphill,
Coriander,
Sweet pomander,
Good Cassander,
Steadfast of thought,
Well made, well wrought,
Far may be sought
Ere that ye can find
So courteous, so kind
As Merry Margaret,
This midsummer flower,
Gentle as falcon
Or hawk of the tower.

SLANT RHYME (also called *approximate rhyme, half rhyme, near rhyme,* and *off rhyme*) *Rhyme that neither looks nor sounds exact. Instead of echoing both vowel and consonant, a slant rhyme echoes only one of them.

With monosyllabic words, if the vowel is the same but the final consonant changes, the rhyme is *assonant* (*myth/whip, hope/cone, break/cape*). If the final consonant is the same but the vowel changes, the rhyme is *consonant* (*myth/bath, hope/cape, break/smack*). If the vowel changes but the consonants surrounding it remain the same, the rhyme is *double-consonant* (*myth/math, hope/hype, break/brook*).

With polysyllabic words, the same combinations hold true for the final accent, but the unstressed syllable(s) at the end usually stay the same, dangling like little tails (*Bible/sidle/stubble/babble*).

Poets differ in their standards of decency concerning proper or improper slant rhymes. Robert Graves insists on consonance. Other sticklers require similar vowels (so that *bat/bet*, both containing short vowels, would qualify, but *bat/boat*, one short vowel and one long, would not). Popular songwriters favor assonance because it rings out more noticeably, especially long open vowels. But some poets are casual, careless, reckless, experimental, or especially open-minded—depending on your view of laissez-faire poetics—in their rhyming. As with most poetic issues, a critic may prescribe and proscribe as much as he likes, but precedent is the ultimate law. If the results are poetry, any deviance from standard practice can be sanctioned; if the results are doggerel or drivel, no literary advocate can rescue the offender.

The ingenious poem below uses both assonant rhyme (*abab*) and double-consonant rhyme (*abba*), deploying two *rhyme schemes at once.

from "FIVE SONGS" (II) / W.H. Auden (1907–1973)

> That night when joy began
> Our narrowest veins to flush,
> We waited for the flash
> Of morning's levelled gun.

But morning let us pass,
And day by day relief
Outgrows his nervous laugh,
Grows credulous of peace,

As mile by mile is seen
No trespasser's reproach,
And love's best glasses reach
No fields but are his own.

SONG Words fit to be set to music; words and melody combined; also called a *ditty*, *lyric*, *lied*, or *chanson*. A song is different from a chant, which is declaimed or intoned rather than sung. Most songs in English are rhymed. (*See* BALLAD, BLUES, CHORUS, MUSIC POEM, RAP, *and* SPIRITUAL.)

FULL FADOM FIVE (from *The Tempest*) / William Shakespeare (1564–1616)

Full fadom five thy father lies.
Of his bones are coral made:
Those are pearls that were his eyes;
Nothing of him that doth fade
But doth suffer a sea-change
Into something rich and strange:
Sea-nymphs hourly ring his knell:
Hark, now I hear them—
Ding dong bell.

NOTE: The burden (or *refrain) is "Ding dong, ding dong bell," which is repeated several times. Robert Johnson (who died in 1634) composed what may be the original musical setting. Counter-tenor Alfred Deller has recorded it.

fadom: fathom, a measure of six (nonmetrical) feet.

SONNET (sahn'-et; Italian, "little song"; or perhaps from the medieval Latin sonitus, "murmur, soft sound or noise") A poem of fourteen lines (give or take a couple), usually *rhymed, usually written in *iambic pentameter; a *song usurped by ideas.

Sonnet

A sonnet often presents an *argument, perhaps a romantic plea in the guise of a legal brief. But it may also contain a description of a memorable scene, a meditation, a miniature story, a portrait, or a list. The *rhyme scheme and *stanza breaks (if any) often determine the structure of the thoughts.

The first sonnets still in existence come from the Sicilian court of Frederick II, sometime between 1220 and 1230. Officials called notaries, who were in effect lawyers, wrote and exchanged them, as did the emperor. Fifty-eight of their sonnets survive, at least twenty-six by Jacopo da Lentini (or Giacomo da Lentino, 1188–1240), who generally receives credit as the inventor of the sonnet—although even his name seems in dispute. Perhaps one of his shorter *nonce forms simply caught on at court and came down to us in much the same fourteen-line form. Jacopo and his colleagues preferred a *rhyme scheme of *abababab cdcdcd* or *cdecde* (called the *Sicilian sonnet*). Sometimes they used repeated end-words, as in a *sestina, instead of rhymes. Here is Jacopo da Lentini's "Io m'aggio posto in core a Dio servire" (translated by John Drury):

> I find room in my heart for serving God
> 　　so that, at last, I might reach Paradise,
> 　　the holy place where, I have heard it said,
> 　　solace and ease and gaiety suffice.
> 　　Without my lady, though, I wouldn't tread
> 　　heavenward for her blonde hair, her bright face,
> 　　because my pleasure would be stale indeed
> 　　if she were not a part of all that bliss.
>
> But no, believe me, I have no intent
> 　　of trafficking in sin while going there.
> 　　I only want to gaze at her, content
> 　　with her sweet look, the deepness of her stare,
> 　　so all my consolation would be spent
> 　　watching my lady's joy reach everywhere.

The immediate poetic ancestor of the sonnet may be a Sicilian song form, the *strambotto* (consisting of eight lines rhymed *abababab*—the same pattern Jacopo da Lentini uses for his octave, or first eight lines).

There are two principal kinds of sonnet: the *Petrarchan* (or *Italian*) and the *Shakespearean* (or *English*). They are characterized by different rhyme schemes and different organizing principles.

The Petrarchan sonnet, named after the Italian Renaissance poet Francesco Petrarca (Petrarch in English, 1304–1374), rhymes *abbaabba* in its first eight lines (the octave) and variously in the last six (the sestet): *cdcdcd, cdedce, ccdccd, cddcdd, cdecde,* or *cddcee.* Here is Petrarch's "Sonnet CLIX" (translated by Marion Shore):

> In what idea, in what part of the sky
> did Nature find the shape she copied there,
> to form a face so radiant and fair
> and show below what she could do on high?
>
> What river nymph has ever loosed to dry
> upon the wind such shining golden hair?
> When was one heart so virtuous and rare?
> although it is the reason that I die.
>
> He who seeks a glimpse of paradise
> here upon this earth must vainly seek
> if he has never gazed into her eyes;
>
> nor knows what sweet destruction Love can wreak
> unless he hears the way she sweetly sighs,
> and hears her sweetly laugh, and sweetly speak.

The Petrarchan sonnet has a two-part structure; the break between octave and sestet is called the *volta* ("turn" or "turning point"). It may or may not be indicated by a stanza break.

One elaboration, the *double sonnet*, consists of twenty-eight lines, arranged in two stanzas. In Anthony Hecht's "Double Sonnet," the rhyme scheme is *abbaabbaabbaabba cdecdeedcedc.* The octave of the Petrarchan sonnet is doubled to sixteen lines (using only *a* and *b* rhymes), followed by a doubled sestet (using only *c, d,* and *e* rhymes).

The Shakespearean sonnet, named after William Shakespeare (1564–1616), rhymes *abab cdcd efef gg.* Here is Shakespeare's Sonnet 130:

Sonnet

My mistress' eyes are nothing like the sun;
Coral is far more red than her lips' red;
If snow be white, why then her breasts are dun;
If hairs be wires, black wires grow on her head.
I have seen roses damasked, red and white,
But no such roses see I in her cheeks;
And in some perfumes is there more delight
Than in the breath that from my mistress reeks.
I love to hear her speak, yet well I know
That music hath a far more pleasing sound;
I grant I never saw a goddess go;
My mistress, when she walks, treads on the ground.
    And yet, by heaven, I think my love as rare
    As any she belied with false compare.

NOTE: *damasked*: arranged ornamentally; *reeks*: is exhaled.

This rhyme scheme was apparently first used by Henry Howard, the Earl of Surrey, who also introduced *blank verse to English. Its structure is four-part, based on three quatrains and a couplet (although actual stanza breaks are entirely optional). There are several possible turning points (although the crux is usually reached with stanza three or the final couplet, which often moralizes or generalizes).

A less common sonnet form, the *Spenserian*, is named after Edmund Spenser (1552?–1599) and rhymes *ababbcbccdcdee*. Here is Sonnet 75 from his sequence, *Amoretti*:

One day I wrote her name upon the strand,
But came the waves and washèd it away:
Agayne I wrote it with a second hand,
But came the tyde, and made my paynes his pray.
"Vayne man," sayd she, "that doest in vayne assay,
A mortall thing so to immortalize,
For I my selve shall lyke to this decay,
And eek my name bee wypèd out lykewize."
"Not so," quod I, "let baser things devize
To dy in dust, but you shall live by fame:

My verse your vertues rare shall eternize,
And in the hevens wryte your glorious name.
Where whenas death shall all the world subdew,
Our love shall live, and later life renew."

NOTE: *pray*: prey; *eek*: also.

Poets have tried out many other rhyme combinations in their sonnets. In "On the Sonnet," John Keats aspires to a "more interwoven" rhyme scheme: *abcabdcabcdede*. Like the Spenserian rhyme scheme, this Keatsian one is pleasantly interwoven, but too hard to remember easily. Neither form has found much favor.

One advantage of the two principal rhyme schemes, the Petrarchan and the Shakespearean, is that their structures are neat and logical, easy to recall in the act of composition. Many sonnets are spontaneous, such as the fifty-five *Sonnets to Orpheus* that Rainer Maria Rilke wrote in less than three weeks in February 1922, a "breathless act ... without one word being doubtful or having to be changed." Rilke improvised his rhyme schemes as he went, using a Shakespearean quatrain (*abab*) to begin his opening sonnet, then shifting to the envelope pattern of the Petrarchan (*cddc*) for the next four lines, and then concluding with a mirroring pattern (*efg gfe*) sometimes used in Petrarchan sestets. He picked what he needed as he went, but he drew from those two great models, writing (or taking down an "enigmatic dictation") furiously, extemporaneously. Of course, many of Rilke's earlier poems had also been sonnets.

The poet is really free to devise any sort of arrangement that works for a particular sonnet. Robert Frost's "Into My Own" consists of seven rhymed couplets, called a *couplet sonnet* (rhymed *aabbccddeeffgg*). His "Acquainted with the Night" is a sonnet in *terza rima (rhymed *aba bcb cdc ded ee*). Robert Lowell and John Peck have written blank-verse sonnets, dispensing with rhyme altogether. And the poet may choose to alter the meter. One of Shakespeare's sonnets (145, "Those lips that Love's own hand did make") is in iambic tetrameter. Rilke uses various line lengths in his *Sonnets to Orpheus*. George Meredith's 1862 sequence, *Modern Love*, contains sonnets of sixteen lines each

S

(rhymed *abbacddceffeghhg*). John Hollander's unrhymed sonnets in his book *Thirteens* consist of thirteen lines of thirteen syllables each. Mona Van Duyn has written "minimalist sonnets" that appear in *Firefall*: "I have shortened the conventional iambic pentameter line in varying degrees, some of the sonnets being held to a one-accent line; but I have kept all other conventions of the Shakespearean, Petrarchan, or Spenserian." Elizabeth Bishop's two-accent "Sonnet," whose first two lines are "Caught—the bubble / in the spirit level," is similarly minimalist.

Free-verse sonnets might hardly qualify as sonnets if they departed from the fourteen-line standard. The "little song" can be corrupted only so much. But an impulse to be "subversive in formal verse," as Julia Alvarez puts it, motivates some poets to explore the form when they might otherwise feel excluded from the grand tradition and put off by the "gigantism of the sonnet," as Robert Lowell characterizes it in *Notebook*, a sequence of blank-verse sonnets. Alvarez writes, "I wanted to go in that heavily mined and male labyrinth with the string of my own voice. I wanted to explore it and explode it too. I call my sonnets free verse sonnets. They have ten syllables per line, and the lines are in a loose iambic pentameter. But they are heavily enjambed and the rhymes are often slant rhymes, and the rhyme scheme is peculiar to each sonnet."

The sonnet has not always found favor in English. In his dictionary of 1755, Samuel Johnson defines "sonneteer" as "A small poet, in contempt." He remarks of the sonnet: "It is not very suitable to the English language; and has not been used by any man of eminence since Milton. ... " It has, however, been used by many eminent men and women since Dr. Johnson.

There are other sonnets scattered throughout this dictionary: an excerpt from William Shakespeare's *Romeo and Juliet* in DIALOGUE, Shakespeare's Sonnet 66 in END-STOP, Seamus Heaney's "The Forge" in FIGURATIVE LANGUAGE, Maxine Kumin's "Poem Found in *The New Hampshire Department of Agriculture Weekly Market Bulletin*" in FOUND POEM, John Crowe Ransom's "Piazza Piece" in FUGITIVES, Molly Peacock's "Where Is Home?" in NEW FORMALISM, Dante Gabriel

Rossetti's "Lilith" in PRE-RAPHAELITE BROTHERHOOD, James Wright's
"Reading a 1979 Inscription on Belli's Monument" in POETRY,
Shakespeare's Sonnet 138 in RHETORIC, Gerard Manley Hopkins's
"The Windhover" in SPRUNG RHYTHM, and Charles Baudelaire's
"Correspondences" in SYMBOLIST POETRY. (*See* CURTAL SONNET,
EUGENE ONEGIN STANZA, SONNET SEQUENCE *and* TAILED SONNET.)

from BLACKS / Gwendolyn Brooks (1917–2000)

PIANO AFTER WAR

On a snug evening I shall watch her fingers,
Cleverly ringed, declining to clever pink,
Beg glory from the willing keys. Old hungers
Will break their coffins, rise to eat and thank.
And music, warily, like the golden rose
That sometimes after sunset warms the west,
Will warm that room, persuasively suffuse
That room and me, rejuvenate a past.
But suddenly, across my climbing fever
Of proud delight—a multiplying cry.
A cry of bitter dead men who will never
Attend a gentle maker of musical joy.
Then my thawed eye will go again to ice.
And stone will shove the softness from my face.

MENTORS

For I am rightful fellow of their band.
My best allegiances are to the dead.
I swear to keep the dead upon my mind,
Disdain for all time to be overglad.
Among spring flowers, under summer trees,
By chilling autumn waters, in the frosts
Of supercilious winter—all my days
I'll have as mentors those reproving ghosts.
And at that cry, at that remotest whisper,
I'll stop my casual business. Leave the banquet.

Or leave the ball—reluctant to unclasp her
Who may be fragrant as the flower she wears,
Make gallant bows and dim excuses, then quit
Light for the midnight that is mine and theirs.

SONNET 6 FROM "REDWING SONNETS" / Julia Alvarez (b. 1950)

I brought a record of common birdsongs
so as to learn to tell the birds apart,
but I gave up trying to follow along.
I'd have one bird down, say, a meadowlark,
chee-up-trill. But right on its tailfeathers
came the peewee with its *pee-ah-wee*,
exactly like the *zee-zee* of the warbler
or the *drink your tea* (so it sounded to me)
of the towhee. Finally, to top it all,
the mockingbird mimicking everyone.
It was bird-Babel worse than biblical
to human ears, which should humble us some
to think our poems no more than mating trills
for the birds: *whan-that-aprill, whan-that-aprill.*

NOTE: "Whan that Aprill with his shoures soote" ("shoures" meaning "showers" and "soote" meaning "sweet") is the opening line of the General Prologue of *The Canterbury Tales* by Geoffrey Chaucer (1343?–1400).

VESTIBULE / John Peck (b. 1941)

All day our paths had crossed, I'd missed you twice
Or three times—then, had come home tired to find
Your sweater on the couch, your shoes kicked off,
The coffee still warm in your waiting cup—
And lightly called your name, only to hear it
Measure the silences; then felt my eyes
Stray back across the sweater's rich abandon,
The shoes more delicate for lying empty,
The porcelain zero of the cup—but then you called,

Upstairs and far away. Your voice brought back
Another room we entered once together,
Catching our breath—bare benches where the Shakers
Sat quiet after field work and prepared
To go together to the larger room.

SONNET SEQUENCE (also called a *cycle*) A group of related poems in sonnet form (usually fourteen lines of *iambic pentameter with a fixed rhyme scheme). The sonnets may be loosely assembled (perhaps according to theme), or they may tell or imply a story.

Many Elizabethan poets wrote sonnet sequences: Sir Philip Sidney *(Astrophil and Stella)*, Edmund Spenser *(Amoretti)*, Samuel Daniel *(Delia)*, Michael Drayton *(Idea)*, and William Shakespeare. In the seventeenth century John Donne wrote his *Holy Sonnets.*

Many sonnet sequences, however, are not wholly sonnets. For example, Marilyn Hacker's *Love, Death, and the Changing of the Seasons* includes several elongated *villanelles and a couple of *rondeaux.

A *crown of sonnets* (also called a *corona* or *coronet*) is a particular kind of sequence. It consists of seven sonnets; the last line of each one must be repeated as the first line of the next; the final line of the seventh sonnet will repeat the opening line of the sequence, so that the crown is (appropriately) circular. The rhyme scheme is not fixed, but some poets choose not to repeat any rhyme sound once it has been used.

A *sonnet redoublé* (or redoubled sonnet) is a sequence of fifteen sonnets. Each line of the first sonnet serves, in order, as the last line of one of the following fourteen sonnets. The first sonnet, sometimes called the *texte*, serves as a kind of supply depot for the rest of the lines.

SONS OF BEN (also called the *Tribe of Ben*) Poets associated with Ben Jonson (1572–1637), such as Thomas Carew, Robert Herrick, Richard Lovelace, John Suckling, and Edmund Waller. These poets took Jonson's work, known for wit and classical polish, as their model. Their poems are elegant, witty, and convivial. The group met regularly with Jonson in the Apollo Room of London's Devil Tavern. They are also known as Cavalier poets (those who supported the monarchy and Charles I, as opposed to the "Roundheads," the Puritans who supported Oliver Cromwell, such as John Milton).

AN ODE FOR HIM / Robert Herrick (1591–1674)

> Ah, Ben!
> Say how or when
> Shall we, thy guests,
> Meet at those lyric feasts
> Made at the Sun,
> The Dog, the Triple Tun,
> Where we such clusters had
> As made us nobly wild, not mad;
> And yet each verse of thine
> Outdid the meat, outdid the frolic wine.
>
> My Ben!
> Or come again,
> Or send to us
> Thy wit's great overplus;
> But teach us yet
> Wisely to husband it,
> Lest we that talent spend,
> And having once brought to an end
> That precious stock, the store
> Of such a wit the world should have no more.

NOTE: The lines are indented to indicate the number of iambic feet they contain: the more indented, the fewer feet. Each stanza is irregular, but they match each other. The Sun, Dog, and Triple Tun mentioned in stanza one are all London taverns.

SPEAKER The *voice that is uttering, chanting, singing, or even thinking the words of a poem; the essential instrument through which a poem's words are channeled and delivered. It may be a careful way of describing the poet herself. It may be a narrator, as in a story.

A poet can, of course, speak through the voice of a character, as Robert Browning impersonates a Renaissance painter in "Andrea del Sarto." Browning says of this practice, "I'll tell my state as though 'twere none of mine." *(See* DRAMATIC MONOLOGUE, SENTENCE SOUNDS, *and* VOICE.*)*

SPEECH STRESS A *stress or *accent that occurs naturally in the course of speaking—as opposed to metrical stress, which occurs when the metrical pattern dictates.

SPENSERIAN STANZA (spen-sare'-ee-un) A stanza, devised by Edmund Spenser and later used memorably in John Keats's "The Eve of St. Agnes" and Percy Bysshe Shelley's "Adonais," consisting of eight lines of *iambic pentameter followed by one line of iambic hexameter, the whole stanza rhymed *ababbcbcc.*

S

from *THE FAERIE QUEEN* / Edmund Spenser (1552?–1599)

> In her left hand a cup of gold she held,
> And with her right the riper fruit did reach,
> Whose sappy liquor, that with fulnesse sweld,
> Into her cup she scruzd, with daintie breach
> Of her fine fingers, without fowle empeach,
> That so faire winepresse made the wine more sweet:
> Thereof she usd to give to drinke to each,
> Whom passing by she happened to meet:
> It was her guise, all straungers goodly so to greet.

(The Bower of Bliss: Book II, canto xii, stanza 56)

SPIRITUAL Religious song made up and sung by African-American slaves in the nineteenth century.

Spirituals combined the African call-and-response with biblical stories, often encoding messages of resistance to bondage and even directions for escaped slaves on their way north to freedom, as in "Follow the Drinking Gourd," which tells how to use what we now call the Big Dipper as a kind of compass. The following poem, "Go Down, Moses," implicitly compares the story of the Israelites in Egypt to slaves in the Deep South.

GO DOWN, MOSES / Anonymous

When Israel was in Egyptland,
Let my people go,
Oppressed so hard they could not stand,
Let my people go.

Go down, Moses,
Way down in Egyptland,
Tell old Pharaoh
To let my people go.

"Thus saith the Lord," bold Moses said,
"Let my people go;
If not I'll smite your first-born dead,
Let my people go."

"No more shall they in bondage toil,
Let my people go;
Let them come out with Egypt's spoil,
Let my people go."

The Lord told Moses what to do,
Let my people go;
To lead the children of Israel through,
Let my people go.

Go down, Moses,
Way down in Egyptland,
Tell old Pharaoh,
"Let my people go!"

SPONDEE, SPONDAIC (spon'-dee, spon-day'-ik; Greek, "solemn drink-offering") A *foot consisting of two stressed syllables (´ ´), such as "hushed crowd" or "skulls crack."

Spondaic meter is virtually impossible in English, since any minor words (such as *and*, *the*, and *of*) and any polysyllabic words (such as *conflagration*) would introduce unstressed syllables into a line. Spondees sound emphatic. They can be substituted for most *iambic feet; for example, "The birds are flying close" could become "Dark birds fly close—thick flocks," three spondees instead of three iambs. A spondee often follows a *pyrrhic foot (two unstressed syllables, a combination called a *minor ionic, as in the phrase "with a rough push").

SPRUNG RHYTHM A term coined by nineteenth-century Welsh poet and priest Gerard Manley Hopkins. Essentially it is a dynamic term for *accentual poetry, the emphatically stressed lines Hopkins found in nursery rhymes and Old English verse. A Hopkins *sonnet in sprung rhythm will count five strong accents but will allow a large, variable number of unstressed syllables.

THE WINDHOVER / Gerard Manley Hopkins (1844–1889)

To Christ our Lord

I caught this morning morning's minion, king-
   dom of daylight's dauphin, dapple-dawn-drawn Falcon, in his
      riding
Of the rolling level underneath him steady air, and striding
High there, how he rung upon the rein of a wimpling wing
In his ecstasy! then off, off forth on swing,
   As a skate's heel sweeps smooth on a bow-bend: the hurl and
      gliding
Rebuffed the big wind. My heart in hiding
Stirred for a bird,—the achieve of, the mastery of the thing!

Brute beauty and valour and act, oh, air, pride, plume, here
   Buckle! AND the fire that breaks from thee then, a billion
Times told lovelier, more dangerous, O my chevalier!

No wonder of it: shéer plód make plough down sillion
Shine, and blue-bleak embers, ah my dear,
   Fall, gall themselves, and gash gold-vermilion.

NOTE: The apparently short lines "riding" and "gliding" actually belong to the lines above them. The poem is a Petrarchan sonnet.

S

STANZA (stan'-zuh; Italian, "room") A group of *lines gathered together as a unit, like a paragraph in prose. Usually it is surrounded by white space above and below, but stanza breaks can also be indicated by indentations, a metrical pattern, or a recurring rhyme scheme (such as couplets). Also called *strophe and verse paragraph (especially for blank verse groups of irregular numbers of lines, and for free-verse line groups).

Here is a list of terms for various stanzas:

Number of lines	General term for Stanza	Specific types of Stanza
1	*monostich	
2	*couplet	*distich, *elegiac distich, *heroic couplet, *ghazal
3	*tercet	*triplet, *terza rima, *haiku, *blues
4	*quatrain	*alcaics, *ballad stanza, Horatian *ode, hymn stanza, heroic quatrain, *In Memoriam stanza, *pantoum, *rubai, *sapphics
5	*quintain	*cinquain, *limerick, *quintilla, *tanka
6	*sixain	*Burns stanza, *stave of six, *sestina, sestet (in *sonnet)
7	septet	*rhyme royal
8	•octave	*ballade, *ottava rima, octave (in *sonnet), *triolet
9		*Spenserian stanza

NOTE: The last stanza of a sestina or a ballade (the envoi or "send-off") contains fewer lines than the other stanzas in the poem.

Some poems combine different stanzas lengths. A *villanelle, for instance, consists of five tercets and a quatrain.

Stanzas of more than eight lines are simply known as nine-line stanzas, ten-line stanzas, and so on. A long stanza (over eight lines) tends to break into smaller units. The fourteen-line *sonnet, for example, can sometimes work as a stanza, but more often it consists of three quatrains and a couplet or an octave and a sestet.

STAVE OF SIX A six-line stanza in *iambic pentameter or iambic tetrameter rhyming *ababcc*; a kind of *sixain (six-line stanza). The stave of six combines an alternating *quatrain and a *couplet.

I WANDERED LONELY AS A CLOUD / William Wordsworth (1770–1850)

> I wandered lonely as a cloud
> That floats on high o'er vales and hills,
> When all at once I saw a crowd,
> A host, of golden daffodils;
> Beside the lake, beneath the trees,
> Fluttering and dancing in the breeze.
>
> Continuous as the stars that shine
> And twinkle on the milky way,
> They stretched in never-ending line
> Along the margin of a bay:
> Ten thousand saw I at a glance,
> Tossing their heads in sprightly dance.
>
> The waves beside them danced; but they
> Outdid the sparkling waves in glee;
> A poet could not but be gay,
> In such a jocund company;
> I gazed—and gazed—but little thought
> What wealth the show to me had brought:
>
> For oft, when on my couch I lie
> In vacant or in pensive mood,

> They flash upon that inward eye
> Which is the bliss of solitude;
> And then my heart with pleasure fills,
> And dances with the daffodils.

STICHIC (stik'-ik; Greek, "row, line") Not divided into *stanzas. A stichic poem is arranged as a continuous block of lines, with no stanza breaks, as in James Wright's "Ohioan Pastoral," which appears in POETRY. The Greek root *stich* means "line," so that a *monostich* is a single isolated line, a *distich* is a couplet, and a *hemistich* is a half-line.

STRESS A syllable that is emphasized (marked by ´ when scanning a poem); also called *accent or *beat.

STROPHE (stro'-fee; Greek, "turning") 1. A *stanza, sometimes used to distinguish one irregular in line lengths.

2. The first stanza of a Pindaric or Greek choral *ode, metrically identical to the second stanza or *antistrophe (an-tih´-struh-fee)*, but metrically different from the third stanza or *epode (eh´-pode)*. Sometimes the strophe is called the "turn" (followed by "counter-turn" and "stand").

SUBJECT What a poem is literally about.

The subject of Wilfred Owen's poems, for example, is war. He writes about the lives and deaths of British soldiers in the trenches during World War I. Subject should be distinguished from *theme, which denotes what the poet is saying about the subject, his attitude toward it, as Owen's themes are pity, the pointlessness of war, and the camaraderie of men.

In *The Triggering Town*, Richard Hugo asserts that a poem has

two subjects, the initiating or triggering subject, which starts the poem or "causes" the poem to be written, and the real or generated subject, which the poet comes to say or mean, and which is generated or discovered in the poem during the writing.

SUBSTITUTION (also *variation*) A *foot that is different from that of the predominant meter of a line; the changing of a foot, replacing the expected foot, such as an iamb (˘ ´) in a line of iambic pentameter, with a different one, such as a *trochee (´ ˘) or *spondee (´ ´), that alters the meter's regularity without destroying the meter; a means of making the rhythm of a metrical line more interesting, more surprising, and often more melodic than a line that moves like a metronome.

SURREALISM A literary and artistic movement that grew out of Dadaism and Futurism and stressed the importance of dreams, the unconscious, nonrational thought, free associations, startling imagery, and strange *juxtapositions.

André Breton's *Surrealist Manifesto* launched the movement in 1924; its early members included Louis Aragon, Paul Éluard, and Pierre Reverdy. Breton defines surrealism as "Psychic automatism in its pure state, by which one proposes to express—verbally, by means of the written word, or in any other way—the actual functioning of thought. Dictated by thought, in the absence of any control exercised by reason, exempt from aesthetic or moral preoccupation." Breton also declared that surrealism was based on belief in "the superior reality of certain forms of previously neglected associations," "the omnipotence of dream," and "the disinterested play of thought." Surrealism also thrived in the paintings of Max Ernst, Salvador Dali, Giorgio de Chirico, and René Magritte. One Surrealist, Jean (or Hans) Arp, excelled at poetry, painting, and sculpture. Michael Benedikt's anthology, *The Poetry of Surrealism*, contains translations of Surrealist poems from French.

Robert Bly, however, remarks that "French surrealism and Spanish surrealism both contain wonderful leaps, but whereas French surrealism often … leaps without any specific emotion—many believe that the unconscious does not have emotions—the Spanish poets believe that it does." Discussing Federico Garcia Lorca's *Poet in New York*, Bly goes on to say, "Powerful feeling makes the mind associate faster, and evidently the presence of swift association makes the emo-

S

tions still more alive; it increases the adrenalin flow, just as chanting awakens many emotions that the chanter was hardly aware of at the moment he began chanting." Bly calls this wild, passionate, associative poetry "leaping poetry." Other Spanish surrealists include Blas de Otero and the South Americans César Vallejo and Pablo Neruda (although much of his poetry is not surrealist).

A BRANCH OF NETTLE ENTERS THROUGH THE WINDOW / André Breton (1896–1966; tr. David Antin)

The woman with the crepe paper body
The red fish in the fireplace
Whose memory is pieced together from a multitude of
    small watering places for distant ships
Who laughs like an ember fit to be set in snow
And sees the night expand and contract like an accordion
The armor of the grass
Hilt of the dagger gate
Falling in flakes from the wings of the sphinx
Rolling the floor of the Danube
For which time and space destroy themselves
On the evening when the watchman of the inner eye
    trembles like an elf
Isn't this the stake of the battle to which my
    dreams surrender
Brittle bird
Rocked by the telegraph wires of trance
Shattering in the great lake created by the numbers
    of its song
This is the double heart of the lost wall
Gripped by grasshoppers of the blood
That drag my likeness through the mirror
My broken hands
My caterpillar eyes
My long whalebone hairs
Whalebone sealed under brilliant black wax

HOME FROM A WALK / Federico Garcia Lorca (1898–1936;
tr. Robert Bly)

> Assassinated by the sky,
> between the forms that are moving toward the serpent,
> and the forms that are moving toward the crystal,
> I'll let my hair fall down.
>
> With the tree of amputated limbs that does not sing,
> and the boy with the white face of an egg.
>
> With all the tiny animals who have broken heads,
> and the ragged water that walks on its dry feet.
>
> With all the things that have a deaf and dumb fatigue,
> and the butterfly drowned in the inkpot.
>
> Stumbling over my face that changes every day,
> assassinated by the sky!

S

SYLLABICS, SYLLABIC METER (sih-lab'-ix, sih-lab'-ik) A
meter in which the number of syllables in a line is counted, not the
accents or lengths of syllables; the predominant meter of French and
Japanese poetry.

English and American poets such as Marianne Moore, Dylan
Thomas, and Kenneth Rexroth began experimenting with syllabic
verse in the first half of the twentieth century. It is a meter that often
doesn't sound metrical in English—both a plus and a minus. On the
one hand, it imposes an order that is not obvious but gives a sense
of regularity more felt than heard. It is a way to regulate the flow of
*free verse or prose, and to avoid the tick-tock of *accentual-syllabic
meter. On the other hand, some critics reject it as a true English meter
because it is hard to hear as a recurring pattern. Unlike *accentual
verse, the native meter of the Anglo-Saxons, syllabic meter is im-
ported and arouses some of the controversy still directed at free verse.

A syllabic poem may be measured in two ways. First, it may have
the same number of syllables in each of its lines. Philip Levine's
"Animals Are Passing from Our Lives," for instance, contains seven

syllables per line. In a syllabic poem with uniform line lengths, it helps to vary the number of accents from line to line, as Levine does.

Second, a syllabic poem may use and repeat a consistent stanza shape with differing numbers of syllables in different lines. The first lines of every stanza have the same syllable count, regardless of how many syllables appear in lines two, three, and so on. Giving the stanzas a graphic shape by indenting certain lines helps to suggest a regular pattern, an intricate meter that otherwise might be hidden. Each stanza of Marianne Moore's "The Fish" has a syllabic pattern of 1-3-9-6-8 and rhymes *aabbX* (the X being an unrhymed line).

Counting syllables, however, can be tricky. How many syllables are in "interesting," for example? Some people say it with three (like "int'resting") and some use four. In "The Fish," the word "opening" in line five is apparently counted as two syllables (like "op'ning"). But this kind of leeway makes meter flexible. Variation is the brains of repetition.

ANIMALS ARE PASSING FROM OUR LIVES /
Philip Levine (b. 1928)

It's wonderful how I jog
on four honed-down ivory toes
my massive buttocks slipping
like oiled parts with each light step.

I'm to market. I can smell
the sour, grooved block, I can smell
the blade that opens the hole
and the pudgy white fingers

that shake out the intestines
like a hankie. In my dreams
the snouts drool on the marble,
suffering children, suffering flies,

suffering the consumers
who won't meet their steady eyes
for fear they could see. The boy
who drives me along believes

that any moment I'll fall
on my side and drum my toes
like a typewriter or squeal
and shit like a new housewife

discovering television,
or that I'll turn like a beast
cleverly to hook his teeth
with my teeth. No. Not this pig.

THE FISH

wade
through black jade.
    Of the crow-blue mussel-shells, one keeps
    adjusting the ash-heaps;
        opening and shutting itself like

an
injured fan.
    The barnacles which encrust the side
    of the wave, cannot hide
        there for the submerged shafts of the

sun,
split like spun
    glass, move themselves with spotlight swiftness
    into the crevices—
        in and out, illuminating

the
turquoise sea
    of bodies. The water drives a wedge
    of iron through the iron edge
        of the cliff; whereupon the stars,

pink
rice-grains, ink-
    bespattered jelly-fish, crabs like green

S

lilies, and submarine
toadstools, slide each on the other.

All
external
marks of abuse are present on this
defiant edifice—
all the physical features of

ac-
cident—lack
of cornice, dynamite grooves, burns, and
hatchet strokes, these things stand
out on it; the chasm-side is

dead.
Repeated
evidence has proved that it can live
on what can not revive
its youth. The sea grows old in it.

—Marianne Moore (1887–1972)

SYLLABLE A speech unit consisting of a single, uninterrupted cluster of sound, as brief as a single vowel (such as *I*) or as long as a vowel or diphthong surrounded by consonant combinations (such as *stretch*, *breathe*, and *sphinx*). For example, *cluster* has two syllables and the first one is accented or emphasized. A monosyllabic word consists of one syllable (such as *crow*, *speak*, and *bench*). A polysyllabic word consists of two or more syllables (such as *breakfast*, *congregate*, and *impervious*).

SYMBOL (Greek, "to throw together") An image that radiates meanings perhaps hard to express in other words but which can be felt, as in the symbols of dreams.

Symbolic language is figurative (in that the literal image suggests something more), but a symbol differs significantly from a *metaphor.

In a metaphor, one thing is compared to another so that its own nature becomes clearer and more vivid; the two things must be otherwise dissimilar, so that the comparison offers a pleasurable surprise ("Why haven't I thought of that before?"). A symbol, however, is an image that plunges to the soul, or the unconscious, of the reader ("I recognize that, but how?"). It resembles a metaphor, but with the difference that the symbolic image is like a metaphorical *vehicle (or likeness) without a *tenor (or subject)—or without a single, definable tenor. It is a kite without someone on the ground holding its string.

William Butler Yeats, who viewed the poet's use of symbols as an imitation of the magician's, declares, "It is only by ancient symbols, by symbols that have numberless meanings besides the one or two the writer lays an emphasis upon, or the half-score he knows of, that any highly subjective art can escape from the barrenness and shallowness of a too conscious arrangement, into the abundance and depth of Nature." Yeats also defined symbols as "images that are living souls."

SYMBOLIST POETRY Nineteenth-century artistic and literary movement that raised the symbol to prime importance.

A good example is the use of *leit-motif,* a repeated melodic phrase that suggests some aspect of a character or a theme (such as yearning), in the operas of Richard Wagner. Symbolists rejected argument in favor of music and image, elements that would appeal more to the unconscious mind than to the conscious, aiming for the depths of the soul instead of the mental surface. The movement, influenced strongly by the works of Edgar Allan Poe, began in France and included poets Charles Baudelaire, Arthur Rimbaud, Paul Verlaine, Stéphane Mallarmé, and Paul Valéry. *The Symbolist Movement in Literature,* by Arthur Symons, popularized symbolism in English, including William Butler Yeats among its poets. Yeats, in turn, looked back to the poet-painter William Blake as an earlier symbolist.

CORRESPONDENCES / Charles Baudelaire (1821–1867;
tr. Richard Howard)

> The pillars of Nature's temple are alive
> and sometimes yield perplexing messages;
> forests of symbols between us and the shrine
> remark our passage with accustomed eyes.
>
> Like long-held echoes, blending somewhere else
> into one deep and shadowy unison
> as limitless as darkness and as day,
> the sounds, the scents, the colors correspond.
>
> There are odors succulent as young flesh,
> sweet as flutes, and green as any grass,
> while others—rich, corrupt and masterful—
>
> possess the power of such infinite things
> as incense, amber, benjamin and musk,
> to praise the senses' raptures and the mind's.

SYNCOPE (sing'-ko-pee; Greek, "to cut short") The contraction of a word, especially to make it fit the meter more neatly, as when "never" becomes "ne'er." In "Eloïsa to Abelard," Alexander Pope often uses syncope, as in the line "But o'er the twilight groves and dusky caves," in which "o'er" stands for "over."

SYNECDOCHE (sih-nek'-duh-kee; Greek, "taking jointly") A figure of speech in which a part of something indicates the whole, like "talking head" for "television commentator" or "mouthpiece" for "lawyer."

It is similar to *metonymy*, which uses an object associated with something, like "the crown" to indicate royalty or a monarch. Both of these devices are useful in poetry, in that they focus more closely on something concrete, like a movie camera zooming in on a significant object. (*See* RHETORICAL DEVICES.)

SYNTAX (sin'-tax; Greek, "arrangement") The arrangement of words in a sentence; the tactics of word order. The first line of Marilyn Nelson's "Diverne's Waltz" ("Diverne stands in the kitchen as they dance") could be rearranged in a number of ways, none as metrically satisfying: "In the kitchen, Diverne stands as they dance"; "Diverne, in the kitchen, stands as they dance"; "As they dance, Diverne stands in the kitchen." In each case, the syntax differs. (The poem appears in QUATRAIN.)

A sentence in an unusual word order would exemplify "wrenched" or "twisted" or "convoluted" syntax. For example, in poem 188 of *The Dream Songs*, John Berryman writes, "Murdered the ruses that would quack me clear / The orchard squeaks."

T

TAILED SONNET (also called a *Caudate* [caw-day'] *sonnet*) A *sonnet with a coda.

To the fourteen rhymed lines of a sonnet, the poet adds an extension, beginning with a short line (usually three *feet) and following it with a rhymed pentameter *couplet. The short line picks up the rhyme of the fourteenth line, thus linking the tail to the rest of the sonnet. The poet can then add a second tail, also beginning with a short line. This full, double-tailed rhyme pattern is *abbaabba cdecde (e)ff (f)gg*—the lines in parentheses being shorter than the lines in the rest of the poem. John Milton and Gerard Manley Hopkins both wrote tailed sonnets.

TANKA (tahn'-ka; also called *waka* and *uta*) Japanese verse form consisting of five lines with a syllable count of 5-7-5-7-7 (or thirty-one syllables in all).

Numerically, a tanka is like a *haiku with two seven-syllable lines added on. As might be imagined, the form is less concentrated than haiku, more casual and conversational, less mysterious, less spiritual. Imagery is important, but there is ample room for statement and declaration, too.

Influenced by Chinese poetry a few centuries old, tanka succeeded the "long poem" (or *chōka*), which alternated lines of five and seven syllables. The new form gained popularity in the seventh and eighth centuries. Here is a tanka by Sami Mansei (early eighth century, translated by Steven D. Carter), which illustrates both the syllabic arrangement and the essential nature of the form:

> Our life in this world—
> to what shall I compare it?
> It is like a boat
>   rowing out at break of day,
> leaving not a trace behind.

The following three tanka show the importance of poetry in relations between members of the imperial court. Carter's translations differ slightly from the 5-7-5-7-7 syllable pattern of the originals, but they are very close.

Emperor Tenji (626–71; ruled from 668):

> At the broad sea's edge
>   the setting sun casts its gleam
>   on banners of cloud:
> this night, the moon of this night—
> so clearly may its rays too shine!

Princess Nukada (seventh century), a poem written when she was longing for Emperor Tenji:

> Waiting for you,
> I languish, full of longing—
> and then the blinds
>   of my house flutter slightly,
> blown by the autumn wind.

Princess Kagami (seventh century), a reply to the poem above:

> If even the wind ...
> I think, in envy of you.
> If even the wind
>   would answer my vain waiting—
> of what could I complain?

TERCET (ter'-sit; Italian, "third") Any *stanza of three lines; some-times confined to three lines that rhyme, either consecutively in a *triplet* (*aaa*) or interlocking with another stanza in a pattern called *terza rima* (*aba bcb cdc*, etc.); also called a *tristich*.

There is some disagreement about the terms for three-line stan-zas. Paul Fussell, in *Poetic Meter & Poetic Form*, offers a reasonable so-lution: "Three lines of any length ending with the same rhyme word are called triplets, or, interchangeably, tercets. It is probably better to use tercet only to distinguish three lines organized other than by a thrice-repeated rhyme." A stanza of three unrhymed lines could thus be called a tercet or a tristich. (*See* HAIKU, TERZA RIMA, *and* TRIPLET.)

THESE ARE THE DAYS WHEN BIRDS COME BACK /
Emily Dickinson (1830–1886)

These are the days when Birds come back —
A very few—a Bird or two—
To take a backward look.

These are the days when skies resume
The old—old sophistries of June—
A blue and gold mistake.

Oh fraud that cannot cheat the Bee—
Almost thy plausibility
Induces my belief.

Till ranks of seeds their witness bear—
And softly thro' the altered air
Hurries a timid leaf.

Oh Sacrament of summer days,
Oh Last Communion in the Haze—
Permit a child to join.

Thy sacred emblems to partake—
Thy consecrated bread to take
And thine immortal wine!

TERZA RIMA (tare'-tsuh ree'-muh; Italian, "third rhyme") *Tercets with an interwoven rhyme scheme, invented by Dante Alighieri for *The Divine Comedy*: *aba bcb cdc ded efe fgf*, etc. The poem (or individual section, called a *canto* by Dante) usually ends with a single line or a *couplet, rhyming with the previous tercet's middle line. But it may also end with a tercet, its middle line rhyming with the opening tercet's first and third lines, making the form circular.

When Dante settled on this interlocking form for his religious epic, he had the Trinity in mind: Father, Son, and Holy Ghost. A kind of Roman Catholic numerology pervades the poem, with its "threefold" arrangement of *Inferno*, *Purgatorio*, and *Paradiso*.

Geoffrey Chaucer introduced terza rima into English with sixteen lines embedded in section III of "A Complaint to His Lady," most of which is written in other forms. Percy Bysshe Shelley's "Ode to the West Wind" is the best known English poem in terza rima, but he also used the form for "Prince Athanase" and "The Triumph of Life." Lord Byron, whose translation of a passage from Dante's *Inferno* follows, wrote "The Prophecy of Dante" in terza rima. W.H. Auden uses it in section II ("The Supporting Cast, Sotto Voce") of "The Sea and the Mirror." Archibald MacLeish uses *assonance instead of true rhymes in much of the terza rima of his *Conquistador*. T.S. Eliot suggests the difficult rhyme scheme merely by alternating *masculine and *feminine endings in "Little Gidding," during a passage that begins "In the uncertain hour before the morning," imitating the Brunetto Latini episode in Canto XV of Dante's *Inferno*.

FRANCESCA OF RIMINI (from *INFERNO*, Canto V) / Dante Alighieri (1265–1321; tr. George Gordon, Lord Byron)

"The land where I was born sits by the seas,
    Upon that shore to which the Po descends
    With all his followers in search of peace.
Love, which the gentle heart soon apprehends,
    Seized him for the fair person which was ta'en
    From me, and me even yet the mode offends.
Love, who to none beloved to love again
    Remits, seized me with wish to please so strong
    That, as thou seest, yet, yet it doth remain.

Love to one death conducted us along,
> But Caina waits for him our life who ended."
> These were the accents utter'd by her tongue.
Since I first listen'd to these souls offended,
> I bow'd my visage, and so kept it till
> "What think'st thou?" said the bard—then I unbended
And recommenced, "Alas! unto such ill
> How many sweet thoughts, what strong ecstasies
> Led these their evil fortune to fulfill!"
And then I turn'd unto their side my eyes,
> And said, "Francesca, thy sad destinies
> Have made me sorrow till the tears arise.
But tell me, in the season of sweet sighs
> By what and how thy love to passion rose
> So as his dim desires to recognise?"
Then she to me: "The greatest of all woes
> Is to remind us of our happy days
> In misery, and that thy teacher knows.
But if to learn our passion's first root preys
> Upon thy spirit with such sympathy,
> I will do even as he who weeps and says.
We read one day for pastime, seated nigh,
> Of Lancelot, how love enchain'd him too;
> We were alone, quite unsuspiciously.
But oft our eyes met, and our cheeks in hue
> All o'er discolour'd by that reading were;
> But one point only wholly us o'erthrew.
When we read the long-sigh'd-for smile of her
> To be thus kiss'd by such devoted lover,
> He, who from me can be divided ne'er,
Kiss'd my mouth, trembling in the act all over—
> Accursed was the book and he who wrote!
> That day no further leaf we did uncover."
While thus one spirit told us of their lot
> The other wept, so that with pity's thralls
> I swoon'd, as if by death I had been smote,
And fell down even as a dead body falls.

NEWS HEADLINES FROM THE HOMER NOBLE FARM /
Paul Muldoon (b. 1951)

I

That case-hardened cop.
A bull moose in a boghole
brought him to a stop.

II

From his grassy knoll
he has you in his crosshairs,
the accomplice mole.

III

This sword once a share.
This forest a fresh-faced farm.
This stone once a stair.

IV

The birch crooks her arm,
as if somewhat more inclined
to welcome the swarm.

V

He has, you will find,
two modes only, the chipmunk:
fast-forward; rewind.

VI

The smell, like a skunk,
of coffee about to perk.
Thelonious Monk.

VII

They're the poker work
of some sort of woodpecker,
these holes in the bark.

VIII

My new fact checker
claims that *pilus* means "pestle."
My old fact checker.

IX

The Rose and Thistle.
Where the hummingbird drops in
to wet his whistle.

X

Behind the wood bin
a garter snake snaps itself,
showing us some skin.

XI

Like most bits of delf,
the turtle's seen at its best
on one's neighbor's shelf.

XII

Riding two abreast
on their stripped-down, souped-up bikes,
bears in leather vests.

XIII

The eye-shaded shrike.
BIRD BODIES BURIED IN BOG'S
a headline he'll spike.

XIV

Steady, like a log
riding a sawmill's spillway,
the steady coydog.

XV

The cornet he plays
was Bolden's, then Beiderbecke's,
this lonesome blue jay.

XVI

Some fresh auto wreck.
Slumped over a horn. Sump pool.
The frog's neck-braced neck.

XVII

Brillo pads? Steel wool?
The regurrrrrrrrrrrrrrrrrrrrrrgitations, what,
of a long-eared owl?

XVIII

The jet with the jot.
The drive-in screen with the sky.
The blood with the blot.

XIX

How all seems to vie,
not just my sleeping laptop
with the first firefly.

NOTE: Toward the end of his life, Robert Frost owned and lived on the Homer Noble Farm, now the property of Middlebury College in Vermont. Paul Muldoon spent a summer in residence there. He calls these sections "snapshots." They are also *haiku, with a syllabic pattern of 5-7-5. Most haiku are unrhymed, but other poets who rhyme theirs (usually just the first and third lines) include Richard Wilbur and James Merrill.

THEME (Greek, "proposition") A poem's attitude toward its *subject; what it says about its subject.

Sometimes the two words, *theme* and *subject*, are used synonymously, but in poetry the theme is an outgrowth of the subject, the poem's comment on that subject. Sometimes, however, theme is used metaphorically in its musical sense, as a recurrent melodic passage. Thus Theodore Roethke talks about poems that are "written to be heard, with the themes often coming alternately, as in music. ..."

TITLE AS FIRST LINE Early in the twentieth century, some poets started using titles as first lines of their poems. Marianne Moore was a pioneer of this device:

NOVICES

anatomize their work

Traditionally, many poems have used their first lines as titles, especially when the poet provided none. Moore and like-minded poets simply dispensed with the redundancy. As a bonus, there is a gap, a definite pause, between title and the next line. It exemplifies a new kind of *enjambment (a run-on from one line to the next). Moore can even play with subtle variations from title to next line, as in the following example:

THE MIND IS AN ENCHANTING THING

is an enchanted thing

Even though this title is an essential part of the body of the poem, it resides outside the stanzaic structure, another source of interesting tension. The reader who skips over the title will be surprised to land in the middle of the opening sentence. As in much Modernist art, a title that serves double duty as the first line also jolts the perceiver into a heightened sense of attention. Poems that use this technique include Sylvia Plath's "You're" (in FIGURATIVE LANGUAGE) and Moore's "The Fish" (in SYLLABIC METER).

TONE The emotional spin a poet puts on his words; the edge or attitude in the *voice of a poem. When we talk to someone, we can hear his tone of voice—how he says something. Sometimes we can even see it (tongue in cheek, for example). In a poem, tone is the coloration of the words, their shading, their warmth or coolness—as in painting. It is also how they sound, their pitch (high or low), harmony (sweet or shrill), and volume (loud or soft)—as in music. *(See IRONY.)*

TRANSLATION The difficult art of capturing a poem in the words of another language.

The translator will often be a poet himself: George Chapman and Alexander Pope translated Homer from the Greek; John

Dryden translated Virgil from the Latin; in our time, Richard Wilbur has translated Molière from the French. The translator's inclusions and omissions, discoveries and losses, compromises and luck will determine the relative success of the translation. Some poets, such as Robert Lowell, refer to their versions of foreign originals as *imitations, permitting themselves the liberty to change the originals for their own purposes, adding images, deleting whole *stanzas, rearranging the order. Arthur Waley, a scholar and celebrated translator of Chinese poetry, calls Ezra Pound's version of Li Po's "Exile's Letter" a "brilliant paraphrase." The poet who takes liberties will probably affix a headnote to the poem, something like "after Baudelaire."

Translation is useful to the poet, who can (1) bring new works from another language into English; (2) make newer, more up-to-date versions of already translated works (since, as Richard Howard has remarked, "translations date; originals do not"); (3) have an inexhaustible supply of raw material for poems (even if the originals are someone else's); and (4) write original poems based on, inspired by, or responding to poems from another language.

In the following translations of Catullus, there is a range of approaches. Walter Savage Landor uses *rhyme, although the original does not, and adds a third line to the original *couplet. Ezra Pound uses the idiomatic "it beats me" as a brilliant play on words, meaning "I don't know," "it hurts me," and "it defeats me." Louis Zukofsky imitates the sound of the original Latin and use related English words, such as *nescience*, for Latin words, such as *nescio*. Charles Martin's version is simple, clear, and close to the original. Frank Bidart's version should be called an imitation, since it departs from the original by adding new material, the metaphor of the "Ignorant fish." Nevertheless, in finding a new, modern, powerful equivalent for what Catullus presents, he revives the poem in the truest, most imaginative sense. After all, for a Roman like Catullus, the image of crucifixion invoked by *excrucior* was as real and immediate as Bidart's image of a fish writhing on a hook.

Odi et amo. quare id faciam, fortasse requiris.
nescio, sed fieri sentio et excrucior.

—Catullus (c. 85-55 B.C.E.)

I love and hate. Ah! never ask why so!
I hate and love ... and that is all I know.
I see 'tis folly, but I feel 'tis woe.

—Walter Savage Landor (1775–1864)

I hate and love. Why? you may ask but
It beats me. I feel it done to me and ache.

—Ezra Pound (1885–1972)

O th'hate I move love. Quarry it fact I am, for that's
    so re queries.
Nescience, say th'fiery scent I owe whets crookeder.

—Louis Zukofsky (1904–1978)

I hate & love. And if you should ask how I can do both,
    I couldn't say; but I feel it, and it shivers me.

—Charles Martin (b. 1942)

I hate *and* love. Ignorant fish, who even
wants the fly while writhing.

—Frank Bidart (b. 1939)

TRIADIC LINE (also called *triadic stanza*) *Free-verse lines
arranged and indented in three steps.

Much of William Carlos Williams's later work appears in the triadic line, although he's free about altering this pattern. He uses it to
demonstrate what he calls the *variable foot*, which stipulates that a
group of words, whether of one syllable or many, can be metrically
equivalent, each foot "variable" in actual length. Skeptics might consider this concept a rationalization, an attempt to graft a metrical
basis onto free verse. Hugh Kenner says of Williams, who had suffered
several strokes: "Up at dawn, he typed, letter by letter, the left hand

guiding and letting fall the right over an electrified keyboard. His eyes followed a line of type with ease but had trouble finding the start of the next line; the three-step indentation he came to favor was in part a way of making a page he could reread."

"The Descent" was Williams' first poem in this new measure.

THE DESCENT / William Carlos Williams (1883–1963)

The descent beckons
            as the ascent beckoned.
                        Memory is a kind
of accomplishment,
            a sort of renewal
                        even
an initiation, since the spaces it opens are new places
            inhabited by hordes
                        heretofore unrealized,
of new kinds—
            since their movements
                        are toward new objectives
(even though formerly they were abandoned).

No defeat is made up entirely of defeat—since
the world it opens is always a place
            formerly
                        unsuspected. A
world lost,
            a world unsuspected,
                        beckons to new places
and no whiteness (lost) is so white as the memory
of whiteness.

With evening, love wakens
            though its shadows
                        which are alive by reason
of the sun shining—
            grow sleepy now and drop away
                        from desire.

Love without shadows stirs now
        beginning to awaken
                as night
advances.

The descent
        made up of despairs
              and without accomplishment
realizes a new awakening:
              which is a reversal
of despair.
        For what we cannot accomplish, what
is denied to love,
        what we have lost in the anticipation—
           a descent follows,
endless and indestructible.

TRIOLET (tree-oh-lay'; French, "little trio") Fixed form from the Middle Ages, eight lines rhyming *ABaAabAB* (the capital letters representing repeated lines or *refrains).

Originally a kind of *rondeau* or *rondel*, this form has been recognized as a triolet since the late fifteenth century. Twentieth-century triolets include Robert Bridges's "When First We Met" and Sandra McPherson's "Triolet" (beginning "She was in love with the same danger"). Barbara Howes ("Early Supper") and Dana Gioia ("The Country Wife") have used the triolet as a *stanza form in longer poems. *(See* RONDEAU *for a chart that shows the now-fixed patterns of the forms, including the triolet, that began as rondeaux.)*

THE COQUETTE, AND AFTER / Thomas Hardy (1840–1928)

I

For long the cruel wish I knew
That your free heart should ache for me
While mine should bear no ache for you;
For long—the cruel wish!—I knew
How men can feel, and craved to view

My triumph—fated not to be
For long! ... The cruel wish I knew
That your free heart should ache for me!

II

At last one pays the penalty—
The woman—women always do.
My farce, I found, was tragedy
At last! —One pays the penalty
With interest when one, fancy-free,
Learns love, learns shame. ... Of sinners two
At last *one* pays the penalty—
The woman—women always do!

TRIPLET A three-line *stanza rhymed *aaa.*

Some critics apply triplet as a general term for any three-line
stanza, rhymed or not. *(See* TERCET *for a discussion of the terminology
that designates a three-line unit.)*

Poets who write in *heroic couplets, such as Alexander Pope, feel
free to insert a triplet now and then. A bracket in the margin typically marks where the three rhymed lines appear. John Dryden likes
to stretch out the third line by an extra foot, so that it becomes an
*alexandrine (iambic hexameter).

UPON JULIA'S CLOTHES / Robert Herrick (1591–1674)

Whenas in silks my Julia goes,
Then, then, methinks, how sweetly flows
That liquefaction of her clothes.

Next, when I cast mine eyes, and see
That brave vibration, each way free,
O, how that glittering taketh me!

TROCHEE, TROCHAIC (tro′-kee; tro-kay′-ik; Greek, "running")
A *foot consisting of a *stress followed by an *unstressed syllable
($ ´ \smile $). Trochaic words include *basket, hoping, purple,* and *rabbit.*

327

Trochee

Trochaic meter, like *iambic, is called *duple meter*—because each foot contains two syllables. The opening lines of William Blake's "The Lamb" are in trochaic trimeter:

Líttlĕ | Lámb, whŏ | mádĕ thĕe?

Dóst thŏu | knów whŏ | mádĕ thĕe?

Trochaic tetrameter consists of four trochees (´ ˘ | ´ ˘ | ´ ˘ | ´ ˘). When the final unstressed syllable is omitted (´ ˘ | ´ ˘ | ´ ˘ | ´), the line is *catalectic, as in these lines from John Donne's "Song":

Go and catch a falling star,
    Get with child a mandrake root,
Tell me where all past years are,
    Or who cleft the devil's foot.

It is an emphatic meter, as heard in Longfellow's *Hiawatha* and countless parodies. William Blake's frequent use of trochaic tetrameter, in poems such as "The Tyger" and "Never Seek to Tell Thy Love," suggests both the childlike simplicity and the mystical power inherent in this measure. It is used for incantation in Shakespeare's *Macbeth*:

I.WITCH.   Round about the cauldron go;
            In the poison'd entrails throw.
            Toad, that under cold stone
            Days and nights has thirty-one
            Swelt'red venom sleeping got,
            Boil thou first i' th' charmed pot.

ALL.   Double, double, toil and trouble;
            Fire burn and cauldron bubble.

Acceptable variations include omitting the final unstressed syllable and adding an unstressed syllable at the beginning of a line (used too frequently, however, this variation will convert the trochaic meter into iambic). *(See* ANACRUSIS *and* CATALEXIS.*)*

FALL, LEAVES, FALL / Emily Brontë (1818–1848)

Fall, leaves, fall; die, flowers, away;
Lengthen night and shorten day;
Every leaf speaks bliss to me
Fluttering from the autumn tree.
I shall smile when wreaths of snow
Blossom where the rose should grow;
I shall sing when night's decay
Ushers in a drearier day.

T

UBI SUNT (uh'-bih suhnt', "uh" pronounced as in "put"; Latin, "where are") Poetic theme in which the poet asks "where are" certain people, where have they gone. The theme began in Medieval Latin, with the formula *ubi sunt* used to introduce a roll call of the dead or missing and to suggest how transitory life is.

The best-known *ubi sunt* poem—François Villon's ballade whose *refrain is "But where are the snows of yester-year?"—appears in BALLADE.

UNSTRESSED SYLLABLE A syllable that is not emphasized, like the *a* in *aghast* or the *ish* in *churlish*; called "offbeat" in Derek Attridge's beat-offbeat system of metrical analysis. *(See* SCANSION.*)*

In an *iambic line, it is hard to find three unstressed syllables together; the ear wants to give the middle one a slight accent. In an *accentual line, on the other hand, only the heavy stresses are counted, so a number of unstressed syllables can accumulate before the next loud thump comes along. *Syllabic verse and *free verse can also have an indefinite number of unstressed syllables between stresses, a condition close to that of *prose (except for the crucial importance of the *line).

VARIABLE FOOT A term coined by William Carlos Williams as a metrical explanation for his own *free verse. A variable foot could contain an indefinite number of syllables, all adding up to a single *beat. Hugh Kenner calls this hypothetical measure a "rubber inch." When Kenner asked if he meant for "each line to take up the same time," Williams immediately replied "Yes" but then added "More or less."

In practice, Williams's poems in the *triadic line do have the feel of a three-beat meter, but that may derive largely from the visual appearance of the lines, arranged in three steps. In his entry on free verse in *The Princeton Encyclopedia of Poetry and Poetics* (1965), Williams says:

> The bracket of the customary foot has been expanded so that more syllables, words, or phrases can be admitted into its confines. The new unit thus created may be called the "variable foot," a term and a concept already accepted widely as a means of bringing the warring elements of freedom and discipline together. It rejects the standard of the conventionally fixed foot and suggests that measure varies with the idiom by which it is employed and the tonality of the individual poem. Thus, as in speech, the prosodic pattern is evaluated by criteria of effectiveness and expressiveness rather than mechanical syllable counts.

VARIATION 1. Changes in words, phrases, or lines that are otherwise repeated. *(See* REPETITION.*)*

2. A *foot that differs from that of the prevailing *meter. For example, in a line of *iambic pentameter, a *trochaic foot would be a variation, as in the first foot of Shakespeare's "Wĭshĭng | mĕ lĭke | tŏ ońe | mŏre rích | ĭn hópe" (Sonnet 29), in which "Wishing" is a *trochee; also called *substitution*.

3. A musical term that can be imitated in a set of poetic "variations on a theme"; one of several different looks at a subject, as in Wallace Stevens's "Thirteen Ways of Looking at a Blackbird."

VERSE (Latin, "furrow," from the verb meaning "to turn") 1. A *line of poetry.

2. Poetry written in lines. The opposite of *prose. *(See* POETRY.*)*

3. In some *songs, a *stanza that has different words whenever the same music recurs; as opposed to a *chorus, which repeats the same words, like a *refrain.

VERSE LETTER (also called *epistle, epistolary poem*, or *letter poem*) A poem written in the form of a letter.

Except in the case of an "open letter" or a "letter to the editor," most letters are addressed to one specific person by another specific person—two characters, one speaking and one listening. A letter in verse can be an actual letter. Marvin Bell and William Stafford exchanged the verse letters that eventually became the book *Segues*. But the letter can also be a vehicle for a *dramatic monologue, in which a character other than the author speaks, as in Richard Howard's "1801." Sometimes verse letters will include dates, salutations, complimentary closes, and "signatures," but often they will not.

V

LETTER / Robert Hass (b. 1941)

I had wanted to begin
by telling you I saw another
tanager below the pond
where I had sat for half an hour
feeding on wild berries
in the little clearing near the pines
that hide the lower field
and then looked up from red berries
to the quick red bird brilliant
in the light. I have seen
more yarrow and swaying
Queen Anne's lace around the woods
as hawkweed and nightshade
wither and drop seed. A new blue flower,
sweet, yellow-stamened, ovary inferior,
has recently sprung up.
                              But I had the odd
feeling, walking to the house
to write this down, that I had left
the birds and flowers in the field,
rooted or feeding. They are not in my
head, are not now on this page.
It was very strange to me, but I think
their loss was your absence. I wanted
to be walking up with Leif, the sun
behind us skipping off the pond,
the windy maple sheltering the house,
and find you there and say
here! a new blue flower (ovary inferior)
and busy Leif and Kris with naming
in a world I love. You even have
my field guide. It's you I love.
I have believed so long
in the magic of names and poems.

Verse Letter

I hadn't thought of them bodiless
at all. Tall Buttercup. Wild Vetch.
"Often I am permitted to return
to a meadow." It all seemed real to me
last week. Words. You are the body
of my world, root and flower, the
brightness and surprise of birds.
I miss you, love. Tell Leif
you're the names of things.

1801 / Richard Howard (b. 1929)

Among the Papers of the Envoy to Constantinople

May it please Lord Elgin, Earl of Kincardine,
to consider the undersign'd, sole author
and inventor of the Eidophusikon,

for the position so lately rejected
by Mr. Turner. On giving the measure
of its Effects, calm & storm both, sunset

or moonlight, the accurate imitation
of Nature's sounds: approaching thunder, the dash
of waves on a pebbly beach, the distant gun—

my Device was pronounc'd by no less a judge
than Richard Wilson, R.A.—the same who cried out
at the sight of Terni Cascade, "O well done,

water, by God!"—was pronounc'd, I say, by him
"highly successful in agitated seas,"
by reason of the high finish carrying

severally their satellites of colour
into the very center of the Pictures.
As it happens, your Lordship, I visited

the same Joseph Turner known to your Lordship
(I believe) only this week, and found a man
pacing to and fro before his pale muslin

on which the sick and wan Sun, in all the doubt
of darkness, was not allow'd to shed one ray,
but tears. Even as he work'd, pouring wet paint

onto paper till it was saturated,
then tore, then scratch'd, then scrubb'd in a frenzy
at the sheet, the Whole being chaos, until

as if by enchantment, the Scene appear'd then,
great ships gone to pieces in order to fling
magical oranges on the waves—but I

digress: even as he shew'd me two books fill'd
with studies from Nature, several tinted
on the spot—which he found, he said, much the most

valuable to him—this Turner discuss'd
the present urgency of your Lordship's need
for an artist who might draw Antiquities,

with suitable finish, before Removal,
by your Lordship's design, from Athens. He said
he could not, himself, endure the Ideal,

but enjoy'd and look'd for only *litter*—why
even his richest vegetation is confus'd,
he delights in shingle, debris, and mere heaps

of fallen stone. Upon communicating
the intelligence that your Lordship's stipend
must include assistance to Lady Elgin

in decorating fire-screens and the like,
the man turn'd back in some heat to his labour
upon what I took to be that mysterious

forest below London Bridge, where great ships ride,
sails filling or falling, disorder'd too
by the stress of anchorage, all beautiful

V

though wild beneath the Daemonic pressure
of his inquiry (with so much of the trowel,
surely a touch more *finishing* might be borne!).

Enough of Turner, I have not to speak here
of him, though what I saw was but the *scribbling*
of Painting, surely. What I would say is this:

I venture to suggest in myself a man
your Lordship, and my Lady, most certainly,
might rely upon for accurate Service,

work of a conclusive polish, not a sketch.
There is, may I make so bold, a point at which
in Turner's Picturesque, as Fuseli says,

two spiders, caressing or killing each other,
must have greatly the advantage, in roughness
of surface and intricacy of motion,

over every athletic or am'rous
Symplegma left by the Ancients. I do not
wish to speak further of the man who renounc'd

your Lordship's commission to copy marbles,
muttering (though plain to hear) "Antiquities
be damn'd, by Thames' shore we will die," and went on

raking at the sea with his untidy thumb;
but only to call your Lordship's kind notice
and gracious favour, for the appointed task,

to the creator of the Eidophusikon,
these many years a loyal British subject,
Yours, &c.

PHILIPPE-JACQUES DE LOUTHERBOURG.

NOTE: "The speaker had settled in England in 1771 on Garrick's invitation to superin-
tend scene-painting at Drury Lane. The Envoy to Constantinople was the seventh Earl of
Elgin, who arranged for the Parthenon frieze to be conveyed to England in 1803." (Richard
Howard) The English painter Joseph Turner lived from 1775 to 1851.

VERSE MIXED WITH PROSE A poetic form that includes both prose and *verse, or paragraphs and *stanzas, or *lines and unlined passages.

There are a number of possible combinations: *verse-prose, prose-verse, verse-prose-verse, prose-verse-prose,* and longer patterns of alternations. Japanese *haibun* intersperses *haiku within a prose work, often a travel journal.

TOURISTS / Yehuda Amichai (1924–2000;
tr. Glenda Abramson and Tudor Parfitt)

Visits of condolence is all we get from them.
They squat at the Holocaust Memorial,
They put on grave faces at the Wailing Wall
And they laugh behind heavy curtains
In their hotels.
They have their pictures taken
Together with our famous dead
At Rachel's Tomb and Herzl's Tomb
And on the top of Ammunition Hill.
They weep over our sweet boys
And lust over our tough girls
And hang up their underwear
To dry quickly
In cool, blue bathrooms.

Once I sat on the steps by a gate at David's Tower, I placed my two heavy baskets at my side. A group of tourists was standing around their guide and I became their target marker. "You see that man with the baskets? Just right of his head there's an arch from the Roman period. Just right of his head." "But he's moving, he's moving!" I said to myself: redemption will come only if their guide tells them, "You see that arch from the Roman period? It's not important: but next to it, left and down a bit, there sits a man who's bought fruit and vegetables for his family."

V

337

VERSET (ver'-set) Long lines in *Biblical verse and in poems such as Allen Ginsberg's *Howl*. A *versicle (ver´-sih-kul)* is a short Biblical passage which may be chanted by a priest and followed by the congregation's response.

VERSIFICATION The art of writing in *lines; in particular, the technical aspects of doing so: *rhythm and *meter, *rhyme, *enjambment and *end-stopping, *alliteration and *assonance. *(See* PROSODY *and* SCANSION.*)*

VILLANELLE (vil-uh-nel'; Italian, folk-song about rural life, from the Latin, "country house") A fixed form, usually nineteen lines in length, consisting of five *tercets and a *quatrain.

The first line serves as one *refrain (repeated in lines six, twelve, and eighteen), and the third line serves as another refrain (repeated in lines nine, fifteen, and nineteen). These refrains *rhyme with each other and with the opening line of each *stanza. The middle lines of each stanza rhyme with each other, so that there are only two different rhyme sounds (*a* and *b*) throughout the entire poem.

The villanelle began as a French adaptation of Italian folk songs about country people. The term had been used widely, for various lyrics with refrains, before the form took its current pattern from Jean Passerat's "Villanelle" after the turn of the seventeenth century. Despite all of the intricate, fussy rules, the villanelle has become a powerful form in twentieth-century poems such as E.A. Robinson's "The House on the Hill," Dylan Thomas's "Do Not Go Gentle into That Good Night," W.H. Auden's "If I Could Tell You," Theodore Roethke's "The Waking," and Elizabeth Bishop's "One Art." Although Passerat's prototype is written in *octosyllabics* (eight-syllable lines), most contemporary poets write their villanelles in *iambic pentameter or perhaps tetrameter.

Some poets, such as Leconte de Lisle and Donald Justice, have omitted two of the inner tercets. Some poets, such as Marilyn Hacker, have added two or three tercets before the final quatrain. Most poets feel free to alter the phrasing and punctuation of their refrains, changing them as they recur. *Enjambment (leading into a refrain, or out of one, or both) can help make this rigid form more flexible and expressive.

The pattern of repeated lines in a villanelle is so distinctive that some poets feel free to omit some or all of the rhymes. In "Little L.A. Villanelle," Carol Muske rhymes the refrains (which end in "rain" and "refrain") but does not rhyme most of the middle lines: "overflowed," "wipers," "mid-scream," "dreamed," "light," and "faster." Rita Dove begins "Parsley," a two-part poem, with an unrhymed villanelle called "The Cane Fields." *(See* CORRUPTED FORM, *"paradelle" and "terzanelle" in* INVENTED FORMS AND STANZAS, *and* PARODY.)

VILLANELLE
(*J'ay perdu ma tourterelle*) / Jean Passerat
(1534–1602; tr. John Drury)

	Villanelle Pattern	Rhyme
My dove has flown away from me:	Refrain One	a
Isn't there something I can do?	Line 2	b
I'll follow her where she may flee.	Refrain Two	a
You miss your darling's company,	Line 4	a
Alas! for me the same is true:	Line 5	b
My dove has flown away from me.	Refrain One	a
As your love proves its constancy,	Line 7	a
My faith will show its mettle too,	Line 8	b
I'll follow her where she may flee.	Refrain Two	a
Your moans recur incessantly;	Line 10	a
I swear my grief is never through:	Line 11	b
My dove has flown away from me.	Refrain One	a
Now that her beauty I can't see,	Line 13	a
Nothing is beautiful to view;	Line 14	b
I'll follow her where she may flee.	Refrain Two	a
Death, so often I've made my plea,	Line 16	a
Take now what is given to you:	Line 17	b
My dove has flown away from me,	Refrain One	a
I'll follow her where she may flee.	Refrain Two	a

V

DO NOT GO GENTLE INTO THAT GOOD NIGHT /
Dylan Thomas (1914–1953)

Do not go gentle into that good night,
Old age should burn and rave at close of day;
Rage, rage against the dying of the light.

Though wise men at their end know dark is right,
Because their words had forked no lightning they
Do not go gentle into that good night.

Good men, the last wave by, crying how bright
Their frail deeds might have danced in a green bay,
Rage, rage against the dying of the light.

Wild men who caught and sang the sun in flight,
And learn, too late, they grieved it on its way,
Do not go gentle into that good night.

Grave men, near death, who see with blinding sight
Blind eyes could blaze like meteors and be gay,
Rage, rage against the dying of the light.

And you, my father, there on the sad height,
Curse, bless, me now with your fierce tears, I pray.
Do not go gentle into that good night.
Rage, rage against the dying of the light.

from FIVE VILLANELLES (I) / Weldon Kees (1914–1955?)

The crack is moving down the wall.
Defective plaster isn't all the cause.
We must remain until the roof falls in.

It's mildly cheering to recall
That every building has its little flaws.
The crack is moving down the wall.

Here in the kitchen, drinking gin,
We can accept the damndest laws.
We must remain until the roof falls in.

And though there's no one here at all,
One searches every room because
The crack is moving down the wall.

Repairs? But how can one begin?
The lease has warnings buried in each clause.
We must remain until the roof falls in.

These nights one hears a creaking in the hall,
The sort of thing that gives one pause.
The crack is moving down the wall.
We must remain until the roof falls in.

ONE ART / Elizabeth Bishop (1911–1979)

The art of losing isn't hard to master;
so many things seem filled with the intent
to be lost that their loss is no disaster.

Lose something every day. Accept the fluster
of lost door keys, the hour badly spent.
The art of losing isn't hard to master.

Then practice losing farther, losing faster:
places, and names, and where it was you meant
to travel. None of these will bring disaster.

I lost my mother's watch. And look! my last, or
next-to-last, of three loved houses went.
The art of losing isn't hard to master.

I lost two cities, lovely ones. And, vaster,
some realms I owned, two rivers, a continent.
I miss them, but it wasn't a disaster.

—Even losing you (the joking voice, a gesture
I love) I shan't have lied. It's evident
the art of losing's not too hard to master
though it may look like (*Write* it!) like disaster.

V

THE CANE FIELDS (Part 1 of "Parsley") / Rita Dove (b. 1952)

There is a parrot imitating spring
in the palace, its feathers parsley green.
Out of the swamp the cane appears

to haunt us, and we cut it down. El General
searches for a word; he is all the world
there is. Like a parrot imitating spring,

we lie down screaming as rain punches through
and we come up green. We cannot speak an R—
out of the swamp, the cane appears

and then the mountain we call in whispers *Katalina*.
The children gnaw their teeth to arrowheads.
There is a parrot imitating spring.

El General has found his word: *perejil*.
Who says it, lives. He laughs, teeth shining
out of the swamp. The cane appears

in our dreams, lashed by wind and streaming.
And we lie down. For every drop of blood
there is a parrot imitating spring.
Out of the swamp the cane appears.

VISION Insight into the unexpected or otherwise unseen; the seeing of things as they might be or as they really, more deeply, are. Visionary poetry is prophetic, mystical, a glimpse into the unknown. The Book of Ecclesiastes Dante Alighieri's *The Divine Comedy*, and Samuel Taylor Coleridge's "Kubla Khan" are visionary poems.

VOICE The characteristic sound, style, manner, or *tone of a particular poet or poem.

On the page, a poetic voice comprises many elements: diction (word choices), *syntax (arrangement of words), attitudes, subject matter, rhythmic proclivities, line lengths, punctuation, the presence or absence of meter and rhyme, and especially the tone. It includes what Wallace Stevens, in "Thirteen Ways of Looking at a Blackbird," calls "the beauty of inflections" and "the beauty of innuendoes." It's also a matter of point of view: the personal voice (however fictionalized) in the first-person "I"; the objective or empathetic voice in the third-person "he," "she," "it," or "they"; the political or communal "we"; the intimate or oracular or accusatory "you."

Sometimes teachers and critics talk about "finding your voice," as if the poet were born without one and had to set about acquiring one. But William Stafford says, "You already have a voice and don't need to find one." A voice-print, after all, is as unique and identifiable as a fingerprint. It might be better to urge a poet to use the voice she was born with, along with the words she has learned and the poems she has loved, to discover what poems of her own she has the power to say.

In *The Poetry of Persuasion*, however, Carl Dennis asserts, "For a poem to be convincing, the primary task of the writer is to construct a speaker whose company is worth keeping, who exhibits certain virtues that win the reader's sympathetic attention." He speaks on behalf of the "persuasive power of an individual poetic voice" and offers advice on constructing such a voice.

Like a novelist, a poet can also let characters speak. It would be foolish to force them all to sound like the writer. A good example of how these kinds of voices work might be Robert Frost's "The Death of the Hired Man." We hear the husband and the wife talk (and the hired man too, through the couple's dialogue). We also hear the voice of the speaker narrating the poem. All of these speakers—characters and narrator—comprise Robert Frost's voice.

A poet can perform other vocal tricks, such as using a reflexive voice to address the reader directly and comment on the technical machinery of the work in progress. In the following poem by Louis Simpson, the speaker interrupts himself in the first and third stanzas, self-consciously thinking aloud as he describes a disquieting scene in Italy. He alludes to Walt Whitman's habit of dropping foreign words into his poems. The poet intentionally breaks the spell, the consis-

Voice

tent narrative or descriptive flow we expect in most poems, and forces the reader to consider what's behind the poem, much as a novelist like Henry Fielding will break off from a novel, such as *Tom Jones*, to address the reader directly. Simpson's interruptions and deliberations make the direct descriptions of stanzas two and four much more jarring than they would otherwise be.

Voice is perhaps the most crucial element of any poem. If a voice is credible and compelling, anything goes. But voice is also a defining feature of a poet's work as a whole. "On the Lawn at the Villa" is conversational, narrative, surreal, political, wryly ironic, and concerned with American mores. All of these characteristics belong to Simpson's voice throughout his collected poems. Even the strong lyrical strain in his work is suggested by the sonic loveliness of the title and repeated line, "On the lawn at the villa." *(See* DRAMATIC MONOLOGUE, IRONY, *and* SPEAKER.)

ON THE LAWN AT THE VILLA / Louis Simpson (b. 1923)

On the lawn at the villa—
That's the way to start, eh, reader?
We know where we stand—somewhere expensive—
You and I *imperturbes*, as Walt would say,
Before the diversions of wealth, you and I *engagés*.

On the lawn at the villa
Sat a manufacturer of explosives,
His wife from Paris,
And a young man named Bruno,

And myself, being American,
Willing to talk to these malefactors,
The manufacturer of explosives, and so on,
But somehow superior. By that I mean democratic.
It's complicated, being an American,
Having the money and the bad conscience, both at
   the same time.
Perhaps, after all, this is not the right subject for a poem.

We were all sitting there paralyzed
In the hot Tuscan afternoon,
And the bodies of the machine-gun crew were draped
    over the balcony.
So we sat there all afternoon.

V

W

WELSH POETIC FORMS The twenty-four "strict meters" of traditional Welsh poetry. The poetry of Wales is renowned for its intricate interweaving of sounds, using *rhyme (both end and internal), varieties of *slant rhyme, *assonance, *alliteration, and cross-alliteration. We catch bits of this intricacy in the English verse of Welsh poets such as Gerard Manley Hopkins and Dylan Thomas.

In *The Burning Tree: Poems from the First Thousand Years of Welsh Verse*, Gwyn Williams notes that "The millennium from the year 600 to 1600 saw the development and decline of poetry in the strict Welsh metres and the perfection and classification of the sound-echoing devices known as *cynghanedd*. Technically the peak came with Dafydd ab Edmwnd in the middle of the fifteenth century. The twenty-four measures, already classified in the fourteenth century, were by him tightened up and made more difficult in order to discourage the half-trained practitioner in verse." Williams adds, "Let it not be thought that the twenty-four measures have since fallen into desuetude or become merely museum pieces. They have been in continuous use, and a knowledge of them is essential to anyone who hopes to win the chair at the National Eisteddfod [*eye-steth´-vod, the "th" as in "this"*]. And at least two of the old measures, the *englyn* and the *cywydd*, are in regular use by a very large number of writers to-day."

Cynghanedd (*kun-yahn´-neth*, the *th* as in "this") is Welsh for "harmony." In verse, it is the tight interweaving of either consonants (alliteration) or rhymes (full or slant). Gwyn Williams cites John Keats's phrase "fairy lands forlorn" as one of the "best examples in English of *cynghanedd*." Without the vowels, the pattern of consonants becomes more obvious: *f-r- l-nds f-rl-rn*, a blend of *f, r, l,* and *n*.

There are three main types of *cynghanedd*: *cynghanedd gytsain* (*git´-sane*), the alliteration of a series of consonants, also called *cross-alliteration*; *cynghanedd sain*, both alliteration and *internal rhyme; and *cynghanedd lusg (leesg)*, internal rhyme.

In "The Wreck of the Deutschland," Gerard Manley Hopkins uses "certain chimes suggested by the Welsh poetry I had been reading (what they call *cynghanedd*)," as in the lines "Warm-laid grave of a womb-life gray" and "a lush-kept plush-capped sloe." In the first example, Hopkins repeats a sequence of consonants, a pattern of *w-m l- gr-* (although he also echoes a long *a* in *grave/gray*). In the second example, Hopkins alternates rhymes and slant rhymes (*lush/plush, kept/capped*; in addition, *sloe* rhymes with the first and last lines of the stanza, *Oh* and *go*).

In *The White Goddess: A Historical Grammar of Poetic Myth*, Robert Graves defines *cynghanedd* as "the repetitive use of consonantal sequences with variation of vowels" and makes up this example:

> Billet spied,
> Bolt sped.
> Across field
> Crows fled,
> Aloft, wounded,
> Left one dead.

There are three classes of Welsh verse: *awdl, cywydd,* and *englyn.* Altogether they comprise the twenty-four "measures" or "strict meters," classified in the fourteenth century by Einion Offeiriad. The *awdl* ("rhyme, rhymed speech; ode, lay") is a line form. The *cywydd* is usually a couplet form. The *englyn* was originally a *tercet; since the twelfth century, six of its kinds have been *quatrains using monorhyme or consonance; most of its lines contain seven syllables, although combinations of ten, six, and seven occur.

W

*Rhyme abounds in Welsh verse. Many lines use internal rhymes, either separate from or echoed by end-rhymes. Both full and slant rhyme are allowed, although a particular form may prescribe or prohibit their use. Sometimes a stressed syllable rhymes with an unstressed syllable, as in *sing/talking*. Sometimes the main rhyme does not end a line but is followed by one to three syllables. These extra syllables after the rhyme are called *gair cyrch* (pronounced *guyr kirch*), or "reaching-out word." They alliterate or rhyme with syllables in the first part of the next line. For example, one could approximate the effect in English:

> The infantry stormed the **hill**—through *bar*bed *wire,*
> a *bar*rage of *fire* and **shrill**
> bullets and shrapnel that **kill.**

The lines comprise an *englyn penfyr*, whose rhyme scheme can be notated as A + *gair cyrch* / A / A. The main rhymes (A) are "hill," "shrill," and "kill." The gair cyrch is "through barbed wire," which is echoed at the beginning of the next line by "barrage" (alliteration) and "fire" (rhyme). Both kinds of echoing occur in the example, but only one is necessary. Gair cyrch resembles the *radif*, or refrain of a few syllables, that follows the main rhyme in a Middle Eastern form called the *ghazal.

In Gwyn Williams's translation of the anonymous "Glyn Cynon Wood," each stanza consists of a pair of *awdl gywydd* couplets, rhymed *a* / *a* + B / *c* / *c* + B, so that the lowercase rhymes recur in the middle of the next line and the upper-case rhymes recur at the end of every other line. Here is the third stanza:

> If a man in sudden plight
> took to flight from foe,
> for guest-house to the nightingale
> in Cynon Vale he'd go.

Frequently in Welsh verse, successive lines begin with the same consonant, a technique called *cymeriad (kuh-mare´-yad).* Another kind of *cymeriad* occurs when the final word of a line is repeated near the beginning of the next line.

The contemporary poet writing in English may find it useful to experiment with some of these Welsh techniques: any of the intricately rhymed line and stanza forms; the standards for using *slant rhymes (matching similar kinds of vowels—short, long, or diphthong); the sound interweaving of *cynghanedd* (especially alliterating a sequence of consonants). If nothing else, it would be good training in the orchestration of sounds. Listed below are the twenty-four measures of Welsh poetry.

NOTES TO THE LIST

- / = line break (two or more letters between virgules indicate internal rhyme).

- *Gair cyrch* occurs one to three syllables *after* the Main Rhyme and is alliterated or rhymed in the first part of the next line.

- Main Rhyme is indicated by a capital letter.

- Other rhymes, indicated by lowercase letters, may be internal rhyme or (in *englyn proest gadwynog*) slant rhymes.

- To approximate the Welsh sounds of these terms, say *ch* as in the Scottish *loch*, *dd* like the *th* in *this*, *th* like the *th* in *thin*. In the pronunciation guides below, *th* must indicate both of these last two sounds. Usually it represents "dd" and sounds like the *th* in *this*; but "thoddaid" includes both (its beginning is unvoiced, as in *thin*, while its middle is voiced, as in *this*).

Englyn Measures (eight kinds) (eng´-lin; plural *englynion*, en-glin´-yon)

- englyn penfyr *(pen´-veer; "short-ended")* 10-7-7 syllables, rhymed *A + gair cyrch / A / A*

W

- englyn milwr *(mih´-loor; "soldier's englyn")* 7-7-7 syllables, rhymed *A / A / A*

- englyn unodl union *(ee-noh´-dl een´-yon; "straight one-rhyme englyn")* 10-6-7-7 syllables, rhymed *A + gair cyrch / A / A / A* (The first two lines = shaft [*paladr*]; second two lines = wings [*esgyll*]; each line uses *cynghanedd*.)

- englyn unodl crwca *(ee-noh´-dl croo´-ca; "crooked one-rhyme englyn")* 7-7-10-6 syllables, rhymed *A / A / A + gair cyrch / A* (Like the *englyn unodl union*, but "wings" come before "shaft.")

• englyn cyrch *(kirch)* 7-7-7-7 syllables, rhymed *A / A / b / b + A* (The first *A* rhyme stressed, second *A* rhyme unstressed: *throw/window*; second *b* rhyme comes in the middle of the fourth line.)

• englyn proest dalgron *(pro´-est dal´-gron)* 7-7-7-7 syllables, rhymed *A / A / A / A* (Slant-rhymed using either all short vowels, such as *hat/hit/bet*, or all long vowels, such as *hate/height/beat*, but not a mixture of both.)

• englyn lleddfbroest *(clethev´-broist)* 7-7-7-7 syllables, rhymed *A / A / A / A* (Slant-rhymed using diphthongs, such as *boil/fuel/vial/vowel.*)

• englyn proest gadwynog *(pro´-est god-win´-og)* 7-7-7-7 syllables, rhymed *a / A / a / A* (First line slant-rhymed with second and full-rhymed with third; second line full-rhymed with fourth: *rod/dead/nod/led.*)

Cywydd Measures (four kinds) (cuh´-with; plural *cywyddau*, cuh-with´-eye)

• awdl gywydd *(ow´-dl guh´-with)* 7-7 syllables, rhymed a / *a + B* (Second *a* rhyme comes in the middle of line 2; main rhyme [*B*] recurs at end of next couplet.)

• cywydd deuair hirion *(die´-ire here´-yon)* 7-7 syllables, rhymed *A / A* (Alternating masculine and feminine rhyme, as in *sword/forward*; the most popular form of cywydd.)

• cywydd deuair fyrion *(die´-ire veer´-yon)* 4-4 syllables, rhymed *A / A* (Seldom used.)

• cywydd llosgyrnog *(clos-geer´-nog)* 8-8-7 syllables, rhymed *a / a / a + B* (Third *a* rhyme comes in the middle of line 3; main rhyme [*B*] recurs at end of the next tercet; rarely used.)

Awdl Measures (twelve kinds) (ow´-dul)

LINE FORMS

• rhupunt *(ree´-pihnt)* three to five sections per line, four syllables per section, rhymed *a a (a a) B* (with cross alliteration in last two sections)

• cyhydedd hir *(cuh-hih´-deth here)* four sections per line, 5-5-5-4 syllabic arrangement, rhymed *a a a B*

(In both of these forms, the next line uses *c* rhymes in place of *a* rhymes. Those internal rhymes remain within the line, while the end-rhyme [*B*] connects not internally but with the next line's end-rhyme.)

STANZA FORMS

• cyhydedd fer *(cuh-hih´-deth ver)* 8-8 syllables per line, rhymed *A / A*

• byr a thoddaid *(bir ah thoth´-ayd)* 10-6-8-8 or 8-8-10-6 syllables per line, rhymed *A + gair cyrch / A / A / A* or *A / A / A + gair cyrch / A*

• clogyrnach *(clog-ir´-nach)* 8-8-5-5-3-3 syllables per line, rhymed *A / A / b / b / b / A* (The last four lines can be a single line, like *a rhupunt.*)

• cyhydedd naw ban *(cuh-hih´-deth naw bahn)* 9-9 syllables per line, rhymed *A / A* (It can go on for many lines with the same rhyme.)

• toddaid *(toth´-ayd)* 10-9 syllables per line, rhymed *A + gair cyrch (b) / b A* (It's used in combination with *cyhydedd hir* or a nine-syllable couplet.)

• gwawdodyn *(gwaw-dod´-in)* 9-9-10-9 syllables per line, rhymed *A / A / A + gair cyrch (b) / b A*

• gwawdodyn hir *(gwaw-dod´-in here)* 9-9-9-9-10-9 syllables per line, rhymed *A / A / A / A / A + gair cyrch (b) / b A* (The *gair cyrch* must rhyme, not just alliterate, with an internal *b* rhyme in the following line.)

• hir a thoddaid *(here ah thoth´-ayd)* 10-10-10-10-10-9 syllables per line, rhymed *A / A / A / A / A + gair cyrch (b) /b A* (The gair cyrch must rhyme, not just alliterate, with an internal *b* rhyme in the following line.)

• cyrch a chwta *(kirch ah choo´-ta)* 7-7-7-7-7-7-7-7 syllables per line, rhymed *A / A / A / A / A / A / A / b / b + A* (It consists of six lines followed by an *awdl gywydd.*)

W

• tawddgyrch cadwynog *(towth´-girch cahd-win´-og)* 8-8-8-8 syllables per line, rhymed *a b / b C / a b / b C*

For further information on Welsh forms, see Gwyn Williams's *An Introduction to Welsh Poetry* and Tony Conran's *Welsh Verse*.

WORD A signifier; the basic unit of the sentence—and of language; the atom of a body of discourse.

A word consists of one or more syllables, clusters of sounds that may or may not be strung together. *Word*, for example, consists of a single syllable; *language* consists of two syllables, the first accented *(lang´-uage)*; *vocabulary* consists of five syllables, with a primary accent on the second and secondary accent on the fourth *(vo-cab´-u-lar´´-y)*. Each syllable, however, contains individual sounds called phonemes, which may or may not correspond to the letters. For example, *word* and *worth* both contain four phonemes, but worth has an extra letter (*th* is a single phoneme).

In addition to its sounds (a matter of pronunciation) and its visual appearance when written (a matter of spelling), a word has one or more meanings and one or more functions within a sentence. The meaning is what the word signifies, what it conveys to someone who speaks the language. Even a nonsense word may have meaning—though a meaning perhaps dependent on sound, like a dog's bark. The function of a word depends on how it is, or can be, used in a sentence. Accordingly, each word serves as a part of speech: noun, verb, adjective, adverb, preposition, conjunction, pronoun, article, interjection. In different contexts, a word can serve as different parts of speech. *Rope*, for example, can serve as noun, verb, or adjective:

> She twirls the rope.
> They rope the steers.
> They walk across a rope bridge.

The following lines from Christopher Marlowe's *Doctor Faustus* include all nine parts of speech:

The clock strikes twelve.

FAUSTUS. It strikes, it strikes! Now body, turn to air,
Or Lucifer will bear thee quick to hell!
O soul, be changed into small water-drops
And fall into the ocean, ne'er be found.

In the lines spoken by Faustus, the parts of speech are as follows:

• Noun (person, place, thing, or idea): *body, air, Lucifer, hell, soul, water-drops, ocean*

• Verb (action or state of being): *strikes, turn, will bear, be changed, fall, be found*

• Adjective (modifying a noun): *small*

• Adverb (modifying a verb, an adjective, or another adverb): *Now, quick, ne'er*

• Preposition (forming a transition from a noun or verb to something that modifies it): *to, into*

• Conjunction (joining words, phrases, or clauses): *or, and*

• Pronoun (substituting for nouns): *it, thee*

• Article (indicating something—*a, an*, and *the* are the only ones, used before nouns or noun phrases): *the*

• Interjection (or exclamation, an utterance like a cry or a shout or a gasp or a curse): *O*

W

PERMISSIONS

"My Word" from *Call Me Ishmael Tonight: A Book of Ghazals* by Agha Shahid Ali. Copyright © 2003 by Agha Shahid Ali Literary Trust. Used by permission of W.W. Norton & Company, Inc.

Sonnet 6 from "Redwing Sonnets" from *Homecoming*. Copyright © 1984, 1996 by Julia Alvarez. Published by Plume, an imprint of Penguin Group (USA); originally published by Grove Press. Reprinted by permission of Susan Bergholz Literary Services, New York. All rights reserved.

"Tourists" from *Great Tranquility: Questions and Answers* by Yehuda Amichai. Translated by Glenda Abramson and Tudor Parfitt. Copyright © 1983 by Yehuda Amichai. Reprinted by permission of HarperCollins Publishers, Inc. and Hana Amichai.

"Photosynthesis" from *The Selected Poems, Expanded Edition* by A.R. Ammons. Copyright © 1987, 1977, 1975,1974, 1972, 1971, 1970, 1966, 1965, 1964, 1955 by A.R. Ammons. Used by permission of W.W. Norton & Company, Inc.

"A Branch of Nettle Enters through the Window," by André Breton, translated by David Antin, *The Poetry of Surrealism*, edited by Michael Benedikt, 1974. Reprinted by permission of the translator.

Chapter One, Stanza One from the book *Eugene Onegin*. Copyright © 1963, 1981 by Walter Arndt (translation). Reprinted with the permission of Ardis Publishers.

"Five Songs II (That night when joy began)," copyright © 1976 by Edward Mendelson, William Meredith, and Monroe K. Spears, Executors of the Estate of W.H. Auden, from *Collected Poems* by W.H. Auden. Used by permission of Random House Inc. and Faber & Faber Ltd.

Marvin Bell, "Stars Which See, Stars Which Do Not See" from *Nightworks: Poems 1962-2000*. Copyright © 2003 by Marvin Bell. Reprinted with the permission of Copper Canyon Press, P.O. Box 271, Port Townsend, WA 98368-0271.

"Get Drunk" by Charles Baudelaire. Originally appeared in *The Prose Poem: An International Anthology* published by Dell/Laurel Editions, edited by Michael Benedikt. Translation by Michael Benedikt, © 1976. Used by permission of Michael Benedikt & agent Georges Borchardt, Inc.

"Lift Plow Plates" from *Islets/Irritations*. © 1983, 1992 by Charles Bernstein. Reprinted by permission of Roof Books.

Permissions

John Felstiner's translation of Paul Celan's "Deathfugue" from *Paul Celan: Poet Survivor Jew*, Yale University Press, 1995. Reprinted by permission of the translator.

All lines from "The Colonel" from *The Country Between Us* by Carolyn Forché. Copyright © 1981 by Carolyn Forché. Originally appeared in *Women's International Resource Exchange*. Reprinted by permission of HarperCollins Publishers, Inc. and Abner Stein Ltd.

Excerpt from "Sir Gawain and the Green Knight," translated by John Gardner, from *The Complete Works of the Gawain Poet*, University of Chicago Press, © 1965 by the University of Chicago. Reprinted by permission of the University of Chicago Press. All rights reserved.

All lines from "A Supermarket in California" from *Collected Poems 1947-1980* by Allen Ginsberg. Copyright © 1955 by Allen Ginsberg. Reprinted by permission of HarperCollins Publishers, Inc. and Penguin Books Ltd.

"The Next Poem" copyright 1991 by Dana Gioia. Reprinted from *The Gods of Winter* with the permission of Graywolf Press, Saint Paul, Minnesota.

"The Red Poppy" from *The Wild Iris* by Louise Glück. Copyright © 1993 by Louise Glück. Reprinted by permission of HarperCollins Publishers Inc. and Carcanet Press Limited.

"Soul Says" from *Region of Unlikeness* by Jorie Graham. Copyright © 1991 by Jorie Graham. Reprinted by permission of HarperCollins Publishers Inc.

"Billet spied" from *The White Goddess* by Robert Graves. Copyright © 1948, renewed © 1975 by Robert Graves. Reprinted by permission of Farrar, Straus and Giroux, LLC, and Carcanet Press Limited

"Narrow Flame" from *Waterborne: Poems* by Linda Gregerson. Copyright © 2002 by Linda Gregerson. Reprinted by permission of Houghton Mifflin Company.

"Eurydice" copyright 1981 by Linda Gregg. Reprinted from *Too Bright to See* with the permission of Graywolf Press, Saint Paul, Minnesota.

"Dear John, Dear Coltrane" from *Songlines in Michaeltree: New and Collected Poems*. Copyright © 2000 by Michael S. Harper. Used with permission of the poet and the University of Illinois Press.

"Letter" by Robert Hass from *Field Guide*, Yale University Press. Copyright © 1973 by Robert Hass. Reprinted by permission of Yale University Press.

"The Forge" from *Opened Ground: Selected Poems 1966-1996* by Seamus Heaney. Copyright © 1998 by Seamus Heaney. Reprinted by permission of Farrar, Straus and Giroux, LLC, and Faber & Faber Ltd.

"lighting by trees" from Lyn Hejinian, *The Cell* (Los Angeles, Sun & Moon Press, 1992), © 1992 by Lyn Hejinian. Reprinted by permission of Sun & Moon Press.

Garrett Kaoru Hongo, "The Hongo Store" in *Yellow Light*, © 1982 by Garrett Kaoru Hongo and reprinted by permission of Wesleyan University Press.

"1801" is reprinted from the collection *Untitled Subjects* (Scribner, 1996) by Richard Howard by permission. All rights reserved on behalf of the author by Writers' Representatives, LLC, New York, NY.

"Correspondences" from *Les Fleurs du Mal* by Charles Baudelaire, translated from the French by Richard Howard. Reprinted by permission of David R Godine, Publisher, Inc. Translation copyright © 1982 by Richard Howard.

"Like Most Revelations" from *Like Most Revelations*, Pantheon Books. Copyright © 1994 by Richard Howard. Reprinted by permission of the author.

356

Permissions

Permissions

"Do Not Go Gentle into That Good Night" by Dylan Thomas, from *Poems of Dylan Thomas*, copyright © 1952 by Dylan Thomas. Reprinted by permission of New Directions Publishing Corp. and David Higham Associates Limited.

Dante's "Amor, tu vedi ben che questa donna," translated by Joseph Tusiani. Reprinted by permission.

"Diverne's Waltz" reprinted by permission of Louisiana State University Press from *The Homeplace* by Marilyn Nelson Waniek. Copyright © 1989, 1990 by Marilyn Nelson Waniek.

"Fontaine: The Grasshopper and the Ant" in *The Mind-Reader*, copyright © 1955 by Richard Wilbur, reprinted by permission of Harcourt, Inc.

"The Lilacs" from *Walking to Sleep: New Poems and Translations*, copyright © 1963 and renewed 1991 by Richard Wilbur, reprinted by permission of Harcourt, Inc.

"Rondeau" and excerpt from "Seed Leaves" from *Walking to Sleep: New Poems and Translations*, copyright © 1964 and renewed 1992 by Richard Wilbur, reprinted by permission of Harcourt, Inc.

"Glyn Cynon Wood," from *The Burning Tree: Poems from the First Thousand Years of Welsh Verse*, translated by Gwyn Williams. Reprinted by permission of Daisy Williams.

"The Descent" by William Carlos Williams, from *Collected Later Poems 1939-1962*, Volume II, copyright © 1948, 1962 by William Carlos Williams. Reprinted by permission of New Directions Publishing Corp. and Carcanet Press Limited.

"January Morning" (3 lines) by William Carlos Williams, from *Collected Poems: 1909-1939*, Volume I, copyright © 1938 by William Carlos Williams. Reprinted by permission of New Directions Publishing Corp. and Carcanet Press Limited.

"Camera Shake with Wide-Angle Field of Snow" from the book *Errors in the Script*, © 2001 by Greg Williamson. reprinted with permission of the Overlook Press.

Charles Wright, "Bygones" from *China Trace*, Wesleyan University Press. Copyright © 1977 by Charles Wright. Reprinted by permission of the author.

"The Fox at Eype," "Ohioan Pastoral," and "Reading a 1979 Inscription on Belli's Monument" from *Above the River: The Complete Poems* by James Wright. Copyright © 1990 by Anne Wright. Reprinted by permission of Farrar, Straus and Giroux, LLC.

"A Lowercase Alphabet" by David Young from *The Names of a Hare in English*, University of Pittsburgh Press. Copyright © 1979 by David Young. Reprinted by permission of the author.

Zukofsky, Louis. *Complete Short Poetry*, page 310. Copyright © 1991 by Paul Zukofsky. Reprinted with permission of The Johns Hopkins University Press.

INDEX OF POETS AND POEMS

Index of Poets and Poems

·

INDEX OF TERMS